Zinn's

CYCLING PRIMER

D0506666

Zinn's CYCLING PRIMER

MAINTENANCE TIPS & SKILL BUILDING FOR CYCLISTS

Lennard Zinn

VELO press

Boulder, Colorado

Zinn's Cycling Primer: Maintenance Tips and Skill Building for Cyclists
© 2004 Lennard Zinn

Printed in the United States of America.
10 9 8 7 6 5 4 3 2 1
Distributed in the United States and Canada by Publishers Group West.
International Standard Book Number: 1-931382-43-3

Library of Congress Cataloging-in-Publication Data
Zinn, Lennard.
  Zinn's cycling primer : maintenance tips and skill building for cyclists / by Lennard Zin.— 1st ed.
      p. cm.
  Includes index.
  ISBN 1-931382-43-3 (paper back : alk. paper)
  1. All terrain cycling—Handbooks, manuals, etc. 2. All terrain bicycles—Maintenance and repair—Handbooks, manuals, etc. I. Title.
  GV1056.Z56 2004
  796.6'4—dc22

                                                                    2004011768

VeloPress®
1830 North 55th Street
Boulder, Colorado 80301–2700 USA
303/440-0601 • Fax 303/444-6788 • E-mail velopress@insideinc.com

To purchase additional copies of this book or other VeloPress® books, call 800/234-8356 or visit us on the Web at velopress.com.

Cover photos by Galen Nathanson. Cover design by Amber Salt.

Design and production by Rebecca Finkel, F + P Graphic Design, Inc.

Interior photos and figures not otherwise noted were photographed or provided by the author. The Anatometer II Plus in Photo 20.1 is manufactured by Benexel Products, a division of Banesh Corporation, patent no. 5,088,504.

To Chama. Thanks for your companionship through the writing of this and all of my prior books. You have been the best possible friend to me.

Contents

Acknowledgments

For the final form this book has taken, my thanks and appreciation go to Dede Demet-Barry, who took such an interest and offered such a compelling vision for it when it was in the "toss a few ideas for various books around" stage, that I was able to visualize it myself and be motivated to act upon it. Thanks also to Michael Robson and the Boulder Nordic Club for grooming the snow in North Boulder Park, so that Dede and I could ski together on gentle terrain and at Boulder's lower altitude, making intelligent conversation possible.

For their contributions that were absolutely critical with content, I appreciate the assistance of Hans Rey, Andy Pruitt, Greg Herbold, Ned Overend, Jonathan Vaughters, Andy Hampsten, Edward Borysewicz, Ugo De Rosa, Davis Phinney, Connie Carpenter, Ron Kiefel, Boone Lennon, John Cobb, Steve Hed, Andrew Juskaitis, Graham Watson, Blair Lombardi, Dean Crandall, Colby Pearce, Jim Bowen, Steve West, Morgan Nicol, Ara Howard, Ron Haney, Tom Slocum, Neal Henderson, Russel Bollig, Ben Serotta, Ulrich Schoberer, Peter Chisholm, Scott Adlfinger, Fausto Pinarello, Kirby Palm, Wayne Stetina, Calvin Jones, Eric Hawkins, Alan Hills, Peter Marshall, Richard Cimadoro, Craig Pearson, John Dunn, Toni Geer, Tami Dick, Bob Anderson, Jean Anderson, Tom Groover, Andrew Gerlach, Scott Loomis, Jeff Broker, Cindy Dallow, Portia Masterson, Zack Miller, Lauren Dundon, Todd Telander, Fulvio Acquati, Tom Ritchey, Stan Koziatek, Wayne Lumpkin, John Tomac, Dave Tiemeyer, Chris Zigmont, Vince Marazita, Steve Driscoll, Paul Morningstar, Doug Bradbury, Scott Boyer, Jose Gonzalez, Jim Pappadoupolis, Mark Langton, Russ Okawa, everybody who has written in to my Tech Q&A Web column, and the late and sorely missed Ed Burke, Ole Aspaas, and Bill Woodul.

Thank you to Sarah, my daughter, for her fine photography and to Sonny and Emily, my wife and my other daughter, for their assistance with the photos as well. *VeloNews* photo editor Galen Nathanson contributed and located many photos also. For their unflagging support of me in this commitment, my undying appreciation goes to Amy Rinehart, Renee Jardine, Rick Rundall, Ted Costantino, Felix Magowan, Dave Peterson, John Ferris, my Boulder seminar friends, the *VeloNews* editorial staff, everyone at VeloPress, and, above all, my family.

Foreword

Over the 20 years I've known Lennard Zinn, he has constantly studied and evolved with the sport of cycling. Most importantly, he is an avid cyclist who continues to ride for fun and fitness long after his racing days ended. He's also a craftsman, a true artisan—Lennard builds bikes for a living. He has written about technical aspects of cycling for *VeloNews: The Journal of Competitive Cycling* for many years. His curiosity about, and love for all things technical extends to everything related to cycling, and that is good news for all cyclists—whether you are just getting started and need answers or looking for an edge after reaching a performance plateau.

Cycling is beautiful but complicated—it is mechanical and technical, yet physical and spiritual. Done well, it's an art form, and admittedly, it's not easy; there's much to learn. It may seem daunting to the newcomer, yet cycling is one of the most popular sports in the world—both in terms of spectators and participants.

So relax, you've found your place.

Lennard knows many of the answers to your questions. But he knows his limits too, and has included other insightful expert viewpoints as well. In cycling parlance he knows when to go to the front and take a pull and when to sit out a turn, letting others share the work. In other words, he knows not only when to ask for advice but who to ask. And, with the patience of a saint, Lennard knows best how to explain it.

Learn. Enjoy! *Andiamo!* Let's go.

CONNIE CARPENTER
*1984 Olympic gold medalist
in Women's Individual Road Race*

Preface

Riding a bike is a great way to play, and everybody needs to play, and feel like a little kid—even more than they need the physical fitness that comes from doing it. A cycling friend of mine, chiropractor John Dunn says, "The world has become a crazier place since September 11, and the difference is palpable in my office. People really need to play now more than ever." Even professionals who ride bikes for their living appreciate the play and rejuvenation that comes with it. Lance Armstrong, after already having won five Tours de France, has said, "A day without a bike ride is an empty day."

As you get older, it's harder to find outlets for play that you used to find everywhere as a kid. And some outlets that you can find can be downright dangerous and injurious as an adult. Fortunately, as long as you keep the rubber side down and are positioned properly on the bike, cycling is easy on the joints and most of the rest of the body.

As a means of playing and of freeing my mind, as well as of maintaining and improving my physical health, cycling is a critical component of almost every day for me. I can't agree with Armstrong about riding absolutely every day, because I also love participating in other sports and do so regularly. However, if I am not outside being active every day, I definitely miss it. And I consider myself very fortunate that cycling has never seemed like a job to me, and that I thirst every day to do more of it. I quit racing not because I was burned out on it, but because I wanted to pursue building bikes and coaching, managing, massaging, and wrenching for my wife's women's cycling team, while of course continuing to ride a lot myself.

Because of its mechanical component, cycling also dovetails nicely with my long-standing interest in physics. Designing bikes has been a passion of mine ever since I embarked on it as a senior seminar for my physics degree in college. It was then that I began to discover how intimately related the design of the bike is to the performance of the rider on it—how the bicycle itself limits or expands what is possible for the rider to do. And in working and playing in this field as racer, rider, bike designer, builder, and mechanic of road and mountain bikes in the ensuing decades, I have learned and constantly continue learning new ways in which the rider can exploit the design features of the bike, and how the bike design can be altered to offer more to the rider.

This book is a compendium of much of that knowledge derived from a career of pursuing my passion for cycling. Contained in it are what I think are the most important ways to increase your comfort, efficiency, joy, and satisfaction in riding. It is chock full of things you can do for your body, to your bike, and with the interface between your bike and your body that will make you ride more comfortably, efficiently, and faster.

My prior books have tended to be all about the bike—about maintaining and improving its parts. While hardware is indeed important, in my own cycling practice it takes a back seat to my body and its state of health. Don't get me wrong—I love fine-tuning my machine so it is light to lift and easy on the eyes and runs like a Swiss watch. However, the fact remains that you can always fix or replace the bike or its parts, but you only get one body and you had better make it last for the duration. If your position on the bike is critically off and you pour on the miles, you will end up injured and unable to ride. Similarly, if you allow your body to adapt only to cycling and do not take care of the resultant muscle, joint, and connective tissue damage and imbalances it can create, you will likewise end up unable to ride and be reduced to a whining mass of complaints. Finally, you can have fun riding a clunky old piece of junk if your body feels good. But if you are in pain, it does not matter how elegant your bike is and how precisely it functions; you will simply not enjoy the ride, which is what this is all about.

This book constitutes my "top 50" list of things you can do to be faster, more efficient, and comfortable on your bike, and it incorporates a long-term approach. It focuses on fitting you precisely to the bicycle and on what you can do for those areas of the body that cycling neglects or even compromises, so that you can ride efficiently, comfortably, and enjoyably late into life. It also goes into specific skills for riding and working on your bike that will pay dividends in your enjoyment and confidence for years to come.

Cyclists young and old should benefit from this book. Efficiency, comfort, fitness, and a well-tuned bike will make anyone faster and lead to more fun. However, now that I'm 46 years old and see how much more difficult it is to stay fast, strong, and pain-free than when I was 22, I think that this book will be of particular assistance to riders over 40. Being comfortable and efficient on the bike is the primary point, while mastering riding skills late in life that it seems any 13-year-old can do is just the gravy. So is upgrading your bike to make it perform better.

How This Book Is Organized

When I attended Colorado College almost three decades ago (geez, has it been that long?), courses there were conducted on a block plan. You took only one class at a time, during "blocks" lasting three-and-a-half weeks, and did a semester's worth of work in that time. Each block was a self-contained, complete course followed by a nice four-day, homework-free break. You could delve into one subject in great depth without the distraction of taking other courses simultaneously. Yet your success in each block depended on at least some of the other blocks you had already completed. Whether you were a physics major or a history major, the knowledge you attained in your field was cumulative, one block stacking on top of another.

The structure of this book is similar. Like math or a foreign language, bicycle knowledge is also cumulative and can be broken down into discrete blocks to be mastered. In this book, each block is a self-contained piece. You can just work on that one portion, and there is no need to read any farther. However, some of the blocks in each section are cumulative, and you may find it necessary to take in a few preceding blocks to bone up on the area first. You can also start right off with the block you want, skipping the information that would be review (unless, of course, a review might be useful!).

Each of the seven sections in this book contains a number of blocks that are completely distinct and relatively independent, yet interconnected, much like study areas in college. For instance, a number of separate blocks in this book address training and adapting your body to ride at a certain performance level, and many of those blocks are cumulative. Meanwhile, the whole area of human performance on the bike is interconnected with other sections (or different "areas of study" of the bike, if you will), like the positioning of the body, mastery of cycling skills, and the mechanical functioning of the bike itself. Just as each block provides a platform to stand on as you take on other blocks, I hope that this entire book serves as a platform for greater cycling enjoyment and satisfaction throughout your life.

When sportswriter Frank DeFord watched Martina Navratilova win professional doubles tennis tournaments in her 50s, he noted the grace and economy of motion of such an experienced older athlete who was blessed with the health and motivation to continue to improve at the sport she loves. He said, "It is where joy meets nobility," and it is in that spirit that I think we all can continue rolling through the countryside on a bike. I love riding, on and off road, with a passion that has remained undiminished over the decades, and it is my intention to be able to ride well for many more decades. Taking the steps outlined in this book allows me to do so, and I hope it does for you as well.

PART I
Initial Setup

BLOCK 1

Saddle Height

There are many formulas out there for determining the position of your bike seat, and those are a great place to start. However, you are unique, and a formula may not work for you. In that case, you would benefit from an anatomic determination of your saddle position.

Seat position is comprised of three components: height, fore-aft position, and tilt. I'll start with height.

Saddle Height

Two simple, heel-on-pedal methods

After warming up on a stationary trainer, clip in and slowly pedal backward until you lock your knee without rocking your hips. Adjust the seat up or down until the bottom of the foot is level when your knee is locked at the bottom of the stroke, with the crank lined up with the seat tube (see Photo 1.1).

1.1

Set the seat height so the foot is level when the knee is locked.

SARAH ZINN

Another method is to set your heel on top of the pedal and slowly pedal backward. Again, adjust the seat up or down until the heel just barely maintains contact with the pedal as you straighten your leg at the bottom of the stroke without your hips rocking. This method only works when you're wearing road shoes, as the heel knobs on mountain bike shoes throw it off.

Two inseam formulas

To use a formula, you need to measure your inseam, and you may need an assistant to help you. The idea is to pull a straightedge, level with the ground, firmly up into your crotch with as much pressure as you'd have sitting on a saddle, and measure from it to the floor.

I use a 3/4-inch dowel rod notched for a tape measure hook and a bubble level taped atop the dowel rod. A 3-foot carpenter's level can be used in a similar manner. Stand with your bare feet placed 2 inches apart. You pull the dowel rod up firmly from both ends into your crotch, and your assistant measures from the floor to the top of the dowel rod (see Photo 1.2). You can also stand against a wall and pull a large book up into your crotch, making sure that you have one edge of the book against the wall to keep the book level. (Pull hard, since it is difficult to compress the soft tissue when grasping the top of the book.) Mark the height of the top of the book on the wall and measure from it to the floor. Whether you use a book or a level, make sure you add in the width of the tape measure itself when you're measuring. Now you're ready to try the two inseam formulas.

Ever since the 1970s, when I read about a study done on Eddy Merckx and other stars of his day, I have multiplied the inseam measurement by 1.09 to determine the distance from the top of the saddle to the center of the bottom pedal spindle when the crank is aligned with the seat tube. It has worked great for me and for hundreds of people I have positioned; I think it's an excellent place to start.

Another formula, dubbed the "LeMond Method," as Greg LeMond uses it, is to multiply the inseam measurement by 0.883 to find the distance from the center of the bottom bracket (that is, the crank axle) to the top of the saddle along the seat tube. The trick with both methods is the difficulty of eyeballing the height of the top of the saddle with the tape measure.

Accurate method of measuring inseam using a bubble level on a dowel

SARAH ZINN

Problems with these methods

None of the four methods above take into consideration the angle of your ankle while pedaling, which is a personal thing.

Other than the first method, none take into account the length of the foot, which, if abnormally short or long, effectively shortens or lengthens the leg. Nor do these latter three methods take into consideration variations in shoe-sole thickness under the ball of the foot and height of the shoe above the pedal spindle when clipped in.

The LeMond Method does not account for crank length, which, if not the same proportion to leg length from person to person, will give a saddle position that's too low or too high. For instance, my inseam is 96.5cm, and using a ratio of 0.21 for the crank length to leg length (see Block 9 on crank length), that yields a crank of 202.5mm, a length only obtainable on a custom basis. The LeMond Method added to my crank length gives a distance from the pedal to the top of the saddle of 105.4cm, virtually the same as the 105.2cm obtained by multiplying my inseam by 1.09. However, if I were to use the longest commercially available crank, 180mm, the LeMond Method would place my seat height a full 2cm closer to the pedal, which I know I could not tolerate.

Neither inseam formula accounts for abnormally thick tissue under the crotch that can compress over time (resulting in a saddle that's too low) or for wearing extra-thick padding, like layers of tights in the winter (resulting in a saddle that's too high).

Anatomical method

Andy Pruitt, director of the Boulder Center for Sports Medicine and the premier expert in the United States on bike fit and cycling-related injuries, determines seat height by measuring the knee angle when the foot is at the bottom

> **A Rule of Thumb for Knee Pain**
>
> Andy Pruitt's rule of thumb on knee pain: "If your knee hurts in the front, raise the saddle; if it hurts in the back, lower it." If you are hurting on a ride, raising or lowering the saddle with this rule of thumb will get you home; it does not mean you should leave it there forever.

of the stroke. This takes into account foot size, shoe and pedal dimensions, and preferred angle of the ankle. For precise fitting, he has pioneered the use of 3-D computer video analysis of pedaling. With reflectors placed on each of the leg joints, the computer creates line segments between the joints, which makes the angles they form easy to measure. Less precise, since the leg is not actually pedaling, but nonetheless very accurate is a goniometer, a long-armed protractor used to measure joint angles (as shown in Photo 13.1).

In Pruitt's dissertation on positioning and injury, the average knee angle of 100 cyclists, with the foot at bottom dead center, was 30 degrees, measured accurately by computer. "The highest saddle that cyclists will acclimate to is 25 degrees of knee bend at bottom dead center, which yields the lowest compressive and shear forces within the knee," says Pruitt. "Any higher and the fulcrum for the leg lever, namely the kneecap, no longer maintains contact with the joint. Nobody will tolerate that; besides which, you cannot push as hard without the fulcrum. The power output is highest with a lower saddle—knee angle of 40 degrees at bottom dead center—but the compressive and shear forces in the knee are too high and the risk of injury is enormous."

Pruitt says that, since track sprinters want more absolute power, which is found in mid-range of muscle, they tend to use knee angles of about 35 degrees at bottom dead center. The knee strain is much higher, but they are only doing short bursts of power output.

The point of anatomic positioning is to take into account your unique characteristics. You can also set up a video camera to monitor yourself on a trainer or rollers. One method is to set the seat too high and lower it until your hips do not rock and your pedaling motion is fluid. 🚲

The work of Andy Pruitt and the Boulder Center for Sports Medicine that he directs can be viewed at www.bch.org/sportsmedicine.

BLOCK 2
Saddle Fore, Aft, and Tilt Position

Knee Fore-Aft Position

The length of a rider's thighbone, foot, and crank determines the saddle's fore-aft position. Andy Pruitt, director of the Boulder Center for Sports Medicine, says, "My experience and 3-D studies we do here consistently show that the center of rotation of the knee must be over the center of rotation of the pedal. Our 3-D digitized video of riders shows that if you do not set up cyclists that way, they will rotate their hips to get over the pedal to get power. If you set up a cyclist with a leg-length discrepancy so that the knee of their long leg is over the pedal, the rider will thrust the short-side hip forward to get the knee over the other pedal."

The knee's center of rotation is not easy to find, and it changes as the knee bends, because the end of the femur (or thighbone) is elliptical. So, it is not useful to try to find this endpoint. Instead, the method Pruitt has settled on, and which I suggest, is to drop a plumb bob from the front of the kneecap and see that it hangs straight over the end of the crankarm (rather than the pedal spindle) positioned forward horizontally (see Photo 2.1). (You'll need someone else to hold the plumb line.) Warm up first and make sure you are seated in your preferred location on the saddle.

Position the knee's center of rotation over the pedal axle by dropping a plumb bob from the front of the knee over the end of the crankarm.

Saddle Fore-Aft Position

Placement of the saddle has to do with the knee's fore-aft position as well as with where you want to bear weight on the saddle, which fits no formula. Variables in sitting position on the saddle include ischial tuberosity (sit bone) spacing and the rider's ability to rotate the pelvis. If riders have widely spaced ischial tuberosities, the saddle should be placed farther forward to get the wide part of it under them. If a rider is flexible and rotates the pelvis forward, this pushes the knee forward, so the saddle will be placed farther back to compensate.

The saddle is a tool for support only; it does not actually determine where the rider sits. Pruitt says, "The pelvis will find the place it needs to be to get the knee over the pedals. I have had women in the clinic with excruciating labial pain who thought I had performed a miracle when I readjusted their saddle. But all I did was push the saddle forward so that their weight was borne on their ischial tuberosities and not on their labia. It did not change where they sat relative to the cranks or handlebars; it just got the wide part of the saddle under them rather than just the narrow part."

The Knee's Center of Rotation

It is obviously difficult to quantify, but it is possible to sit farther forward or back and change where you apply pedal force on the crank circle. The knee's center of rotation will not be over the pedal's center of rotation as determined by gravity, but it will be "over" the pedal as determined by the direction of force.

Some great climbers, like Andy Hampsten and Greg LeMond, set up their bikes with their knee 2cm aft of the pedal spindle when using a plumb bob. However, both riders liked to push from behind and use their gluteus and hamstring muscles more. They rotated the position on the crank circle where they applied force farther back, but they were still directing the power straight from the center of rotation of the knee straight into the center of the pedal.

Similarly, when Chris Boardman, holder of the world hour record, raced with aerobars, he rotated his entire road position (which was set up with his knee slightly aft of the pedal) forward, around the crank center. Thus, his shoulders came forward and down as his butt came forward and up, to bring his back to a level, aerodynamic position. But he then applied power lower and farther back around the stroke than when riding his standard road bike. This sort of adjustment to body position and pedaling makes sense for time trialers and triathletes (see Blocks 5 and 6).

Saddle Tilt

Set the saddle so that it's level. Period. Use a carpenter's three-foot level (see Photo 2.2), or eyeball it using a windowsill for reference.

That said, not all saddles are created equal. If the saddle is flat on top, a level works fine. If the saddle is bowed in the middle, however, using a level would ensure that the front and

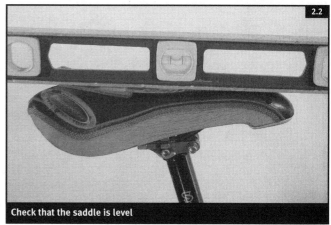

Check that the saddle is level

back are at the same height, but the whole thing may be V-shaped. In general, you want the nose section of the saddle to be level (again, eyeball it against a windowsill or something else that's horizontal).

If the saddle nose is tipped upward, the pelvis tends to roll back, which causes several problems. It creates more curvature and pain in the lower back, confines the diaphragm and hence constricts breathing, and increases pressure on the perineum. Compression of this area can cause pain and even long-term injury (in both men and women), and the rider has less bike control.

The opposite position is no better. If your seat is tipped down, it will throw you against the bars and put too much strain on your arms. If your saddle is tipped up or down for reasons of comfort, it indicates a problem with your bike position. Level it and go through the steps addressing positioning on the bike in Blocks 1 through 8 (and perhaps Blocks 9 through 13 as well), and see if your comfort improves. If you still feel the need to tilt the saddle, perhaps a different saddle is in order.

Recheck the Saddle Height

Whenever you shift your saddle fore or aft or change its tilt, double-check your saddle height (see Block 1). In general, for every centimeter the saddle goes back, its height (the distance from the saddle to the bottom bracket) increases by a half centimeter, and vice versa. And obviously, leveling a formerly downward-tipped saddle raises its front.

After you reset the saddle height, go back to the fore-aft setting to dial it in exactly.

Road versus Mountain Bikes

Saddle position should be the same for road and cross-country mountain bike riding (as opposed to downhill-only riding), but if you are measuring seat height from the bottom bracket and have a difference in crank length between the two bikes, add or subtract that difference. The two positions will also vary based on the thickness of the shoe's sole, the pedals used, cleat position, and frame angles. Due to mountain biking's emphasis on climbing and control when descending, the seat position should never be forward of neutral (front of knee over end of crank), but it could be a centimeter or two aft.

The work of Andy Pruitt and the Boulder Center for Sports Medicine that he directs can be viewed online at www.bch.org/sportsmedicine.

BLOCK 3

Handlebar Reach

Now that you have your saddle position dialed in, you can find your proper handlebar reach, but first make sure that your road bars are the same width as your shoulders.

I will present one formula for handlebar reach for you to use as a starting point, but do not take it to be the ultimate answer, as a formula cannot take into account your individual characteristics. As fit guru Andy Pruitt says, "Handlebar position is the most personal fit component." It is also the least exact, having to do with the number of years you've been riding, your hamstring and lumbar flexibility and strength, the degree of pelvic rotation you ride with, back and neck problems, torso length, and arm length.

Ugo De Rosa's Handlebar-Reach Formula

For over half a century, Ugo De Rosa has been custom building legendary De Rosa bicycles, many of them for top professional riders. In the early 1970s, De Rosa was the personal framebuilder for Eddy Merckx, who is renowned for being finicky about position.

De Rosa's method is based on the principle that, when you are holding road bars adjacent to the stem, the straightened arms and back form a 90-degree angle (see Photo 3.1). In this configuration, your torso and arms form two sides of a right triangle, and the length from the tail of the saddle to the center of the bar forms the hypotenuse. You can then use the Pythagorean theorem to find the proper distance from the saddle to the bar.

To get the torso measurement, mark a wall with a pencil held level, sticking out from the base of your sternal notch, the notch at the base of your throat (at the top of your rib cage, where your collarbones meet). Make sure you are standing up straight when you make the mark. Measure up the wall from the floor to the mark, and subtract the inseam measurement that you determined in Block 1. Better yet, use the same dowel and bubble level as you did in Block 1 (see Photo 3.2).

For the arm measurement, sit on the bike and grasp the top of the handlebar with your arms straight (Photo 3.1). Have a friend measure from the center of the bar to the front of the crease at the shoulder between your arm and your torso.

> **3.1**
>
> When holding the top of the bars, the torso and arms form a 90-degree angle, and the torso is just below 45 degrees from horizontal.
>
> SARAH ZINN

> **3.2**
>
> Measure from the sternal notch to the floor using a level dowel.
>
> SARAH ZINN

Now apply the Pythagorean theorem, where *a* is your arm length and *b* is your back (i.e., torso) length. Then:

$$a^2 + b^2 = c^2,$$

where *h* (hypotenuse) is the distance from tail of saddle to center of handlebar, and is thus equal to:

$$h = \sqrt{(a^2 + b^2)}.$$

"Two of the greatest riders I worked with, Merckx and Francesco Moser (also a world, Giro d'Italia, and Paris-Roubaix champion and world hour-record holder), were the same height, but Merckx has a 92cm inseam and Moser's is 87cm. I made Moser's bike smaller yet longer than Merckx's," says De Rosa, who used this method to figure out the bar to saddle distance for them.

Two Methods to Avoid

Two common methods for finding bar position are useless; I mention them here so you will shy away from them. One is to put your elbow against the forward tip of the saddle and have your middle fingertip reach the handlebar. This usually gives a reach measurement that is too short, and it depends on the forearm length, which has nothing to do with the length of other body segments or with flexibility. Furthermore, this method factors in the length of the saddle and where you prefer to bear weight on it, neither of which affect reach to the bar.

A better, but nonetheless poor, method is to look at the front hub while sitting on the bike holding the bars in the drops and position the bar so it obscures your view of the hub. This method factors in the height of the bar (which should be adjusted separately from reach), the front-end geometry of the bike, the arm bend you choose at the moment, and the tip of the head, none of which have to do with proper reach.

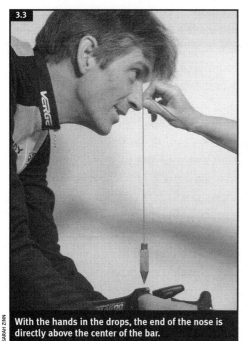

With the hands in the drops, the end of the nose is directly above the center of the bar.

On-Bike Methods

One reliable on-bike method is to look at the rider's back to see that it is 45 degrees above horizontal (or slightly less for faster riding in groups, and slightly more for climbing—see Block 25) when the rider is holding the bars on top with a bit of elbow flexion. Another technique is to first position the rider on the bike with hands in the drops, elbows comfortably bent (15 degrees), and the rider looking ahead. Then drop a plump bob from the end of the rider's nose. Look for the plumb bob to drop over the center of the handlebar (see Photo 3.3) or 2cm at most behind it (and never ahead of it).

Greg LeMond recommends positioning the bar so that the knee is horizontally 1 to 2 inches behind the elbow at the closest pass when riding in the drops with the arms deeply bent at 65 degrees to 70 degrees. It is hard to estimate this angle, but the following technique yields the same result: If the gap is 2 inches from LeMond's method, when the forearm is horizontal the knee will barely touch the back of the upper arm at its closest pass (see Photo 3.4). (Of course, you have to push your elbows inward when doing this experiment to line them up with the knees). This reach is longer than most people will initially tolerate, but after they have been riding long miles for many years, most will find it comfortable.

Listen to your body. Former U.S. National Team Coach Eddie Borysewicz writes, "If you develop soreness in your trapezius muscle (upper back), the stem is too short; when your deltoids and triceps (front of shoulder and back of arm) hurt, it is too long."

Other Reach Factors

Reach also depends on your degree of pelvic rotation. Many riders have reduced pedaling efficiency, collapsed breathing space, and lower-back pain because they sit on their saddle as if they were sitting in a chair and then bend forward at the waist. Instead, if you slide back on the saddle and rotate your pelvis forward and down so you roll forward on the front part of your crotch, you can pedal and breathe more effectively, and your

When the arms are horizontal with the hands in the drops, the knees graze the triceps muscle.

back will have less of the reverse curvature that is so detrimental to it (see Block 20 on back pain). You will need to position the bar farther away, since you will be extending your torso farther forward. Your choice of saddle will be critical for comfort.

Reach also depends on what kind of riding you are doing. How aggressive you can get with your riding position depends on the duration spent in that position. Whether you are racing criteriums or doing long-distance touring will make a big difference in the position that you can tolerate and that is most efficient for your riding.

Also be aware that road bars come with different amounts of forward extension, so you do not have to set reach with stem length alone.

Bar Reach on Mountain Bikes

If you are using bar ends on your mountain bike, I recommend using the same reach from the saddle to the handlebar as you do on your road bike. Then your bar ends will give you a similar reach to when you grab the tops of your road brake hoods. If you are not using bar ends, you may want to move the bar a bit farther forward.

Changing Reach

Because you have already set your seat position, change the reach by changing stems. Now that most stems come with a removable front faceplate, it is much easier to change stems than it was prior to 1995 or so, when you had to remove the handlebar tape or grips and levers. The range of lengths and angles available has also increased.

The stem choice will be dictated by the change in length and height (discussed in the following pages) that you want. On my Web site, www.zinncycles.com, I have a stem calculator page designed by Alan Hills (at www.zinncycles.com/stemFit.aspx) that you can refer to. You input your frame's head angle and the dimensions of your current stem to find its current rise and reach. To these numbers, add or subtract how much longer or shorter and higher or lower you want your bar to be. Then plug in dimensions of other stems and spacers to see which one brings you closest to your desired position.

You switch the stem by first removing the handlebar and the headset top cap and loosening the bolts clamping the stem to the steering tube. Then, assuming you've got a threadless headset, slide the stem up and off of the steering tube. You will have to readjust the headset when you replace the stem; to see how, consult Chapter 11 of either *Zinn and the Art of Road Bike Maintenance* (VeloPress, 2000) or *Zinn and the Art of Mountain Bike Maintenance* (VeloPress, 2001). On a new bike or fork, it behooves you to leave the steering tube long and use lots of spacers until you dial in your position, at which point you can cut it to length. 🚲

The peerless craftsmanship of Ugo De Rosa and his family can be viewed online at www.derosanews.com.

The work of Andy Pruitt and the Boulder Center for Sports Medicine that he directs can be viewed online at www.bch.org/sportsmedicine.

BLOCK 4
Handlebar Height and Tilt

Handlebar Height

Criterium racers will always want their bars lower than tourists do. But in general, someone who includes hill climbing in a regimen of frequent bike riding and who has no significant back problems will like 3cm to 8cm of drop from the top of the saddle to the top of the handlebar. This wide range accommodates various body sizes as well as diversity in flexibility and pelvic rotation.

According to Neal Henderson, coordinator of sport science at the Boulder Center for Sports Medicine, "When the angle between the thigh and the torso is less than 30 degrees, a rider will often have impairment in breathing and the glute and hip flexor muscles will be outside of their optimal force-producing ranges." It is also inevitable that a rider will prefer a higher bar as he or she ages; our bodies simply are more sensitive to a lower bar than when we are racing at age 20. Also, as I mention in Block 25, climbing is often improved with a higher handlebar.

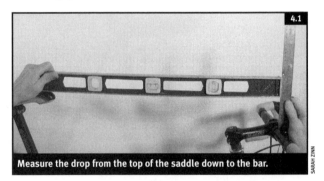

Measure the drop from the top of the saddle down to the bar.

Choose your setting

Measure the drop from saddle to bar by placing a long straightedge with a level on it on the saddle (see Photo 4.1). Extend the straightedge forward horizontally and measure down from its underside to the top of the bar. Andy Pruitt, director of the Boulder Center for Sports Medicine and the premier U.S. expert on bike fit, recommends a ballpark height difference equal to the width of your clenched fist.

Riders outside of the bell curve of average height, body proportions, or flexibility require special measurements. For instance, people shorter than 5'3" will perhaps want a 0cm to 3cm drop. This modification has to do not only with their height but even more with the fact that standard-length crankarms are relatively long in proportion to their legs. Whereas an average crankarm length might be about 21 percent of inseam length, the 165mm or 170mm cranks of a person with a 65cm inseam will be more than 25 percent of his or her leg length. This means that, relative to the "average size" rider, the shorter rider's knees will come up higher and constrict to a greater degree the angle between the torso and the thigh at the top of the stroke. So if your thighs hit your chest, raise your bar. (See Block 9 on selecting crank length.)

The converse is true with tall riders, as 175mm or 180mm cranks are only 17.5 percent to 18 percent of the length of the legs of someone with a 100cm inseam. The knee will be bent less sharply at the top of the stroke, and the angle between the torso and thigh will be wider. For example, I am 6'6" tall and flexible, thanks to stretching and thousands of miles of riding a year over several decades. Given these factors, I prefer greater seat-to-bar drop than most riders. In general, people taller than 6'4" prefer a drop range of 6cm to 10cm, depending on crank length (my own personal road bikes have crank lengths ranging from 180mm to 203mm, and I prefer a lower bar on the bike with the shorter cranks).

The role of body proportions and flexibility cannot be underestimated either. The backs of Tour de France champions like Greg LeMond and Bernard Hinault were closer to horizontal than that of Lance Armstrong, but LeMond and Hinault have longer thighs relative to their lower legs than Armstrong does. A long thigh means a short lower leg, so their knees come up lower. Furthermore, Armstrong has a congenital back condition that requires his position to be more upright.

If a rider tips his pelvis forward, he compresses the iliac arteries (the main source of oxygenated blood to the legs) less than someone whose lower back is rolled back. Thus, a lower, longer position is not only possible but also more efficient for the more flexible person.

The bottom line is to fine-tune the bar height and listen to your body's feedback, not to your buddies who think your bars should be positioned like the world road champion's.

Raise or lower the bar

If you have an old bike with a quill stem and threaded headset, loosen the vertical bolt, smack it with a hammer to free the wedge, slide the stem up or down, and retighten the bolt.

Raising or lowering a stem for a threadless headset requires removing the stem from the fork steering tube and adding or removing spacers below it (note the spacer stack below

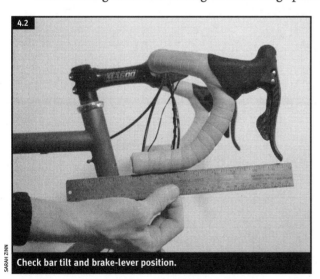

4.2

Check bar tilt and brake-lever position.

SARAH ZINN

the stem and the single spacer above it in Photo 4.2). The other way to raise or lower a stem is to change its angle, either by flipping it over (provided it is not a "zero-degree" stem, that is, 90 degrees from the steering tube) or by replacing it. As mentioned in the previous block, you can consult the Stem Size Tool on my Web site, www.zinncycles.com, to assist in choosing the dimensions of a different stem to get you where you want to be.

You will have to readjust the headset when you install a stem. For instructions, consult Chapter 11 of either of my books *Zinn and the Art of Road Bike Maintenance* (VeloPress, 2000) or *Zinn and the Art of Mountain Bike Maintenance* (VeloPress, 2001).

Mountain bikes

The above discussion applies equally to mountain bikes (for cross-country riding) and to road bikes. The bar drop and reach yield good control and prevent the weight from being shifted so far back on a steep climb that the front wheel becomes unweighted and you cannot steer properly.

For technical descents, the bars can come upward a bit to move your weight farther back. Given mountain biking's emphasis on climbing, a longer stem can then counteract the higher position and help keep the front wheel down when going up. To eliminate maneuvering problems, make sure that the elbows and knees don't overlap.

Bar tilt is obviously irrelevant to a straight mountain-bike bar, but it does apply to bar ends. A bar end angled at 15 degrees allows you to stretch out as well as to pull up when standing, analogous to holding onto the tops of the brake levers on a road bike.

Handlebar Tilt

Threadless headsets eliminate the ease of raising and lowering the handlebars that a quill stem provides, and they start the stem out lower than even a fully inserted quill stem. Furthermore, the trend toward small frames for reasons of low weight and stiffness, and integrated headsets for style, have decreased the height of the top of the stem, unless a rider inserts a stack of spacers under it or flips it over so it angles upward. These last two options are anathema to many roadies who are attached to the bike looking a certain way.

Until recently, the style was to position the handlebar hooks level with the ground. But the trend is now to angle the bars up (with hooks pointing toward the rear brake or lower) and to mount the brake levers higher on the curve of the bar. This helps counteract the longer seat-to-bar drop on the new bike designs. Photo 4.2 shows the bar slightly tilted up, and the brake levers slightly higher than the old standard of meeting the straightedge along the bar hook. 🚲

BLOCK 5

Bike Setup for Aerodynamic Time Trialing

For riding time trials on flat or rolling terrain and for many triathlon events, aerodynamic efficiency can be a bicyclist's overriding concern. Certainly, you need to be able to generate power effectively on the bike, but the major force you must overcome is the drag of the air through which you are passing.

So how do you and your bike become more aerodynamic? The primary way is by positioning your body properly, since the aerodynamic drag from the bike itself accounts for less than a quarter of the total drag force opposing you and the bike together. And because there is not much you can do to change the shape of your body (other than perhaps wear an aero helmet and suit, which is covered in Block 38), you reduce its drag primarily by riding in a lower, narrower position.

Narrow Arms

By narrow arms, I mean bringing the arms closer together, as in a downhill ski racer's tuck, by adjusting the elbow pads inward on aerodynamic handlebars (see Photo 5.1). This reduces the frontal area of your body and directs more of the wind around it.

5.1

1997 Tour de France and 2000 Olympic champion Jan Ullrich in the March 2004 Tour of Murcia time trial: He is using a standard helmet due to a rule change outlawing nonprotective aerodynamic head fairings that went into effect January 1, 2004; no aero helmets had passed the safety standard as of this spring race.

GRAHAM WATSON

There are obvious reasons why bicycles have traditionally positioned the rider's arms out at shoulder width or wider—the main one is that it's easier to control the bike and support the body that way. So, you should understand that you lose a measure of control the farther inward you bring the elbows. Consequently, move the elbow pads inward gradually rather than all at once. Get comfortable with the control you have at each setting before making the next adjustment. If you have a power meter (see Block 18), check that you can produce as much power at each arm position as you do in your normal road position before going still narrower. Be patient. This may take several weeks or even months, but the gains in speed will be noticeable and perhaps even dramatic.

How far inward a rider should ultimately bring the elbows is a matter of debate. Ideally, you want them positioned as narrow as your knees (which should also be narrow; read on). Clearly if you can bring your elbows in until your forearms touch, you will have closed (as much as you can) the hole that lets air in under your chest. On the other hand, if by doing so the air that comes around them still gets scooped in between the knees, you have gone too far, and you have made it harder to breathe and steer to boot! This is certainly a matter of body shape and pedaling style, and you will not be able to answer the question completely without being tested in a wind tunnel. However, if you set yourself up on your bike in front of a large mirror, you can see yourself as the wind "sees" you and you may find ways to improve your position.

Wind tunnel tests have shown that bringing the arms inward makes more aerodynamic difference than lowering the handlebars to drop the shoulders. However, new research by Lance Armstrong's former aerodynamics guru, John Cobb, suggests that you might ride faster with wider elbows. See Cobb's suggestions in Block 6 on triathlon positioning.

Narrow Knees

You do not want to narrow the distance between your knees at the expense of pedaling efficiency or to the point where you experience knee pain; however, the farther inward your knees are positioned when you pedal, the more aerodynamic you will be. The legs are large objects, and pedaling with them positioned outward scoops a lot of air and slows you down. Bringing in the knees makes at least as much difference as bringing in the arms. This is certainly something to do consciously, but you may find that your consciousness alone will not do the trick. Again, this is great to do on a trainer facing a large mirror as well as looking down at your legs while riding on the road.

If you find that one knee swings out with each pedal stroke, you should consider corrective methods (see Block 11). If you pedal with both knees out and are not naturally bowlegged, it may be that your body position (see Blocks 1 through 4) or your foot position on the pedal (see Blocks 7 and 8) could be corrected.

If your knees swing outward to avoid hitting your chest, there are three ways to correct it. You can reduce your crank length (see Block 9); this may be great for short riders and a poor idea for tall riders because of lost leverage. You can raise your handlebar to get your chest higher and out of the way, but at some aerodynamic cost. Or, you can move your seat forward, and, to maintain the same distance to the pedals, it will need to come up as well— about half the distance you moved it forward.

This third option, which will move your chest up and forward relative to your knees, is usually the preferred one. And, like raising your handlebars, it will open the angle between the thigh and the lower back, which may yield comfort and blood-flow advantages as well. Assuming your upper body is already at optimum reach, if you move your seat forward, move your handlebar forward as well. "We go up 2cm and forward 2cm with the seat when switching from a road position to using aerobars," says Andy Pruitt, director of the Boulder Center for Sports Medicine. If you are competing in events sanctioned by either the UCI or USA Cycling, remember that their rules dictate that the tip of a rider's saddle must be set back horizontally a minimum of 5cm behind the center of the bottom bracket.

Low Shoulders and Flat Back

Lowering your shoulders to the height of your lower back is as low as you can go and lower than you want to go. But moving in that direction reduces frontal drag. Work down gradually without compromising power output, comfort, and control, and being sensitive to hamstring flexibility and lower-back pain (stretching, Block 22, will help).

During my stint on the U.S. National Team, Coach Eddie Borysewicz used to tell me, "Flat back, not cat back!" Indeed, you want to flatten your back as much as possible because you will be able to breathe and pedal more effectively. If you are hunched over, you'll partially collapse your chest and your lungs will have less room to breathe. While Jan Ullrich in Photo 5.1 has his back arched, notice that his chest and diaphragm area are open to facilitate breathing. Some riders, but not many, will have a flatter back than this when their elbows are this much lower than their saddle.

Reducing the arch in your back requires rotating your pelvis forward. You can do this consciously (bring your belly button closer to the top tube, like Ullrich in Photo 5.1), and moving the seat forward as described above will also do the trick. Understand that it will put more pressure farther forward on the saddle, under the perineum. The saddle should be level (even though tipping it down might reduce this pressure) so you do not slide forward and throw more weight onto your arms, but saddle choice may be critical for you to feel comfortable with a forward-tipped pelvis. While it seems like a poor idea for symmetrical pelvic movement, Cobb recommends that riders with crotch discomfort rotate the tip of the saddle 1/8 inch to one side or the other to move the pressure off of the center of the perineum. "It's better a little asymmetry than agonizing crotch pain," he says. If you do this, try to choose the direction your body favors; some riders find that their saddle turns a bit to one side in normal usage anyway.

A flat back requires that you have enough reach from the seat to the handlebar to stretch out properly. A plumb line dropped from the front of the shoulder should come out at the back of the elbow (Photo 5.1). In that position, you won't be reaching too far, will support your weight well, and should have enough extension.

Low Chin

The last thing for aerodynamic efficiency is to drop your chin. You want to be comfortable looking ahead down the road with your chin low, to block air flowing under your chest and to keep the head from sticking up high and increasing frontal area. You do not want to be bobbing your head or otherwise squirming around, as this is aerodynamically inefficient. Keeping your head down will block air from filling under your chest, but you won't be able to see ahead—not a wise trade-off. Also, modern aero helmets smooth the air over the head when your eyes are forward, and putting your head down sticks the tail up in the wind. So keep your eyes forward and your chin low for the best combination of aerodynamics and safety. You may find that a change in eyewear is necessary so that the top rim of your glasses does not obscure your vision. ⚙️🚲

John Cobb was Lance Armstrong's aerodynamics adviser throughout his first five Tour de France victories and is manager of Bicycle Sports cycling and triathlon stores (www.bicyclesports.com).

BLOCK 6
Bike Setup for Triathlons

Your ideal bike setup will depend on the kind of events that you are riding and training for. If you are doing draft-legal, International Triathlon Union (ITU)–sanctioned, Olympic-style racing, your bike setup will differ from one you would use for most triathlons, in which drafting is illegal. Since the former type of racing is available only to professional triathletes in ITU World Cups, points races or the Olympics (also, to some elite juniors in ITU feeder-type programs), the draft-prohibited racing is where the concerns of the vast majority of triathletes will lie. And within that group of events, bike-leg distances vary greatly, which also affects bike positioning.

Draft-Legal Racing

Although only a very small subset of all triathletes participates in draft-legal racing, positioning in that type of race is the simplest to describe. Draft-legal race poisitioning is similar to what we have already discussed in this book since the demands are similar to normal road racing. Moreover, the ITU's rules are quite restrictive, making a standard road bike with standard positioning your best bet for a draft-legal triathlon.

One critical ITU rule reads: "The front-most point of the saddle will be no more than 5 centimeters in front of and no more than 15 centimeters behind a vertical line passing through the center of the chain wheel axle, and a competitor must not have the capability of adjusting the saddle beyond these lines during the competition." This rule effectively eliminates the forward positioning otherwise so prevalent in triathlon. Furthermore, drafting largely eliminates the advantage of an aerobar, and safely drafting, braking, shifting, and steering all while in a pace line is best done with a drop bar, which is all the ITU allows. ITU does permit a clip-on in draft-legal races, but it must be very short, because the rules mandate that the end of the aerobars shall not extend beyond the brake levers (and no more than 15cm beyond the front wheel axle).

If you follow the positioning instructions in the first four blocks in this book, you will be well set up for draft-legal racing. In the event that you get out in front or off the back of the group, you will definitely want an aerobar. The best bar choices as of this writing that fall within the ITU guidelines are the Profile Jammer GT, Syntace XXS, and Oval A700 Slam clip-on bars. Short clip-ons banned by the UCI from road racing, such as the Cinelli Spinaci and its clones, also work but only if you add elbow pads, because you can't get power pulling against the clip-ons without elbow pads.

Draft-Prohibited Racing
Elbow pads and hands

According to John Cobb, aerodynamics guru and longtime triathlon consultant, to get the most power, you want the elbows almost shoulder-width apart, the pads halfway between your wrists and your elbows, and your forearms approximately level (see Photo 6.1). The conventional wisdom for over a decade has been to place the elbows as narrow as possible to reduce aerodynamic drag. Cobb, as much as anyone, developed this conventional wisdom with his work in the Texas A&M University wind tunnel. Now, however, he is straying from it.

In his wind tunnel work with riders including Lance Armstrong and his U.S. Postal Service Team, Cobb looked not only at straight-on aerodynamic drag but also at drag produced when the wind comes at the rider from side angles. Additionally, he has simultaneously measured how much power riders are generating while measuring their wind drag in various positions. In studying power data as well as drag data, he found that elbows positioned wider increase power and oxygen uptake because in narrow positions the lateralis (lat) muscles alongside the chest overpower the diaphragm and reduce breathing space.

6.1

An efficient bike setup for draft-prohibited triathlons that allows room to breathe while positioning the legs and the upper body for high power output and low aerodynamic drag

GRAHAM WATSON

Furthermore, he claims that wider elbows result in an aerodynamic cost in a straight-on headwind of only less than 0.1 pound of drag at 30 miles per hour. And in side winds, there is no difference.

Cobb's argument for moving the elbow pads away from the elbow and closer to the wrist has to do with power increases he has measured when doing so. To illustrate, he suggests placing your left elbow and forearm lying on a desk or flat surface. With your right hand, hold the left hand down on the desk as you try to lever your left up off the desk. Notice what your left upper arm and shoulder muscles are doing. Now slide the left elbow back off the desk so the desk edge is closer to the wrist than to the elbow, and push up against the right hand. See how much more your left shoulder is engaged and how much more power you can get from it. "You will be instantly aware of a speed increase with the elbow pads up there," says Cobb.

As for hand height, Cobb suggests making a fist and having the top of the thumb joint level with the bend in the elbow, at the base of the biceps muscle (Photo 6.1). He cites perennial Tour de France runner-up Jan Ullrich, who time trials with his forearms tilted down (Photo 5.1), as an example one should *not* follow since he feels Ullrich loses power that way. However, Cobb's comments notwithstanding, Armstrong also adopted the tilted-down forearm position for the 2004 season.

Cobb claims that a rider generating 225 watts (which he says equates to about five hours for an ironman-distance bike leg for a 150-pound triathlete) can pick up an enormous 10 percent increase in power with the pads positioned forward and wider. "I guarantee you he will," he says. "We've done a bunch of testing with this. Lance may not pick up that much, but just 3 to 4 watts is a big deal to him." The five-time Tour de France winner and multiple-time wind tunnel visitor moved his elbow pads forward, midway between his elbow and wrist, as per Cobb's recommendation. "He won't move his elbow pads out any wider, though," muses Cobb. "He doesn't believe me on that one."

Short-course positioning

A position that works for time trialing (see Block 5) generally works for short-course triathlons as well. Because of the need to jump off the bike and run, a position even farther forward can be beneficial, and UCI rules on time trial positions do not stand in the way. The steep seat-tube angles of 78 degrees or so found on many triathlon bikes will generally work fine. The forward position allows you to have your back closer to level without restricting movement because it offers a wider angle at the hip between the thigh and torso and avoids having the knees hit the chest. This is particularly important for triathletes with relatively short femurs (thighbones), as their knees consequently come up higher. Start in a position in which, when the crankarm is horizontally forward, a plumb bob dropped from the front of the kneecap comes out about 2cm forward of the end of the crankarm. The height of the seat as determined in Block 1 (see Photo 6.1) and a level saddle should work well.

As for positioning the bar, the front of the shoulder should be over the back of the elbow when in the aero position (as in Photo 6.1). This is the same recommendation as for time trialing (see Block 5). For improved aerodynamics in short-course events, you should be able to tolerate a lower handlebar and elbow pads than you could during an ironman race or a long training ride.

If you find that your hip angle is still too compressed to drop your upper body down and out of the wind, you can move the saddle forward and upward; make corresponding adjustments to the bar height and reach, though.

Cobb has had great success in positioning his clients by duplicating the angles of their joints while running with those used while they're cycling. He does this by videotaping them as they run on a treadmill, analyzing individual frames of the video, and duplicating those joint angles when they're on the bike. Elite runners run with far more knee bend than average runners; they use hip rotation to get longer strides, and more knee bend keeps them from bouncing up and down; this dictates a relatively low and far-back positioned saddle to optimize efficiency. The average triathlete, however, has slower foot speed and less knee bend, and the high, forward position on the bike comes closest to matching those angles and will improve pedaling power as well as ease the transition from cycling to running.

The "Slam" Position

Noticing the deep knee angles of elite runners led Cobb to a revolutionary new concept in triathlon positioning. In his Slam Position, the rider is much farther back and lower than in conventional triathlon positioning, and Cobb claims that it has dramatically reduced the bike times of many elite triathletes.

Slam positioned, the saddle nose of a 5'9" athlete would end up 8.5cm to 9cm behind the bottom bracket center, and the knee can easily end up 5cm behind the pedal spindle when the crank is horizontally forward. A shorter clip-on aerobar, such as the Cobb-designed Oval Slam or the Profile Jammer GT, is required to work with this position, because the saddle is so far back. Cobb has found that the Slam Position is aerodynamically equal to or slightly better than a forward position.

According to Cobb, the tilt of the seat is important in the Slam Position; "you have to jack the nose of the seat up high; it requires a big leap of faith," he says. He suggests raising the nose 1/4- to 1/2-inch higher than the back of the saddle and then rotating the nose 1/8 inch to whichever side feels more natural, in order to move saddle pressure off the center of the perineum. He adds that, "if you have problems with hand numbness, you can move 15 to 20 pounds off of your hands right away by doing this."

Cobb states that the Slam Position is particularly good for athletes with long femurs, crotch pain, hand problems, or chronic hamstring soreness. He believes that the Slam Position also works for road racing by taking pressure off the hamstrings and thus easing spinning at high revolutions per minute. And deeper knee bends have always been associated with higher power outputs (see Block 1); the downside is more stress on the knees. "Lance Armstrong is lower than he used to be," Cobb adds. He claims that the average race speeds of triathletes using his new seat position and elbow pad position are up one mile per hour!

Ironman-Distance and Longer Events

Whether you are using a forward position or one that's farther back, you should raise the aerobars slightly when adjusting the bike for a long event such as an Ironman. That change opens the diaphragm and reduces tension on the hamstrings, strain on the lower back, and pressure on the nose of the saddle. Greater comfort adds up to greater speed when you are out on the bike for so many hours. That said, not everybody does it, particularly elite competitors. Two-time Ironman® World Champion Tim DeBoom says, "I don't really change my bike setup [for the Ironman]. I set it at the beginning of the year and it sticks."

John Cobb was Lance Armstrong's aerodynamics adviser throughout his first five Tour de France victories and is manager of Bicycle Sports cycling and triathlon stores (www.bicyclesports.com).

BLOCK 7
Setting Up Clip-in Pedals and Shoes

It is critical for comfort and efficiency that you transmit your physical efforts directly onto your pedals. If one or both of your feet roll to one side or the other, if their placement on the pedals forces the knees to twist or move laterally, or if your feet hurt when you ride, you will pedal ineffectively and develop injuries. You may address these issues by changing the position of your cleats (road and mountain bike cleats are shown in Photo 7.1) and/or with wedge-shimming the cleats; however, sometimes these measures are insufficient. If pain or other problems persist after you've followed the instructions below, proceed to Block 8, which addresses how to customize your shoes.

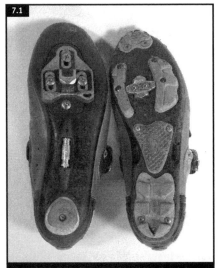
7.1

Road bike cleat (Campagnolo cleat shown here, at left) on a road cycling shoe, and mountain bike cleat (right) on a mountain bike shoe: The cleats can be moved fore-aft, side-to-side, and rotationally when the screws are loosened.

The Initial Fore-Aft Cleat Position

In the neutral fore-aft foot position, when the foot is level the ball of the foot is over the pedal axle. However, "this [neutral starting point] only works for European shoe sizes 40 or 42 [U.S. sizes 8 or 9]," according to bike fit guru Andy Pruitt. He explains, "A cycling shoe becomes an orthotic [that is, a corrective device] by taking a flexible foot and making it into a rigid lever," which makes cycling more efficient. If the shoe size is larger than 42, the lever is too long (and often too flexible) with the ball of the foot over the pedal. Greater efficiency is achieved by shortening the lever by sliding the cleat back so that the pedal axle is behind the ball of the foot (Photo 1.1).

The opposite is true if the shoe size is less than 40; increase the lever length by pushing the cleat forward of the ball of the foot.

It is not always a simple matter to put the cleat exactly where you want it, since the cleat-mounting holes might not be in the right place. That's because shoe companies do not sell as many pairs of large or small shoes as they do mid-size ones. To cut costs, the manufacturers make a sole mold for each mid-size sole; but small and large shoes are often built onto a sole designed for the next size up, and those soles have the extra length and width trimmed off. In other words, the cleat-hole drill pattern for your shoe may be dictated by cleat placement for another size shoe, and it may be hard to position the cleat where you want.

Rotational Position of the Cleats

Your foot should sit on the pedal the way it wants to, not how somebody else's feet are angled. Do you walk duck-footed, straight, or pigeon-toed? Expect your shoe to rotate similarly when pedaling.

To find the neutral position for your pedal cleat, sit on a table with your feet hanging down and the edge of the table against the backs of your knees. Your knees should be shoulder-width apart, making your feet about pedaling-width apart. Sit up straight with 90-degree angles at the hip, knee, and ankle. The way your feet line up when hanging off the table is probably how they will naturally line up on the pedal.

Now lean forward at the waist; your feet may rotate inward or outward, and perhaps even swing inward toward each other. Your feet will rotate in a similar way if you straighten your legs. This is why you want to have a floating pedal! Your feet should be free to twist back and forth as you pedal. The foot twists because the two condyles (the rounded, bony cartilage-covered protuberances) on the end of the femur are not the same length, so the knee hinge twists as it bends. Furthermore, as the hip joint closes, the femur may also rotate inward due to the forward position of the hip joint in the pelvis.

You want to have at least 3 to 6 degrees of float from your neutral foot angle to accommodate foot rotation during the pedal cycle. Pruitt recommends that there also be an endpoint to the float (a rise in resistance before the release point), so that your muscles are not trying to control the float. He prefers 10 degrees of float at most. Mount the cleats so that you have as much float to the inside before hitting the release point as you have to the outside from your foot's natural pedaling position.

Foot Tip on the Pedal

The tip of the foot to the inside or outside is an important issue for cyclists. Studies have shown that 85 to 92 percent of humans have forefoot varus, also known as supination. That is, in the foot's neutral position, the big toe rises higher than the little toe, because that configuration is part of a normal walking gait. If your knee swings inward as you push the pedal, that indicates forefoot varus, since pushing down forces the foot to go from tipped up at the inside edge to flat on the pedal, and the knee goes inward with it. Conversely, forefoot valgus is the opposite condition, also called pronation, in which the little toe is higher than the big toe.

If you know the correction you need, you can tip the cleat inward or outward with varus or valgus wedges so your knees go up and down like pistons rather than waving around. Plastic cleat wedges are available at bike shops or via the Web. They look similar to the cleat shims in Photo 11.1, but they are thicker on one edge. To correct for forefoot varus, wedge up the cleat on the medial (inboard) side. Some shoes, like Specialized Body Geometry models, have this correction built into the sole. People with forefoot valgus are in the minority but need a wedge on the lateral (outboard) side of the shoe.

Relative Cleat Height

Shimming up one cleat can partially alleviate differences in leg length. See Block 11 for more information.

Stance Width

The width of a rider's stance (which is also known as the Q-Factor in cycling vernacular) can be reduced by moving the cleats laterally on the shoe, or by interchanging cranksets or at least bottom brackets. If the shoes are set for a certain stance width and you make it wider, then you force a rotation in the knee and hip joints. For instance, in the 2003 Tour de France, Lance Armstrong developed painful tendinitis in his hip due to unknowingly changing his stance width on a new bike. Fortunately, Pruitt diagnosed it on TV and called Armstrong's coach, Chris Carmichael, and asked, "Why is Lance pedaling pigeon-toed?" After his feet were moved inboard, Armstrong held on for his fifth straight Tour title.

Women often need a narrower stance due to rotation and angulation in the bones of the upper and lower leg, but limitations in bike frame, crank, bottom bracket, pedal, and derailleur design typically do not allow it.

Some people require a wider stance. Riders with total hip replacements, for instance, have reduced range of motion, and a wider stance helps them. If they cannot internally rotate their hips, then there is no way to pedal straight. To create a wider stance, you can move the cleats inboard, insert washers on the pedal axle threads, or use a wider bottom bracket.

If the legs could be brought inward very close to each other, the rider's aerodynamics would improve, but most riders cannot pedal this way. Pruitt, who has been working with the U.S. National Team for decades, notes that after the team's breakthrough in the 1984 Olympics in Los Angeles, it selected riders for the team pursuit (in this event on the track, two four-man squads start on opposite sides of the track and chase each other) who were more aerodynamic than other riders because they could bring their feet farther inward. If two riders tested similarly for power output and VO_2 max, the more flat-footed, knock-kneed, and pigeon-toed rider was selected for the team pursuit squad. The team pursuit bikes were built with very narrow bottom bracket shells and short bottom bracket spindles, and only riders with this body structure could tolerate pedaling with the narrow stance width. ⊘

The work of Andy Pruitt and the Boulder Center for Sports Medicine that he directs can be viewed online at www.bch.org/sportsmedicine.

BLOCK 8
Orthotics

Just as they support you when you are standing, your feet are the basis of all of your cycling efforts. They must be supported, cradled, and angled properly to apply the repeated forces required. If you ride a lot and have any pains from your lower back down that persist after following all of the previous blocks' bike and cleat setup instructions, it is critical to address how your cycling shoes support your feet.

It seems to me that some of the now-common foot, knee, and hip problems were rare in the 1970s and early 1980s, when we were all racing on quill pedals with toe clips and leather-soled shoes, once riders got their cleat rotational angles adjusted correctly. In my case at least, the foot and knee issues I have been dealing with since the advent of clip-in (also known as clipless) pedals and rigid shoe soles never appeared with the old system.

To avoid problems with my iliotibial (IT) band—the large tendon running on the outside of the leg from the hip to the top of the calf—my foot needs to be tipped inward slightly, or the tendon gets pulled too tightly and hurts like mad where it rubs the side of my knee. With the old system, my foot was free to roll inward or outward when using toe clips with slotted cleats, and the metatarsal—the joint at the base of each toe—of my big toe always deformed my shoe down into the center of the quill pedals to accommodate the way my foot rolled inward. Clip-in pedals, on the other hand, clamp the shoe sole flat on the pedal, preventing the foot from rolling to either side. These pedals offer greater convenience and efficiency, but increase the importance of proper foot placement and support.

Like most people, I prefer today's pedals and more rigid shoes with improved closures to toe-clip systems. However, I have to either customize my shoes or use shoes custom-built for me to ride without pain. I have had success in eliminating my IT band troubles by wedging my cleat on the outboard (lateral) side. Now I instead use custom orthotics (also known as custom foot beds) that cant (tip) my feet inside the shoes and also support the metatarsal arch to eliminate my neuroma pain, which is a sharp, "hard handshake" pain between the metatarsals caused by them rubbing together. Photo 8.1 shows these orthotics, both of which have a pronounced arch, a metatarsal-arch pad, and a dropped area under the first metatarsal and big toe. I also have custom shoes that have soles molded to my feet, but the orthotics allow me to use any shoe and pedal system by simply moving my custom foot beds from shoe to shoe, without having to do further customization. With any shoe, though, I still have to watch out for cleat wear (see more information on this below).

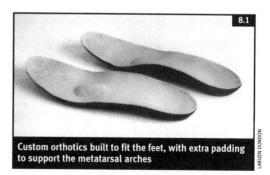

8.1

Custom orthotics built to fit the feet, with extra padding to support the metatarsal arches

LARIEN DUNDON

Custom Orthotics

Custom orthotics (Photo 8.1) can address pain in the feet as well as in the knee and hip. Russel Bollig (see Photo 8.2), owner of Podium Footwear in Boulder, Colorado, has built custom orthotics for many cycling stars, including Lance Armstrong and Tyler Hamilton, as well as for top athletes in other sports. "People usually come to me because they have pain," Bollig says. "Foot injuries, like ball of the foot pain (metatarsal pain), constitute the majority of cases. The second most-common complaint I see is the foot collapsing on the medial arch, rolling inward (pronating) and causing knee pain. In about half of the cases, this results in medial (that is, inboard) knee pain (associated with the knee coming in toward the top tube from the foot rolling in), but we also see it all over the knee and in the back, depending on what the leg is doing."

Pedorthist Russel Bollig looking at the footprint of a cyclist on a glass plate in an illuminated mirror below

Orthotics will help improve biomechanics, just as a good bike fit will. If there is less unwanted motion in the foot and ankle, then there is less unwanted motion in the knee.

If a rider has difference in leg length of less than 3mm, a lift can be built into the orthotic rather than between the cleat and the shoe. Leg-length discrepancy can be indicated by hip pain and should be diagnosed by a medical professional (see Block 11).

The problem of numb feet can also be relieved by custom orthotics, but not just any orthotic in a cycling shoe will do. It should be made specifically for cycling; don't try to stuff a running-shoe orthotic in a cycling shoe. The benefits of a cycling-specific orthotic include narrowness and low volume. These elements are especially important in the heel (in cases where a heel "post"—or angular support—is not needed), so that the heel can sit at the bottom of the shoe without lifting out. The best person to see for a cycling orthotic is someone who has experience making them and who understands cycling biomechanics; it could be a pedorthist (also known as an orthotic maker), podiatrist, chiropractor, or physical therapist.

How orthotics are made

A pedorthist needs a cast of the foot in order to build an orthotic. "I prefer to cast people's feet myself, but half of my business I receive through the mail, usually from health-care professionals," says Bollig.

One way to determine the orthotic's shape is to have the cyclist stand on a heated moldable plastic piece or isolation foam placed on a soft casting pillow. The plastic or foam solidifies to the shape of the foot. Another option is to use a foot impression box with dry foam inside into which the feet press and leave an imprint, like a footprint in sand. Some pedorthists have the cyclist wear a fiberglass resin-impregnated sock that encases the foot until the resin solidifies. With the latter two methods, the pedorthist pours plaster into the foot impression or cast to make a positive of the foot. Then he or she vacuum-forms hard plastic onto the plaster form to create the orthodic.

If you stand during casting, it is called a neutral or semiweight-bearing cast, whereas if you sit it is called a nonweight-bearing casting. Most podiatrists will do nonweight-bearing casting by wrapping plaster strips around the foot without weight on it while maintaining the foot in a neutral position. Which techniques are used may depend on treatment goals, examination findings, and the orthotic maker's experience or preference. The technique is not as important as the orthotic provider. As long as you go to a professional who specializes in meeting cyclists' needs, you should be okay. You can expect to need to go back a few times to make modifications, however.

What problems can orthotics cure?

I first sought Bollig's assistance for extreme pain (neuroma) between my metatarsals. He fitted me with orthotics that had pads placed under my metatarsals to support my metatarsal arch (Photo 8.1), which alleviated the pain. The orthotics also greatly increased my comfort and efficiency by supporting my high arch. Furthermore, tipping the orthotic inward and supporting the lateral border of the foot (the space on the outside of the foot ahead of the heel seen on a wet footprint) prevents my IT band problems from recurring. Finally, removing material under my first metatarsal and big toe prevents my other toes from curling under. Without this, the smaller toes are trying to support my foot, because my abnormally short first metatarsal is not up to the task. (This is called Morton's Foot Type, meaning the second toe is longer than the big toe).

Another example is Lance Armstrong, whose foot, Bollig says, works inefficiently and has sesamoiditis—an inflammation of the ossicles (small bones) under the first metatarsal joint. (Ossicles are generally a class of moveable bones. A sesamoid is a type of ossicle that acts as a fulcrum in the function of a foot tendon. Sesamoids also bear body weight and act in proprioception, to help you with walking balance as well as to clip into your pedals without looking.) "Lance's whole right foot wants to roll outward, so we have to wedge him from the outside, which puts more pressure yet on the sesamoids. But we have to do it to force him inside to make the leg efficient." To correct the biomechanical problem, Bollig made a crater with thin, soft foam under the sesamoids, even though forcing the foot onto that area is creating a foot injury to get efficiency. "But Lance would rather have the pain than the inefficiency," says Bollig. "He told me in 2003 that it just has to get him through a couple more Tours! I cast his feet a couple of different ways, made several sets of orthotics, and we kept improving on them. Finally, he e-mailed me with, 'Bingo, that's it!' "

Prefabricated Insoles

Over-the-counter arch supports offer a great place to start and may work for you without the investment in custom orthotics. Think of an orthotic as a shoe gasket—a soft thing to fill spaces as a gasket does in an engine. A custom orthotic fills in all the void spaces to ensure a better-fitting shoe, but if there is no injury, a prefabricated arch support might improve the fit of that nice shoe just enough.

Cleat Wear

Some pedals with broad, plastic cleats (Look and Campagnolo are two examples—see the road shoe in Photo 7.1) require the user to monitor cleat wear or they can have problems. If the cleat wears on the outside when walking, the foot may roll to the outside when riding, which can create IT band, knee, and muscle problems. Even a cleat that allows play between the foot and the pedal can cause knee pain. Check your cleat wear frequently.

BLOCK 9
Determining Ideal Crank Length

Be forewarned that determining optimal crank length might upset your world a bit, because it may indicate a far different crank length than you are currently using. And that could be costly, not only for new or even custom cranks but also for a custom frame whose bottom bracket height and seat tube length is adjusted for the crank length.

I base the recommendations in this block on the assumption that crank length should vary in proportion to the rider's leg length. (See my reasoning below.) Once you accept that premise, then all that remains is to find the constant of proportionality between leg length and crank length. What this constant is may be up for discussion, but the idea that the constant exists at all is crucial; if you accept that, the actual constant will probably lie within a relatively narrow range.

So here is the formula I recommend:

crank length (mm) = inseam (mm) X 0.216

Or, more conservatively for tall riders:

crank length (mm) = inseam (mm) X 0.210

Another formula, from fit guru Bill Boston (www.billbostoncycles.com), comes up with similar results. Boston suggests measuring in inches your femur (thighbone) from the center of the hip joint to the end of the bone. This number will be your crank length in centimeters. For instance, if you have a 20-inch femur, you would have a 20cm (200mm) crank.

9.1

Different length strokes for different folks: 200mm, 220mm, and 175mm right-hand crankarms.

Andy Pruitt, fit expert of many cycling superstars, has a few other things to add. "Crank length formulas using femoral length or leg length are fine," he says. "But if your style is mashing, use longer cranks, and if you are a spinner, shorten them a bit. Mountain-bike cranks should be a bit longer for that moment to get you over a rock. Use 2.5mm or 5mm longer (than your normal road crank) for purely time trial usage, and vice versa for the track." One study done at Marshall University in Huntington, West Virginia, showed that *everyone, regardless of body size*, rode faster over short distances with each increase in crank length. Pruitt warns, however, that you can hurt yourself if you use cranks that are too long for your legs. In that configuration, the compressive and shear forces in the knee joints "go up exponentially" due to the sharper knee bend. (Compressive forces in the knee are stationary, felt behind the knee. Shear forces are the result of fore-aft sliding of the condyles—the rounded, cartilage-covered ends of the femur—as they rotate on the cartilage pad atop the knee platform.) So, do not stray much beyond the long side of this proportional relationship.

Cranks that are too short are not dangerous, however. You may lose some power since you are not using your muscles through the same range of movement, but you will put less stress on your knees.

Other Adjustments

Before I get into the whys and wherefores of these formulas for determining crank length, I want to tell you other ramifications that adjusting the crank length has on your bike position. If you increase your crank length, you should, at a minimum, lower your saddle (and perhaps your stem) by the same amount. You could argue that you should also push the saddle forward and increase your stem length by the same amount as well. This adds some complexity, because the seat and handlebars should also go up one-third of the distance of the forward movement to maintain the same pedal-to-saddle distance and saddle-to-bar drop (see Block 2).

The inverse is true if you switch to a shorter crank. Raise the saddle (and perhaps the bar) the amount of the length change and perhaps adjust the saddle aft as well. You may find that your saddle-to-bar drop must be reduced with a longer crank since your knees come up higher and your hip angle is reduced. The opposite occurs with a shorter crank.

With a longer crank, your pedal clearance in a corner will be reduced, and vice versa with a shorter crank. So, ideally, the height of the frame's bottom bracket should be higher with the longer crank and lower with the shorter one. And to account for the portion of the seat height measurement constituted by the crank, with increases or decreases in crank length the seat tube should be shortened or lengthened accordingly from the bottom by raising or lowering the bottom bracket without raising or lowering the top end of the tube.

Proportionality between Leg and Crank Length

Why do I say that there's a proportional relationship between leg length and crank length? Because no other conclusion makes sense. Muscles and joints work most effectively when operating in a certain range of motion. Short riders should not have to force their muscles through an extreme range of motion. On the other end of the spectrum, 7-foot basketball players do not bend their legs any less when they jump than shorter players do, so why should they use minimal knee bend and operate their muscles only through a tiny part of their range when they ride a bike?

To test this hypothesis, I conducted crank-length tests and published the results in *VeloNews* in 1995 and 1996. These tests were either inconclusive or seemed to indicate that all riders, regardless of size, put out more maximum power with superlong (220mm) cranks, and that all riders had lower heart rates at low power outputs with supershort cranks (100mm to 130mm).

My experimental method in those tests was lacking, but I was simply unwilling to stop there, since I knew from personal experience that increasing crank length for a tall rider like myself (6'6") makes a difference. In the late 1970s, for instance, when I went from 177.5mm to 180mm cranks, the improvement in my racing results was marked. In 1980, when I was on the U.S. National Team, Coach Eddie Borysewicz told me that I should be using even longer cranks, and increase them still more for time trials and hill climbs, but at the time I never found longer cranks. Since then, I have continued to experiment with my own crank lengths. Lately I've been using the range of cranks that Bruce Boone built for those 1996 tests (eight cranks evenly spaced between 100mm and 220mm) and find that I am very happy with 202.3mm cranks.

Thus encouraged, I have conducted other crank studies in recent years. However, in understanding what went wrong in those 1995 and 1996 tests, I developed higher experimental standards for a test worthy of publication, and my subsequent studies still have not met them. Being neither a physiology researcher nor funded to do these sorts of studies, I find it hard to conduct a test that eliminates all other variables besides crank length. It requires lots of time, willing (that is, paid!) subjects, and equipment. It is an unrealistic undertaking with no budget in order to write a single article of the many required each month for a cycling magazine.

Anyway, I have conducted all these recent tests on the road with tall riders (6'5" and taller) because it was simpler and cheaper to use my own stable of bikes than to always switch cranks on other people's bikes. And my tall customers, who are willing to follow my crank-length recommendations and purchase the custom cranks and frames that I have made for them, have also graciously acted as test subjects. The experimental and empirical data shows that tall riders generally go faster and generate more power with custom cranks that are far longer than standard lengths. That conclusion is reinforced by many people raving about how much more comfortable, natural, and powerful they feel on cranks proportional to their leg length. On mountain bikes, my tall customers report being able to smoothly power over obstacles they could not have before. As an added benefit, the higher bottom bracket I built into the frame to accommodate the long crank makes it almost impossible to hit the chainrings on logs and ledges.

The results indicate clearly enough to me that crank length must be proportional to rider size in some way. Whether you decide it is proportional to leg length, thigh length, overall height, or something else is a minor point. The same goes for the constant of proportionality. It could be other than 0.210 or 0.216, but regardless, simply selecting a single constant will indicate to a lot of people that they should be using a crank vastly different in length from their current crank. That is the hard part for a lot of people to accept.

No matter our size, we are by and large all stuck on cranks of the same length. The 3 percent difference between a 170mm and a 175mm crank hardly constitutes a choice; and while the 180mm length is available, you can find it only in top-end component groups and even so it does not broaden the range much. Accepting the premise that cranks should be scaled up or down depending on rider size opens up a whole can of worms that a lot of riders, bike makers, and component companies would just as soon stay closed. Obviously, economies of scale for producing cranks go out the window if you have to supply a range from, say, 120mm to 220mm. The same goes for bike frames; the cost and complexity of producing frame jigs goes up if a manufacturer increases the bottom bracket height with every increase in frame size in order to accommodate crankarms proportional to the size of the rider.

There are obvious, practical reasons to stick with the status quo. However those reasons may have more to do with what is best for the rider's pocketbook than what is best for the rider's performance and comfort.

The Constant of Proportionality

If you have accepted the idea of a proportional relationship between the leg and crank length, how would you come up with the constant of proportionality relating them? I propose that one way would be to look at what works for a wide range of riders. For instance, the world is full of successful bike racers with 80cm (31.5-inch) inseams. Thirty years ago, they probably would have been racing on 170mm cranks. Nowadays, they would likely be on the extremely popular 172.5mm crank. To illustrate this trend, 50 percent of the high-end carbon road cranks that crank maker FSA sold in 2003 were 172.5mm, 35 percent were 175mm, and only 15 percent were 170mm. Campagnolo's approximate 2003 sales numbers were 60 percent in 172.5mm, 10 percent in 175mm, and 30 percent in 170mm. Shimano reported 50 percent in 172.5mm, 30 percent in 175mm, and 20 percent in 170mm in 2003. These figures show big changes from around 1970, when the vast majority of high-end road cranks were 170mm.

Sales figures show what is fashionable and could perhaps also indicate that people are taller than they were 30 years ago, but if we continue to consider a rider with an 800mm (80cm) inseam, a 170mm crank would be 21.3 percent of his leg length ($170/800 = 0.2125$). Furthermore, a 172.5mm crank would be 21.6 percent of it, while 165mm would be 20.6 percent, and 175mm would be 21.9 percent. So, if you multiply a rider's inseam in millimeters by 0.213 or 0.216, you will determine a crank in the same proportion as a 170mm or 172.5mm crank for a rider with an 80cm inseam.

If you want to be conservative on the long end, you could go with 0.210 as the constant. This is what I have been doing for a number of years with my very tall custom-frame clients, who almost universally prefer them to the lengths they had used in the past. For instance, a 6'8" rider with a 1,000mm (100cm, or 39.4-inch) inseam would use a 210mm crank with a 30cm-high bottom bracket.

On the other hand, using a constant of 0.210 gives surprising numbers on the short end, such as a 168mm crank length for our rider with the 80cm inseam. So you could argue for a constant of 0.216, since that yields 172.5mm for an 80cm inseam, consistent with what we see in pro racing. The 6'8" rider's crankarm becomes 6mm longer (216mm) with the 0.216 constant than with 0.210, but notice that we are now haggling over a few millimeters while being *centimeters* longer than the normal range of crank length into which the tall rider would have been when locked. If you use the same constant for both riders, their knees and hips will go through the same range of bend, and their muscles will reach the same extension and contraction.

Testing for the Ideal

Try various cranks and see how you measure up against other riders with whom you are competitive, or time yourself up a climb you frequently clock. Adjustable-length cranks are available, but they are extremely heavy and increase your stance width, making it difficult to retain your objectivity.

Block 12 gives an intriguing experimental method for determining your bicycle setup, and crank length is a big part of it. I recommend at least looking it over to see if it is something you are willing to try. 🚲

Custom-length cranks can be found at www.zinncycles.com.

BLOCK 10
Choosing the Correct Frame Size

Awell-fitting bike frame is fundamental to an enjoyable cycling experience. If your frame does not fit properly, it is impossible to set up your entire bike to fit your body without making extreme adjustments of components that will compromise stability, weight distribution, or performance. But if your bike fits you well, you'll be more comfortable, which will not only increase your riding enjoyment; it will also encourage you to ride more, which improves your fitness and performance!

Measuring Frame Dimensions

First of all, it is important to understand how bike frames are measured before taking your own body measurements. Since the vast majority of readers will be buying a stock frame (as opposed to a frame custom-made to their measurements), I'll describe how to measure frames so those readers will know how to compare them. It is not generally enough to read manufacturer specification (spec) lists, since the measurement method varies from manufacturer to manufacturer, and you want to compare apples to apples.

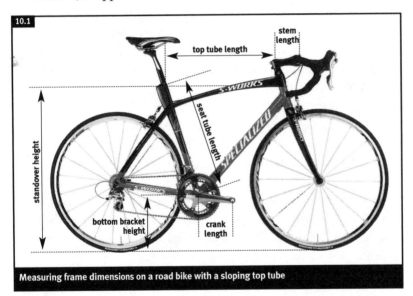

10.1

Measuring frame dimensions on a road bike with a sloping top tube

In this era of sloping top tubes (also known as compact geometry), it is a lot more difficult to measure a bike frame than when top tubes were level. You can get around this by extending a taut string in a horizontal line starting at the intersection of the top tube's upper edge and the head tube and drawing the string back to the seat post. The distance along this line (see Photo 10.1), from the center of the head tube to the center of the seat post, is the top tube length. (You will notice that this length, the "effective top tube length," is greater than the length measured center-to-center along the top tube itself. Elementary geometry demonstrates this, since the head tube and seat tube are approximately parallel, the shortest distance between two parallel lines is perpendicular to them both, and the sloping top tube is closer to perpendicular than is the effective top tube.)

The distance along the seat tube from the center of the bottom bracket to this horizontal line is the center-to-top seat tube length (Photo 10.1). To convert this measurement to a center-to-center seat tube length, subtract half the diameter of the top tube (or around 2cm on many current frames) from the center-to-top seat tube length.

Obviously, on a frame with a horizontal top tube, measure its length from the center of the head tube to the center of the seat tube. The seat tube length is simply measured from the bottom bracket center to the top tube's top edge or centerline where it intersects the seat tube centerline, depending on whether you want a center-to-top or center-to-center measurement.

Once you have measured the frame properly, you can compare it to other frames measured in the same way.

But note that if you plan to install extra-long cranks, you also want to be sure that the bottom bracket is high enough. You can measure this yourself from the ground to the center of the bottom bracket when the wheels are on (Figure 10.1). Without that, you will need to refer to the manufacturer's specifications list. You will also need to rely on the spec list for frame angles, since you will not be able to measure them.

Finding Frame Dimensions that Fit Your Body

The next step is to calculate your ideal frame size based on your body measurements and compare it with the frame's dimensions. I think the simplest way is to use the free fit calculator page I put up on my Web site, www.zinncycles.com. It instructs you to take three body measurements, click on one of three possible characterizations of your riding level, and indicate whether you want recommendations for a road or mountain bike frame. It spits out a recommended seat tube length, top tube length, and bottom bracket height. It also suggests a seat height and reach setting for the complete bike.

In the appendixes of *Zinn and the Art of Road Bike Maintenance* (VeloPress, 2000) and *Zinn and the Art of Mountain Bike Maintenance* (VeloPress, 2001), you'll find a manual frame fit method that will yield similar results to my online fit page. Finally, Block 13 lists a number of other frame fitting resources.

Once you have a frame that fits you, you can choose and adjust components so that you are riding in a comfortable and efficient position. To set up your components properly, follow the instructions in Blocks 1 through 9, and perhaps 11 and 12. Or, pursue some the of the bike-fit options outlined in Block 13. 🚲

BLOCK 11

Adjusting for Leg-Length Discrepancies

After following the fit instructions in all of the preceding blocks, you may still have asymmetrical movement or be in pain. For instance, one knee may swing outward on each pedal stroke, your hip may hurt, or you may sit far off to one side of the bike. These may be symptoms of a leg-length discrepancy.

The fixed position on the bike and repetition of movement aggravates the effect of a leg-length discrepancy that you might not notice while walking. Many promising cycling careers have been cut short by debilitating pain in the lower back, hips, and legs due to differences in leg length. Even the greatest cyclist of all time, Eddy Merckx, suffered mightily due to this condition and constantly fiddled with his bike position to try to alleviate his back pain.

Functional length discrepancies can occur in even-length legs due to an asymmetry in the angles of the ankles at the bottom of the stroke. This can often be alleviated with orthotics and awareness. Another type of functional length discrepancy results from shortened muscles pulling the pelvis up on one side. It can be caused by such incidents as injuries or years of slinging a heavy backpack over one shoulder. Functional leg-length discrepancy is treatable by some chiropractic methods (see Block 20).

Static leg-length discrepancies, on the other hand, are part of your bone structure. These must be addressed in the bike and shoe setup.

Measuring Leg-Length Discrepancies

You can tell if you have a significant leg-length difference by having a friend pull on your legs while you lie on your back. If your ankles do not line up, you have a length difference, although the exact difference and whether the discrepancy is functional or static won't be clear.

The gold standard of measuring the discrepancy is taking X rays of the legs while the rider is standing. This method allows you to find the length difference in each leg segment and in total.

The High Sierra Cycle Center (HSCC) in Mammoth Lakes, California, specializes in treating cycling leg-length discrepancy problems and can accurately measure leg-length differences while the rider is on the bike. Measurement plates rise up and brush the bottom of the heel when the rider is sitting squarely on the saddle with the knee locked out. HSCC's Tom Slocum says, "95 percent of the time, I am within 1/16-inch of an X-ray length difference measurement."

A goniometer, a long folding protractor used to measure the angles of human joints, can also help determine the extent of the problem when the rider is on the bike. Using a digital goniometer positioned on the side of the rider's leg, Slocum claims that in some patients he sees differences as large as 15 degrees from one knee angle to the other. The Boulder Center for Sports Medicine (BCSM) uses 3-D computer video analysis to find joint angles when the rider is actually pedaling. The computer creates line segments between reflectors placed on each leg joint and measures the joint angles from both the side and the front (to determine, for instance, if one knee is swinging outward).

Corrective Measures
The Boulder Center Method

After determining with X rays the amount and location of the leg-length difference, BCSM staffers start to correct the discrepancy by placing shims between the cleat and the shoe (see Photo 11.1). For a tibial (lower leg) length difference, they shim up the shorter side by the amount of the difference. With a femoral (upper leg) length difference, they shim the cleat up half the length difference and shift the cleats fore and aft as well. The cleat on the shorter leg is moved forward, and the one on the longer leg is moved back. The saddle may also be moved fore and aft to get the knee over the pedal spindle.

BCSM Director Andy Pruitt corrected for a length difference he discovered in the legs of professional rider Axel Merckx, Eddy Merckx's son. The elder Merckx sighed, "Where were you when I was racing? I have the same thing, and I could have done a lot better if it had been treated!"

The High Sierra Method

The HSCC attempts to balance the leverage from side to side as well as to correct for the length difference with cleat shims. At the heart of its system are Synchronizer crankarms

11.1

Cleat shims

that offer two adjustability features. First, the chainring spider is movable relative to the crank so that the chainrings need not be centered about the bottom bracket. Secondly, the square taper-hole insert that slips onto the bottom bracket spindle can be rotated inside the left crankarm so that the arms need not be 180 degrees apart.

The HSCC staff measures the client's leg-length difference on the bike as described previously, and a video camera helps determine if and when the pedaling rider drops one heel more than the other. "Then," says Slocum, "we install a block (that is, a cleat shim) the full amount of the length difference. We want to get the same knee and ankle bend at the bottom of the stroke on both sides."

Slocum reasons that a block under one cleat changes the leverage in different parts of the stroke and should be adjusted for as well. For example, if you put a 1cm block under one shoe, when it is at 6 o'clock (the bottom of the stroke) you have effectively shortened the crank by 10mm. At 12 o'clock, you have lengthened it by 10mm. The HSCC attempts to balance the loads by offsetting the chainrings. When the longer leg's crank is at 6 o'clock, Slocum reasons that it can take a heavier load because the "lever" is 10mm longer, so the chainrings are offset upward to make a higher gear. When the short leg's crank is at 6 o'clock, the consequent downward chainring offset creates a smaller gear.

As for altering the angle between the crankarms, "When most people pedal, one side may pick up at the top a little sooner than the other side. We call that 'timing,' " says Slocum. "By changing the relative crankarm angle as little as two degrees (and) up to 10 degrees, we can change that timing sequence so both legs feel like they're firing at the same point and there is no lag time from right to left."

Slocum finds no consistency among individuals as to whether the short leg needs to be advanced or delayed relative to the long leg. He determines how to adjust the relative angles in three ways: by looking at the video of the rider pedaling, by looking at SpinScan power-output curves generated on a CompuTrainer computerized trainer as a function of position in the stroke, and by talking with the individual about what he or she feels.

The 1984 Olympic road-race gold medallist, Alexi Grewal, has a length discrepancy due to breaking his leg on the growth plate when he was 16. When the leg emerged from the cast, it was a centimeter longer than the other one. Like Merckx, he feels he would have had greater racing success with proper treatment, and he has found relief for his back problems with HSCC's adjustable-offset cranks. (HSCC makes the cranks as well as adjusts them, and diagnoses and sets up the rider.)

Everybody with a leg-length discrepancy adapts to it differently, with individual adjustments. The nice thing about cleat shims and High Sierra cranks is that you can tweak the setup yourself. You must find your own, unique solution.

You might also check out Blocks 7 and 12 for more hints on this process, since some people with differing leg lengths have found relief merely by adjusting crank lengths. 歊

The work of Andy Pruitt and the Boulder Center for Sports Medicine that he directs can be viewed online at www.bch.org/sportsmedicine.

The work of Tom Slocum and the High Sierra Cycle Center he directs can be viewed online at www.hscycle.com.

BLOCK 12
Haney's Way: Another Setup Method

Bike-fitting formulas and standard methods don't work for everyone. Lance Armstrong, for example, is a rider for whom a formulaic fit fails. And former Team Coors Light pro rider David Farmer was dropped from the U.S. National Team program because he could not tolerate the bike position dictated to him. Those two riders are on the fringes of the anatomy bell curve and require an individualized fit. Fortunately both were persistent enough to find the fit resources they needed and became successful professionals.

I recommend determining your own bike fit "by the book" (preferably this one!) if you have problems and cannot find a position that feels good, then I get the advice of an expert in the field of matching bodies with bikes, like Tom Coleman of Wobble-naught Fitting Systems in Boise, Idaho, or Andy Pruitt at the Boulder Center for Sports Medicine in Colorado. Or, if you know you have a leg-length discrepancy, try Tom Slocum at the High Sierra Cycle Center in Mammoth Lakes, California. See Block 13 for more resources.

However, making such a journey might not be in the cards for you, or you might have already done so and still have problems. In that case, provided you are willing to devote sufficient time and energy to it, the method below will find a completely unique fit for you, from the positions of the components to the length and stance width of the cranks.

Finding Your Unique Position

I have a friend, Ron Haney, who is passionate about bike riding but had become incapacitated by pain when doing it. He is a professional musician with a degree in mechanical engineering—a unique combination of skills and knowledge that gave him insight into his pain. Effective breathing is at least as critical to wind-instrument players as it is to cyclists and it depends on good posture and biomechanics. Furthermore, most musical instruments are asymmetrical, and the body must be positioned asymmetrically in order to play them. A bicycle, on the other hand, supports the rider symmetrically. Haney's understanding of postural and biomechanical asymmetry, which he gained by playing his instrument, led him to discover the degree to which he was sitting asymmetrically on his bike and how to correct it. I learned this method from him.

In 1993, Haney's back pain on the bike had become so debilitating that he made the trek from Washington, D.C., to Boulder to see Pruitt, who used X rays to measure an 8mm discrepancy in the length of Haney's legs. Pruitt set him up with a block (or cleat shim—see Block 11) under the cleat of his shoe on his short leg that was half the height of the leg-length difference. Haney's back pain went away, but his performance suffered. His quest then led him to Mammoth Lakes to see Slocum, who first replaced Pruitt's half-thickness block under the cleat with a full-thickness one. Slocum also installed his Synchronizer cranks, which allow the chainrings to be offset from the crank center and the angle of the crankarms to be adjusted so they are not at 180 degrees from each other. Haney experimented with the position of the eccentric rings and with the crank angle, using the same length crankarms on each side. His comfort and performance improved.

However, not being one to do anything halfway, Haney continued to experiment. He initially followed Slocum's suggestions, but ultimately "adjusted myself out of Tom's system," as he expressed it. Haney wanted to have the "least amount of odd stuff" (such as eccentric chainrings, cleat blocks, and offset crank angles) and the most natural pedaling style possible. He eventually eliminated all of those things, rides more comfortably and powerfully than ever, has no back or neck pain, and maintains great flexibility.

Getting centered on your bike

Set up a trainer with your bike held exactly vertically; eyeball the bike relative to a vertical line on the wall or a hanging plump bob. Level the height of the front and rear hubs above the floor, not by placing a block under the front wheel, but rather by placing a rotating lazy

12.1

Pedaling on wooden rectangles with mirror in position to view heel drop

Susan bearing under it and shimming it until the front and rear tires are the same height. Placing the wheel on a phone book open to the proper height is a good second best, since the wheel can turn by twisting the page. Finally, place a large mirror alongside the bike, as in Photo 12.1.

As you ride the trainer, watch your pedaling in the mirror to see if one heel drops more than the other on each downstroke (see Photo 12.1). Haney learned this from Slocum, who looks for heel drop symmetry with freeze-frame video of the foot angle on each side at the 3 o'clock pedal position. But doing it alone and without videotape, it's too difficult to determine the heel drop relative to a horizontal crank as the cranks spin past, and Haney came up with the following ingenious method to see it.

Start with a piece of plywood the thickness of your cycling shoe soles. Cut two rectangles somewhat larger than your feet. Mount cycling cleats on the rectangles (Time cleats, as in Photo 12.2, or Speedplay cleats that mount on a flat surface are obviously preferable for this), and clip them into the pedals. Although Haney worried that he would

not be able to pull up without wearing cycling shoes, he found that he generated exactly the same amount of power while pedaling barefoot on a CompuTrainer with the wood rectangles as he did wearing his cycling shoes. He concluded that, for him at least, generating power on the upstroke was "a fallacy," except under extreme efforts and sprinting.

An additional benefit of the wooden rectangles is that your feet are free to find their ideal fore-aft, rotational, and lateral positions relative to the pedal spindle. (This obviously simplifies the positioning of cleats on your

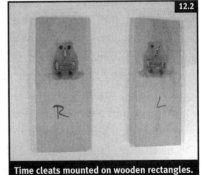

12.2

Time cleats mounted on wooden rectangles.

shoes.) Haney found that the ball of his foot tended to gravitate directly over the pedal spindle (see Photo 12.1) and that his feet came inward as far as they possibly could, indicating that anything he could do to reduce his Q-Factor, or the width of his stance, would be an advantage.

It's easier to see the plywood's angle than that of a cycling shoe, but it's still hard to catch the exact instant when each crank is horizontal. Instead, look at the crank angle when the foot is parallel to the crank (Photo 12.1). You can usually find a spoke on the front wheel lined up with the crank at the moment the foot becomes parallel with it; rotate the front wheel a few degrees as needed to get a spoke to line up better. If a mirror on the side is set up right, you can look through the wheel and see the angle of the opposite foot as well.

If, for example, your right heel drops more than the left, you are sitting asymmetrically to the right side of the bike. You can also check for pedaling symmetry by lightening up on each foot on the upstroke and slapping it back down onto the wooden rectangle; when you are centered, each foot will slap just as loudly as the other.

Also notice if one hand pushes harder on the handlebar than the other, so the front wheel is directed off to one side. Haney's left-pointed front wheel corresponded to numbness in his left hand when he rode. Notice if you are less stable when riding while drinking from a bottle held in the left hand than in the right. This may indicate that you are sitting off to the right side of the bike and are unconsciously pushing forward with your left hand to compensate (which moves the front wheel back under your center of gravity). When you grab the bottle with the left hand, you may actually have to pull back on the handlebar with the right hand to maintain stability.

Another way to check if you are laterally centered on the bike is to look straight down the axis of the bike as you pedal, especially with no hands (see Photo 12.3). When you focus both eyes on the top of the front tire, your stereoscopic vision makes it appear as though you are "seeing" two rims, one sticking out on each side of the bike. If you are centered, you will see the same amount of rim sticking out to either side. To emphasize this effect, try using 3/4-inch diameter orange dots with sticky backing (you can get them in the labels section of an office supply store). Put one dot on top of the front tire with the bike on the stand, one on the rim on the far side, and one on the hub. They really clear up how things line up when you sight down the front wheel.

Using this method and an adjustable-length crank, Haney initially adjusted away the angle difference between the crankarms and the eccentricity of the chainrings by using

12.3

Ron Haney, balanced and centered

cranks of different lengths, starting with a 165mm crank on the left and a 172.5mm crank on the right. He was centered on the bike and had no back pain, but he was not satisfied with cranks of different lengths. He found, however, that as he increased the crank length, he needed a smaller block under the cleat and less difference between the crankarms to maintain a centered position and pain-free riding.

With each crank combination, he was trying to get centered, having started out too far to the right. He found that each increase in crank length pulled him farther to the left. With asymmetrical lengths, a combination of a 180mm crank on the right and a 177.5mm crank on the left came the closest to centering him. Finally, a 181.5mm crank on both sides with no block under either cleat did the trick—he had achieved a centered, comfortable, powerful position without a cleat block, asymmetrical cleat fore-aft positions, off-angle cranks, or eccentric chainrings.

Some riders may have asymmetrical canting of the foot as well. If the crank is too short or long, the rider will be off to one side of the bike, and one foot may tip inward and one outward. When a rider finds the proper crank, the need for asymmetrical canting shims under the feet may also disappear.

Also, if you are more comfortable with your saddle twisted to one side or the other when you ride, you may find that you are more comfortable with it straight if you start riding a crank that is closer to your ideal length.

Saddle position

So far, this somewhat complicated method of observing your own pedaling has only addressed cranks and foot position, and not the seat or bars. Hang on, that's coming!

As Haney worked more with his side-to-side weight balance on the bike, he began to discover things about fore-aft balance as well. As he varied his crank lengths, he obviously had to adjust his saddle position and then consequently his handlebar position. But how? When you make such large adjustments to crank length, there is no formula that tells you what to do with your seat and bar.

The breakthrough in fore-aft balance came partially from Haney's study of yoga, which he had undertaken for years as a way to alleviate his back pain. It turns out that a particular yoga pose when done on the bike (on a training stand) can reveal a lot about your position.

First, sit on the bike. Clasp your hands behind your back, palms together (see Photo 12.4). Now swing your hands upward as you bend forward and then look down the cen-

terline of the bike (Photos 12.3 and 12.4). As you bend over, your butt comes up off of the saddle, so it is just you and the pedals. The goal here is to balance. Your pedals may be either turning or vertically stationary. Be careful riding with your hands behind your back; you can lose your balance! Put your nose to the stem (or as close as you can) and see how you line up. As you become more flexible, you will be able to position yourself lower and lower, and the farther forward you bend, the more your saddle wants to go back and down. If your saddle is too far forward or too high, you won't be able to bend over as far (the body should support itself) because the saddle will be wedged into your crotch. Now it may be interesting to reflect on how professional riders' positions have evolved since the early 1960s to being farther back and lower today.

Balanced and centered, palms touching behind back

Haney discovered an amazing thing from this exercise, namely that he could pedal with no hands while standing (see Photo 12.5)! However that is only possible with a crank length that centers him laterally and a saddle position that centers him fore and aft. The rider's center of mass (COM) must be directly over the bottom bracket. With a traditional position, it is hard to figure out where the COM is, but it is definitely ahead of the bottom bracket.

12.5

Pedaling while standing up on the pedals (no hands)

Handlebar position

As the saddle position gradually reveals itself in the process of doing this exercise, the bar position will as well. Most likely, you will notice that your hands want to extend farther forward and down. You can even grab broomsticks in your hands, suspending the bristles above the floor while pedaling, to determine the position of the brake hoods.

As you approach the ideal crank length, your position will improve. But it doesn't happen overnight. You'll start out more upright, and eventually get lower and more stretched out. You need to work this out slowly or you will have problems. As with yoga or stretching, you are increasing your flexibility as you go, and your position will adjust, too. Work on keeping your gaze horizontal as well.

Once you are balanced fore-aft and laterally over the bottom bracket, then the harder you pedal, the more weight you will have on your feet, since your butt and hands actually do not need to be on the saddle and bar to maintain balance. Thus, this position sets you up for maximal load. The easier you pedal, the greater the weight on the bar and saddle, and the less comfortable the position becomes. And you not only become more comfortable the harder you push the pedals, but you also become more aerodynamic (lower and level) as a byproduct of the biomechanics. For instance, Haney finds that he can do a time trial with a short clip-on bar such as a Cinelli Spinaci without forearm pads because his body is already balanced without resting his arms on the pads, and a short, little clip-on gives him all the forward extension he needs.

Taking Another Cut

The method above probably seems pretty far out, not to mention time consuming and expensive due to the cost of special cranks. Well, Haney has come up with a simpler, no cost, off-the-bike method that yields similar results. If you undertake the procedure described below, and it reveals intriguing results, then you may be motivated to pursue the on-bike method above.

For this procedure, you need one or two cinderblocks (depending on their dimensions) and some wood blocks of varying thickness. Easy enough?

First, you have to know your stance width, or Q-Factor, meaning the space between the first metatarsal (the bump behind your big toe directly above your pedal spindle) of each foot when pedaling. You can determine the stance width most easily by clipping one foot into the pedal. Measure from the side of the foot at the first metatarsal to the center of a water-bottle cage bolt on the down tube. Take the same measurement with the other foot to the center of the same bottle bolt, and add the two measurements together. This is your stance width.

Now that you have that measurement, lay one cinderblock down on its edge and stack the second one identically on top so that the edges line up. Place a thin sheet of wood roughly the same size as the block on top of the stack, so that the front and one edge line up with the block edges. Measure out half of your stance width from the blocks and draw a line on the floor parallel to the blocks through this point. Measure the same distance in from the edge of the wood sheet, and draw a line on the sheet parallel to the edge through this point. Draw a line on the floor perpendicular to the blocks, and line the front edge of the wood sheet atop the cinderblocks on it (see Photo 12.6).

12.6

Experimenting with crank length using cinderblocks

Stand barefoot with one foot on the floor and one atop the wood sheet on the cinderblock stack. Line the toes up against the front of the wood sheet and the line square with it on the floor. Set the edge of each foot's first metatarsal bump against the corresponding line parallel to the blocks.

Almost all of your weight is on the lower foot at first, with the toes of your upper foot only carrying a tiny bit of weight and the heel raised off of the block. Look down, and you will see that your head is centered over your lower foot. Now, press your upper heel downward to the block, trying to feel that both feet carry the same amount of weight (Photo 12.6). As you push your heel down, you will notice that you bend forward and push your butt back, your hands come up, and your body moves laterally toward the blocks. Look down and see if your gaze lines up down the face of the cinderblock (try alternately closing each eye and inter-polating between them).

The stack of blocks represents your crankarms. What you are trying to find is a height of the stack so that, when both heels are down and both feet have even weight on them (as at the vertical crank position while pedaling), your body is centered between your feet. In other words, when you find the right crank length, which will be equal to half of the height of the block stack, your gaze will line up right down the edge of the block.

This is where the other pieces of wood of various thicknesses come in. They should be roughly the size of the rectangular face of a cinderblock. Use them under the top wood sheet, once again lining up their front and inside edges with the rest of the blocks, to shim the block stack up or down and keep repeating the experiment. Hard to believe as this may be, you will actually find a point where the stack height is just right so that when your weight is balanced on both feet you bring your gaze right down the edge of the block. Shorter people may need to only use one cinderblock with a stack of wood blocks on it.

Rock back and forth laterally to find the point of even weight on your feet. If your "crank length" is too short (that is, the block stack is too low), your head will stay more over the lower foot. At the same time, your butt will not come back very far, you will not bend for-ward much, and your hands will come up to an unequal height. If the block stack ("crank length") is too tall, your head will move to the upper foot's side of center, your butt will push far back, you will bend forward more, and your hands will stick farther out ahead, perhaps with the other one now higher. Once you find the right stack height, turn around and reverse your feet to check it the other way around.

Incidentally, you can use a bathroom scale as one of the shim blocks and ensure that half of your weight is on that foot. Unfortunately, if your weight is exactly evenly divided between your feet, this method does not work, unless you also allow your Q-Factor to become as narrow as your body prefers (walking or hanging from a chin-up bar, your feet may be closer together than a bike forces them to be). It will not work, because your head will always come over above the up foot. Since you cannot actually bring your feet significantly closer together on a bike without having a special frame and crankset made, it is better to use perceived even weight distribution between your feet.

Standing centered this way relative to the block, look at the horizon level with your eyes. Your position is similar to when climbing a set of very steep stairs. Your head and hands go forward and your butt back to counterbalance you (Photo 12.6).

Now, the critical discovery Haney made is that when you hit the right crank length (block height), the distance from your butt to your hands is exactly the same as on the bike, and the relative heights of your butt and hands will be the same, too. You will need a friend to dangle a plumb bob from the back of your butt and mark it on the floor while you dangle ski poles, broomsticks, or plumb bobs from your hands that he or she can also mark on the floor. This not only finds your seat-to-bar reach but also the position of the bar forward of the bottom bracket and of the back of the seat behind the bottom bracket. The centerline of the bottom bracket is the line between the first metatarsals of the feet. Furthermore, the measurement from the floor to your sit bones and to your palms will likely be the same as the height of the bar and saddle vertically above the shoe insole at the ball of the foot when clipped into the pedal at the bottom of the stroke.

Doing this yourself at home

There is nothing complex about this method. Clearly, you could do it yourself at home, and you may now be intrigued enough to consider it. I imagine that few of you will actually embark on this unless you have pain when riding and have exhausted other means at your disposal to alleviate it. If you do, at least you have another alternative now, and it is one in which you are in control.

If you are considering it, try the following simple test to look at the asymmetry in your riding position. First, put your bike on a trainer and ensure that it is vertical. Get on the bike and pedal to get positioned as you normally would be. Place a broomstick across the top crest of your pelvis (hip bones) and look for rotation and tilt of the broomstick. Roll the broomstick up and down over the crests of the bones to ensure that it is in the right spot and to see what it does against the fronts of the bones versus atop the bones. If the broomstick is tilted or rotated fore-aft significantly, consider either embarking on this setup method or looking into leg-length discrepancy measures with an expert like Andy Pruitt or Tom Slocum (see Block 11).

Some Tips

When changing seat height, measure from the top of the seat tube to a mark on the seat post for accuracy, rather than to the saddle; you are looking for relative differences, once you have established a baseline position. When checking fore-aft changes, measure from the saddle tip to the clamp on the seat rails.

Remember that, because of the seat angle, when you raise the saddle, it also goes back about one-third that distance at the same time. Similarly, when you are moving the saddle back, the distance to the pedal increases by one-third that aft adjustment. And the inverse is true when moving the saddle downward or forward.

Bar adjustments work the same way; because of the head angle, when you raise the stem, the bar comes back toward the saddle about one-third that distance and vice versa. If you know where you want your bar to be and your current stem will not get you there, you can use the stem calculator tool on my Web site at www.zinncycles.com/stemFit.aspx. To use this tool, you input the dimensions of your current stem and your bike's head angle. It tells you your current rise and reach relative to the top of your headset. Knowing that you want your bar, say, 15mm lower and 7mm farther forward, you can add or subtract those numbers from the current rise and reach relative to the top of your headset given by the tool. Then input dimensions of different stems you are considering and add or subtract headset spacers to see which combination gets you the desired rise and reach. If you want to change the rise a lot, try flipping the stem; for instance, reverse the angle so −17 degrees becomes +17 degrees. 🚲

Adjustable cranks are available from www.hscycle.com, www.velotron.com, and www.SRM.DE.

Custom-length cranks can be found at www.zinncycles.com.

BLOCK 13
Other Bike Fit Resources

In addition to the bike fit instructions in Blocks 1 through 12 in this book, there are many resources available for professional fitting assistance as well as for instructions and calculators you can use on your own. I've listed them here in no particular order.

Fit Kit

Probably the best-known bike fitting system in the United States is the Fit Kit, which has been around since 1982. The system consists of measurement tools, charts, software, and the Rotational Adjustment Device (RAD) pedal cleat adjustment system that determines optimal cleat angle. New to the Fit Kit line is the Quick Fit, which usually takes about ten minutes for measuring and assessment and for which most dealers charge $25 to $35; but note that it is only suitable for mid- to low-end bicycle purchases. Shops usually charge $75 to $250 for a Fit Kit Performance Fit, which covers bicycle fitting, cleat alignment, and fine-tuning. A session of this type can take up to two hours and is suited to mid- to high-end bicycle purchases and for determining custom bike geometry. The www.bikefitkit.com Web site includes a dealer locator.

Serotta

For three decades, Ben Serotta has been perfecting his bicycle fit system. Serotta has designed his fit tools, methodology, and training programs based on his study of thousands of

13.1

Using a goniometer to determine the thigh/torso angle of a rider on a Serotta Size Cycle

COURTESY OF SEROTTA

cyclists and from consulting with medical professionals in the cycling field. The Serotta Size Cycle (see Photo 13.1) is a fully adjustable stationary bicycle around which the system is built. Since 1998, Serotta has trained more than 500 technicians (mostly bike shop employees) from across the country to use the system. According to Serotta, "The cost of fitting varies on the depth of the procedure . . . and on the dealership and level of experience. Basic bike fittings usually start at about $75, while full-on Size Cycle fittings generally start at about $100, but can go as high as $300 or more depending on the extent of the evaluation, which can include many aspects of body and foot alignment, or an aerodynamics assessment. The average full fitting cost is about $150." See www.serotta.com for more information.

Bikefitting.com

Bikefitting.com started as BioRacer, a fit system and custom frame and clothing manufacturer based in Holland and Belgium. The Bikefitting System is sold in about twenty-three countries worldwide, and it's available in the United States through both Merlin and Litespeed to dealers as a Litespeed- or Merlin-branded fitting product, or without the Merlin or

Litespeed logo. Every dealer uses the system differently and utilizes various elements of it—some all, some only one or two parts, and it can be customized to each dealer's desires.

The system includes large, wall-mounted measuring devices (see Photo 13.2); a size cycle (see Photo 13.3); a cleat adjuster; and the Internet connection to Bikefitting.com. The latter not only offers analyses for positioning on an existing bicycle but also creates a drawing for construction of a full custom frame. In addition, it features a plug-in for the best fit on standard geometry bicycles from Litespeed, Merlin, and many other brands. More information and dealer locators can be found on the www.merlinbike.com and www.bikefitting.com Web sites.

Bikefitting.com's measuring wall includes sliding implements built into the wall to ensure measurement accuracy.

Dealers charge anywhere from $100 to $300 for a "pro fit" depending on whether they are fitting a rider with a new bike or dialing in a current bike, and they usually apply some or all of that cost to a new bike purchase.

Bikefitting.com's adjustable size cycle

Wobble-naught

Based in Boise, Idaho, Wobble-naught Fitting Systems uses high-tech tools to measure muscle forces and pedal stroke mechanics and a big screen for the rider to observe their muscles as they pedal. Company founder Tom Coleman owns another company, called Myo-facts, which provides Wobble-naught fitters with Noraxon sEMG (surface electromyography) equipment, which records muscle signals via electrodes hooked up to the rider. Graphically, in real time on an 80-inch wide screen, riders see what their muscles are doing and they can improve pedaling technique while watching their power output increase. The system is also wireless and telemetric, so Coleman can even follow riders outside from up to 100 meters away and inform and instruct them by radio.

Wobble-naught and Myo-facts utilize an Ergomo power meter (see Photo 18.5) integrated with the sEMG to measure wattage. Crosshair lasers help measure the bike and set the cleats to the millimeter. These lasers are also used to point out alignment needs. Coleman says, "The key is to provide a better 'model' for riders to understand themselves. Humans learn by sight over being told, by experience rather than by words or reading."

Another unique Wobble-naught option is a "dynamic" custom foot bed called SOLE that conforms to the rider's foot and pedaling style. The plastic foot bed is warmed up and placed in the shoe, and it conforms and cools to the foot as the rider pedals, rather than being molded to the static foot.

The basic Wobble-naught fit using computer-aided design and lasers costs $100 (prices may vary), and takes about one-and-a-half hours to complete. These fits are available from Coleman (out of George's Cycles) in Boise and through Wobble-naught/Myo-facts authorized technicians in many locations nationwide, in Canada and in South Africa, and upon request at race camps. The Myo-facts sEMG software costs an additional $100, and requires about one hour. Telemetry on the road is additional. The SOLE foot bed costs $40. For $36, www.wobblenaught.com (where you can also find a dealer locater) offers a solution that allows the home user to obtain an accurate fit. The user will need someone to assist in taking precise measurements of their anatomy and bike, and the site provides digital photos and MPEG videos to aid in understanding the measurement descriptions. You must print out a blank measurement data sheet and record the measurements before inputting them into the system, since the time clock on the system limits data-entry time.

Boulder Center for Sports Medicine

One of the most eminent bicycle fitters in the United States is Andy Pruitt, director of the Boulder Center for Sports Medicine, former race doctor for the Tour Du Pont, and an accomplished cyclist in his own right. Top pro cyclists from all over the world make the trek to Boulder, Colorado, to "go see Andy." According to Pruitt, "We do basic fits, but really we specialize in the medical-grade fit, both traditional and using 3-D computer video. Most of our patients/clients have orthopedic issues. Sometimes they come just for comfort or performance, but most of the time they have failed to resolve their pain with a traditional fit somewhere else and seek us out." A recent example of an out-of-state client from is mountain bike World Cup and world champion Gunn-Rita Dahle from Norway.

The "3-D" Pruitt is talking about is three-dimensional digital imagery. The process involves placing reflective markers on the hips, knees, ankles, and feet and filming the pedaling rider from the front and side using six infrared cameras (see Photo 13.4). A computer digitizes the film into moving stick figures that are then analyzed for efficient pedaling motion. Pruitt X rays a rider's leg bones to detect leg-length discrepancies and corrects for them appropriately, and he can provide custom foot beds to put inside the shoes. The basic Performance Fit is $185. The 3-D Digital Imaging Fit, which includes a medical office visit, costs $400. X-ray charges are additional. Check out www.bch.org/sportsmedicine for more information.

13.4

In its 3-D Digital Imaging Fit, the Boulder Center for Sports Medicine creates a digitized moving image on the computer screen of the rider's legs by placing reflective dots on the hip, knee, and ankle joints and filming the pedaling rider from the front and side using six infrared cameras.

COURTESY OF BCSM

Body Scanning CRM

Body Scanning CRM stands for Customer Relationship Marketing, which indicates that it is more than just a fit system for bicycle retailers. The software package allows a dealer to capture not only fit information but also customer information that they can use to follow up with clients. All the measurements are done with a laser, for accuracy and speed, and its bike adjustment gauge transfers measurements to the bike. The Body Scanning CRM system is in its infancy in the United States but was developed in Germany. It has been in use for five years within BICO (www.bicoplus.de), Germany's second largest bicycle dealer cooperative, which consists of more than 400 stores. See the www.bodyscanningcrm.com Web site for more information. Pricing is up to the retailer.

Tiemeyer Dynamic Bike Fit

Working with USA Cycling and USA Triathlon team athletes since the early 1990s while at GT bicycles, aeronautical engineer and framebuilder David Tiemeyer has developed Tiemeyer Dynamic Bike Fit. While the client pedals on various geometries on the Tiemeyer Position Cycle (see Photo 13.5), performance data are quantified under controlled conditions of heart rate and cadence. The system produces graphs of power output, frontal area, and predicted speed in each position, as well as a drawing of the optimized frame geometry. The cost of the Dynamic Bike Fit is $50 per hour and takes two to three hours depending on the number of positions analyzed. The cost of the service can be applied toward the purchase of a new Tiemeyer frame. A free sizing calculator is posted at www.tiemeyercycles.com, giving frame geometries for nine types of frames.

A rider receiving a Dynamic Fit from David Tiemeyer tries various Position Cycle setups while her power output is monitored.

DAVID TIEMEYER

Personal AccuFit

With framebuilder Bill Boston's Personal AccuFit system, you can do fittings for up to two riders with unlimited bike setups for each rider for $30. At greater expense, AccuFit Professional is for bike shops that fit lots of riders. AccuFit Designer is for framebuilders and includes a system that not only fits the rider but also helps design the frame, the mitering angles, exact tube lengths, and jig setup instructions. See www.billbostoncycles.com for more information.

Bike Dealers

The Bicycle Ranch (www.bicycleranch.com) in Scottsdale, Arizona, is a bike dealer that offers a high-end fitting system incorporating European coaching experience, the Serotta Certified Fitting Program, and the inputs of biomechanists, doctors, and physical therapists. It claims to be "one of the most in-depth series of fitting services available anywhere in the world" and costs $90, $150, or $300, depending on the level of fit.

In addition, there are numerous highly qualified fit experts at bike shops throughout the country, many certified on some of the above fitting systems, and many with their own fit methods. Ask for referrals from local cyclists. Depending on the dealer, they may charge for fitting services or include the cost in the price of a bicycle.

Furthermore, recognizing the importance of good fit to create happy customers, some big bike companies provide fit systems through their dealers.

Online Fit Resources

While do-it-yourself online fitting services do exist, note that you'll always need another person to take the measurements.

As I have mentioned in other blocks, there is also a free frame size calculator on my Web site, www.zinncycles.com. It calculates frame dimensions, crank length, saddle height, and other setup parameters for road and mountain bikes based on measurements you input.

Some of the above fit systems have online versions as well, and a Web search will certainly unearth other online resources.

Print Resources

A plethora of books out there contain bicycle fitting information. The late Ed Burke's *High-Tech Cycling*, 2nd ed. (2003) has a chapter on it, as does *Mountain Bike Like a Champion* by Ned Overend and Ed Pavelka (1999). Greg LeMond and Kent Gordis devote considerable space to correct fit in *Greg LeMond's Complete Book of Bicycling*, 2nd ed. (1990), as does Eddie B. in *Bicycle Road Racing: The Complete Program for Training and Competition* by Edward Borysewicz and Ed Pavelka (1985). *Andy Pruitt's Medical Guide for Cyclists* by Andrew L. Pruitt, Ed.D. with Fred Mathen (2001) has a chapter on each of a number of bike fit aspects. I have included an appendix on fit in *Zinn and the Art of Road Bike Maintenance* (VeloPress, 2000) as well as in *Zinn and the Art of Mountain Bike Maintenance* (VeloPress, 2001). There are doubtless numerous other books that contain fit sections that I am unaware of. There is no sense suffering in pain or having questions about your riding efficiency because resources abound for you. 🚲

PART 2

Fine-Tuning Your Body

BLOCK 14
Nutrition

Primary to any human-powered activity is what goes into the human doing the powering. If you don't put the right kind of fuel, or enough of it, in your car, you don't expect it to run properly. You can hardly expect your body to behave any differently; it runs efficiently on some foods and poorly or not at all on others, and its caloric intake must equal or exceed its caloric output or else that output will not last long.

And daily nutrition is at least as important to improvements in training as it is during or just before a competition or endurance cycling event. Cindy Dallow, Ph.D., a registered dietitian and marathon runner, has found in her practice that "most cyclists were not eating enough—not enough calories and especially not enough carbohydrates." Along with a proper balance of macronutrients (carbohydrate, protein, and fat), a cyclist must provide the body with sufficient micronutrients (vitamins, minerals, and enzymes).

Carbohydrates, Bonking, and High-Protein Diets

When I was bike racing on an international level in 1981, racers constantly sought out large quantities of carbohydrates, especially pasta. Now at the turn of the millennium, *carbohydrate* has become a dirty word; heck, many foods of questionable nutritional value, including pork rinds, beer, and vodka, are now advertised as healthy because they are low in carbohydrates! Magazines at the grocery checkout counter promote high-protein diets like The Atkins Diet, 40-30-30, The Paleo Diet, and others, and people are flocking to them.

40-30-30 refers to the relative percentages of carbohydrate, protein, and fat in the diet; that contrasts with the 60 percent carbohydrate and 20 percent maximum fat recommendations implicit in the federal government's "food pyramid." The Paleo Diet is based on the theory that the human digestive system evolved over hundreds of thousands of years, and that the cultivation of grain has existed only for a few thousand. Following this reasoning, it makes sense that eating like a hunter-gatherer might best provide the sustenance your body needs.

I am not questioning the weight loss and other health benefits that people report having achieved with high-protein, high-fat diets, especially since I myself have noticed health benefits from following more of a hunter-gatherer type diet for a number of years. However, if you want to perform at your best in an endurance sport, the fact remains that the most effective fuel is carbohydrate. In virtually every study of sports nutrition ever done, athletes performed better on high-carbohydrate diets than on high-protein or high-fat diets. You need to ingest adequate carbohydrates in order to store enough glycogen for your muscles to keep firing and avoid "bonking." (Bonking is the uncomfortable and disheartening sudden drop in performance that occurs when the body runs out of fuel during demanding physical activity.)

"The thing I see the most with cyclists is not getting enough carbs and not seeing how to," says Dallow. "They are often relieved to hear that they can eat carbs after hearing all the bad stuff about them in the news these days!"

In case you are thinking, "Yes, but what about burning fat instead of carbohydrate?" there simply is no science to back up the idea that the body can burn fat alone during endurance sports. Admittedly, there is compelling anecdotal evidence that burning fat works. For instance, Mark Allen won the Hawaii Ironman® a number of times while reportedly eating a high-fat diet and doing almost all of his training at low intensity; he intended to train his body to burn fat as its primary energy source. Since there is so much fat in the human body (even in skinny people like Allen), if you could train your body to depend on fat alone for energy during a race, you wouldn't have to worry about bonking. There's no question that while training at low intensity the body derives a higher percentage of its energy from fat than it does while training at high intensity; but no study has shown that training can increase the percentage of fat burned when you're racing at a high intensity. Studies have shown that the total amount of fat burned per unit of time is the same in low-intensity as in high-intensity training; the ratio of fat to carbohydrate burned is simply greater at low intensity because lower caloric demand requires less carbohydrate burning. According to Dallow, "It takes twenty minutes to break down the body's fat tissue, so the body will automatically switch to carbos when the workout intensity goes up."

Carbo Loading

Classic carbo loading involves first starving yourself of carbohydrates for a few days in advance of a big race to deplete your muscles' glycogen levels. Then, 1 to 3 days before the event, you eat large quantities of almost solely carbohydrate, which "supersaturates" your muscles with glycogen. These high levels of glycogen in the muscles, unobtainable by merely stuffing yourself on carbohydrate without depleting yourself of them first, allow you to exert yourself harder for a longer time before bonking. Nonetheless, you must delay glycogen depletion during the event by eating some carbohydrate along the way. A good way to do this in high-intensity events is with carbohydrate- and electrolyte-replacement drinks and carbohydrate-rich energy gel packets. For lower-intensity events, eating energy bars, muffins, and fruit works fine.

Along with some of the new fad diets has come the idea of fat loading, rather than carbo loading, to extend the duration of effort without bonking. But there is no scientific evidence that you are able to exert yourself longer after fat loading. It appears that only stored fat breaks down into energy, and your body's supply of stored fat is so large that fat loading would not appreciably affect it immediately. Furthermore, fat takes too long to break down to depend on it as an energy source in high-intensity exercise.

How Much Should You Eat?

It is probably obvious that the goal is to match your energy intake with your energy output. If your food intake exceeds your caloric output, your body either (literally) flushes those calories out of the system or stores them as fat. If the caloric output exceeds the intake, the body has to make up the difference or it can't keep going, so it burns tissue stored either as fat, protein (that is, muscle), or both. So, if you want to lose weight, you don't have to be a rocket scientist to see that all you need to do is burn more energy than you consume. Tour de France superstars like Lance Armstrong and Tyler Hamilton carefully watch their energy output in the spring and intentionally eat fewer calories in order to drop weight from their lean frames prior to their annual July engagement. Armstrong and Hamilton have the benefit of numbers from physiological tests of basal metabolic rate (BMR) and energy consumed on the bike (measured by a power meter), which added together equal total energy consumption (see Blocks 15 and 18). You may not be able to measure your energy consumption as precisely as they do, but qualified dietitians can accurately estimate an athlete's caloric demands from charts based on height, weight, and activity level, and new, easy-to-use BMR systems can be found in many sports medicine and health club settings.

Dietary consultation starts with assessing what an athlete eats; the athlete fills out questionnaires at each meal. Inputting this information into a computer can result in a precise count of the calories derived from carbohydrate, protein, and fat, but it can also be done fairly accurately using only charts. A dietitian can gauge food intake compared to standard recommendations for endurance athletes based on age, gender, fitness level, and training regimen. This process is particularly useful in clearing up misconceptions. "I see people who think they are on high-carbohydrate diets but actually are on high-fat diets," says Dallow. "For instance, cookies and donuts are high-fat foods, not high-carbohydrate. And contrary to popular belief, beer is actually not a high-carb food either; there are 8 grams of carbohydrate in an 8-ounce beer compared to 43 grams of carbohydrate in 8 ounces of cranberry juice. I'm not against beer; health-wise and training-wise, there's nothing wrong with moderate alcohol consumption, but avoid it one or two nights before a race since it will dehydrate you."

How and When to Eat Carbohydrates

Many cultures have beliefs about eating foods in particular combinations and in which order specific foods should be eaten. In many cases, the beliefs on these subjects may be completely contradictory from one culture to another. "I could write a book on all of the myths about food," chuckles Dallow. "You can eat protein, carbohydrate, and fat in the same sitting and in any order. If you feel good afterward, then that is a good indicator. People need to relax about it."

That applies to when to eat what at a sitting. However, according to Amy Roberts, former dietitian for the Boulder Center for Sports Medicine, "It is important when you eat relative to exercise—especially that you have some carbohydrate within the first half hour after exercise and again a couple of hours later to refill your glycogen levels optimally." Roberts points to studies that have shown that if you wait to eat beyond that half-hour window, your body robs its own resources, usually muscle tissue, to replenish muscle glycogen. The glycogen level replenished this way tops out with only about half as much stored compared to if you had eaten sooner and blocks further replenishment from the next meal. All in all, your recovery time is extended by not eating carbohydrate within the first half hour after exercise. She suggests consuming over 100 grams of carbohydrate during the hour before exercise (100 grams of carbohydrate is about two energy bars); the equivalent of 4 to 8 ounces of sports drink every 15 minutes during exercise longer than one hour; and over 100 grams of carbohydrate within a half hour after exercise, and again two hours after exercise. Furthermore, Dallow says that adding a bit of protein—such as yogurt, a bagel with cheese or milk, a sports bar, or pizza—to those carbohydrates may help stimulate the body to store glycogen.

A Sample Diet Recommendation

An average 150-pound male athlete who rides two hours a day needs approximately 540 grams of carbohydrate and a total of 3,000 calories per day. What does that mean in terms of real eating? For example, 3,200 calories per day could be composed of the following: 20 servings from the bread group (a serving is 1 slice of bread or ⅓ cup of rice), 5 vegetable servings, 10 servings of fruit (a serving is ½ cup of juice or 1 piece of fruit), 3 to 4 servings from the dairy group, 4 to 6 servings from the meat group (a serving is 4 to 6 ounces of meat), and 12 servings from the fat group. This high-carbohydrate plan would benefit a cyclist. Don't worry about making a conscious effort to take in the fat—you get lots of it in the other foods, so attaining these 12 servings of fat requires no focus whatsoever.

Chiropractor and avid cyclist Craig Pearson says, "I think Lance Armstrong may lose some of his competitive advantage now that other riders mimic the measures he takes with his diet. Now other teams also travel with their own cook and monitor what the riders eat." Pearson says that, because of the demands of the sport, cyclists particularly need to take in Omega 3 fatty acids, certain enzymes, and B-complex vitamins.

"I believe that people should enjoy food and work the foods they love into their diet," says Dallow. "A few Twinkies here and there are not a big deal, and I give people tips about snacks. People worry too much about if this food will make them do this or that. I think people need to relax and enjoy their food, including having a glass of wine with it if they feel like it." 🚲

Nutrition and lifestyle coach Cindy Dallow, Ph.D., R.D., works with Partners in Nutrition, LLC.

BLOCK 15
Assessing Your Condition

If you want to get faster, you just ride more, right? Well, depending on your current condition, riding more may or may not improve your cycling. For the couch potato, riding more is the obvious and necessary first step. But for someone who already maintains a relatively high level of fitness, performance improvements are harder to come by and require conditioning for specific systems in the body. But it is hard to focus the training if you don't know the current status of these systems. Neal Henderson, a physiologist, certified triathlon coach, and coordinator of sport science at the Boulder Center for Sports Medicine, says, "It is best to start with testing; without baseline data, you're shooting in the dark a bit."

What is baseline data and how do you get it? A sports science lab can perform a number of physiological tests that, taken together, tell a fairly complete story about your body and its current capabilities. Armed with the results of these tests, you (and perhaps a coach) can come up with a highly specific, personalized training program designed to move you toward whatever your athletic goals happen to be. (I cover how to design the program in the next block.)

We are fortunate here in Boulder to have the Boulder Center for Sports Medicine; anyone can set up an appointment there and get the tests described below. But the type of equipment at the center is no longer rare and exists not only in sports medicine clinics. You can arrange to be tested in many health clubs, university athletic departments, and private coaching centers. And two of the most important tests, namely your basal metabolic rate and lactate threshold, can be approximated on your own, without a lab.

Body Composition (Body Fat)

The idea behind the body composition test is to determine what percentage of your body is comprised of fat. Obviously, the lower your body-fat percentage, the faster you can be, especially riding uphill, since you are carrying less weight that does not contribute toward powering the pedals. On the other hand, the higher your body-fat percentage, the more you can improve your cycling, with training, compared to a thinner person!

The test methodology can be simple or complicated. The easiest is a skin-fold test. At a number of points around the body, the thickness at the base of a pinch of skin is measured with a caliper. The numbers are averaged and plugged into a formula, yielding a body-fat percentage.

A specific-gravity test for body composition is more complex. Sitting in a suspended chair, you are lowered into a vat of water. A scale from which the chair hangs measures your weight in the air and in the water. As fat is less dense than muscle, the lower the submerged weight relative to the mid-air weight (that is, the better you float), the higher your body-fat percentage.

However, air in your lungs increases your flotation, so a correction must be made. First you take a giant breath and blow it all out into a tube to measure your "vital capacity," or the volume of air your lungs hold. When you exhale underwater as completely as you can, a certain percentage of the air remains in your lungs and reduces the measured weight. A formula incorporating your vital capacity adjusts for that air and gives a more accurate measurement of body-fat percentage.

The gold standard body-fat test is dual-energy X-ray absorption (DEXA). Two different wavelengths of X rays are sent into the body, one of which is absorbed better by fat. The difference in how these wavelengths pass through the tissue shows the percentage of fat in the body.

Basal Metabolic Rate

The basal metabolic rate (BMR), also called resting energy expenditure (REE), is particularly important if you are trying to lose weight. For this test, you lie down in a dark room for an extended period with a breathing apparatus over your nose and mouth that measures your inhaled and expired gases. By measuring the rate of oxygen going into you versus the rate of carbon dioxide coming back out of you, a technician can determine the rate at which you consume calories at rest.

That's your BMR (or REE). This number is about 60 percent to 80 percent of your total daily caloric need; when factored in with your present athletic status, daily activities and training load, age, sex, weight, and body-fat percentage, it gives an accurate prediction of the total number of calories your body burns per day. Then your diet can be adjusted accordingly, for instance to include fewer calories if you want to lose weight.

Even without a BMR test, you can consult a chart for a person of your age, sex, and build to roughly predict your daily caloric requirements.

Respiratory Quotient

The respiratory quotient (RQ) is the ratio of the volume of carbon dioxide the body produces versus the volume of oxygen it consumes. By looking at the relative percentages of carbon dioxide and oxygen you expire, the technician knows what fuels your muscles are burning. The reactions that produce adenosine triphosphate, or ATP (energy for the cells), result in different relative amounts of oxygen and carbon dioxide in the expired breath. The exact number depends on whether the body is burning carbohydrate, fat, or protein. An RQ of 0.7 would mean that only fat was being metabolized, while an RQ of 1.0 would indicate that only carbohydrate was being metabolized. (When the body burns carbohydrate, six oxygen molecules combine with a carbohydrate molecule to yield six carbon dioxide molecules, ATP, and water. So, the ratio of oxygen consumed to carbon dioxide expired is one-to-one.) Protein is also burned as a fuel, but during intense exercise the amount is negligible.

At low power output, the body burns mostly fat, and at high power, mostly carbohydrate. At VO$_2$ max (your highest aerobic intensity—see below), you produce more lactate than your body has the capacity to clear. In that case, RQ goes above 1.0 because, in buffering the acid associated with the lactate, the body produces (and exhales) extra carbon dioxide.

Maximum Oxygen Uptake

The maximum oxygen uptake test, commonly known as VO$_2$ max, is renowned, likely because it is difficult to endure. It measures the volume of oxygen (in milliliters) that the body takes in per kilogram of body weight per minute when working at its maximum intensity. Therein lies the difficult part; to get the reading, you have to ride as hard as you possibly can until you cannot go anymore.

As in the REE and RQ tests, the total volume of inhaled and expired gases and their relative percentages are monitored through a mask that the rider wears over his lower face. Throughout the test, technicians measure heart rate, may check blood pressure, and record the rider's subjective assessment of perceived effort on a scale from 1 to 10. The standard procedure is for the rider to pedal an ergometer while maintaining discrete power output levels for certain durations at a fixed cadence. If you make it through one period (which usually lasts one minute) without letting your cadence drop, then the ergometer's resistance is notched up so that your power output jumps another 25 or so watts. You try to hold the same cadence at that level for the next period of time, and so on. Ultimately, you get to the point at which you can no longer maintain the cadence through the entire period. Just before this point, your body was taking in the maximum volume of oxygen it could per minute; it's the maximum heart rate/maximum lactate point shown at the far right of the graph in Figure 15.1. You divide this figure by your body mass, and you have found your VO_2 max!

This figure is a good predictor of performance in a large population; those with the highest max VO_2 will likely be the fastest. But among elite athletes, it is a much less accurate

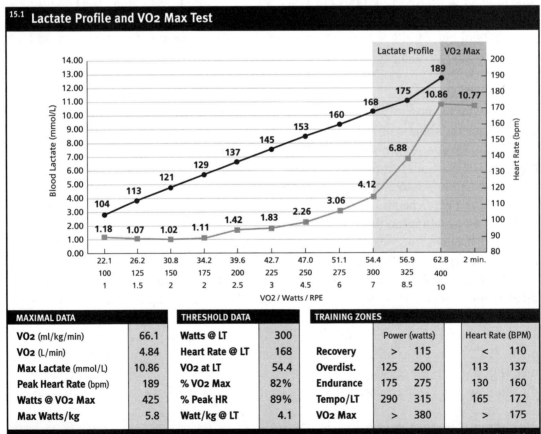

15.1 Lactate Profile and VO2 Max Test

MAXIMAL DATA		THRESHOLD DATA		TRAINING ZONES				
					Power (watts)		Heart Rate (BPM)	
VO2 (ml/kg/min)	66.1	Watts @ LT	300					
VO2 (L/min)	4.84	Heart Rate @ LT	168	Recovery	>	115	<	110
Max Lactate (mmol/L)	10.86	VO2 at LT	54.4	Overdist.	125	200	113	137
Peak Heart Rate (bpm)	189	% VO2 Max	82%	Endurance	175	275	130	160
Watts @ VO2 Max	425	% Peak HR	89%	Tempo/LT	290	315	165	172
Max Watts/kg	5.8	Watt/kg @ LT	4.1	VO2 Max	>	380	>	175

This is a graph from a lactate threshold test that continued to VO2 max. The heart rate and power data at VO2 max and at LT is listed in the left and center tables: From this graph, the heart rate and power output for the five defined training zones is calculated (see Block 16) and both are shown in the Training Zones table (above right).

SOURCE: BCSM

determinant of performance than lactate threshold (LT), especially the power output at LT. VO_2 max is ultimately limited by genetics and does cap an athlete's aerobic capability. But it can be increased, with training, up to that genetically predetermined point. What is more important is how close to the VO_2 max an athlete can work for extended periods and how much power he or she can put out at that level. This is measured in the LT test described below.

Lactate Threshold

If you are in a position to do only one test, then the LT is the one to do. Most sports physiologists would agree that this test, also known as a lactate profile, is the most critical for determining a training program and also is the best predictor of an athlete's endurance performance at a given point in time.

How lactic acid affects the body

When the body breaks down carbohydrate in the absence of oxygen (that is, anaerobically), it produces lactic acid, or lactate. The lactate is a by-product of the reaction that produces ATP, which fuels the muscle cells.

Lactic acid, which is often blamed for muscle cramping, breaks down immediately to form lactate and a hydrogen ion, which is an acid. Henderson says, "It is the accumulation of the acid ions that you feel interfering with muscle contractions; it's not the lactate!" With training, the body produces less lactate at a given intensity, and it also produces enzymes to break lactate down and convert it into usable energy. Lactate is not just a waste product; your heart actually uses it as a fuel. Training will also improve the body's ability to buffer the acid produced from the dissociation of the lactic acid.

Above the LT, also called the aerobic threshold, the body is doing so much work anaerobically (without oxygen, in a reaction that produces ATP and lactate) that it cannot maintain the pace for an extended period. This is because the lactate (actually, the acidic hydrogen ion) concentration interferes with muscle contraction. At LT, a trained athlete can maintain the pace for an hour or two.

How the test works

Like the VO_2 max test, a lactate threshold test starts at a low intensity. But as the power is stepped up every four minutes or so, the technician takes a blood sample from the athlete. This sample is analyzed for concentration of lactate, usually measured in millimoles of lactate per liter of blood. As the intensity of the effort increases, the concentration of blood lactate stays fairly constant and then begins to climb. As the effort continues to ramp up, the lactate concentration ultimately increases dramatically until the athlete reaches VO_2 max.

When working at low to moderate intensities, the body produces and then consumes and clears out lactate at the same rate. This equilibrium produces a flat line on a graph of heart rate (or power output or perceived effort) versus lactate concentration (the left end of the graph in Figure 15.1). The graph slopes up as the intensity climbs beyond this equilibrium. When you reach your LT, you are producing lactate faster than you can remove it, and the graph's slope steepens. LT is actually precisely the heart rate and power output at which the lactate concentration has gone up exactly one millimole per liter from its baseline level.

Benefits of knowing your LT

Knowing your LT is a great tool. It allows you to not only predict the power output you can maintain for long periods in a race, but also allows you to set up a training program designed specifically to raise your threshold (see Block 16 for this program). Untrained people will produce more lactate than they can clear at exercise intensities as low as 40 percent of their VO_2 max. Training allows you to shift the curve so that your LT is at 80 percent to 95 percent of your VO_2 max, and you increase VO_2 max to boot. It should be obvious that you would be riding much faster then!

Finding the lactate threshold yourself

If you have a heart monitor, or, better yet, a power meter on your bike, you can estimate your LT fairly accurately. Henderson says, "One good indirect indicator of your threshold is your respiration rate. Once you've passed your LT, your respiration rate really increases. If you incrementally speed up and note the heart rate [or power output] where your respiration really picks up, you'll be pretty close to your LT [about 5 to 10 beats above]."

You can also determine your LT during a time trial. In a half-hour time trial, your average heart rate will usually be 5 to 10 percent above your LT, and you will do a one-hour time trial at an average heart rate and power output that is at or up to 10 percent above LT. 🚲

Neal Henderson, M.S., C.S.C.S., is coordinator of sport science at the Boulder Center for Sports Medicine (www.bch.org/sportsmedicine).

BLOCK 16
Raising Your Lactate Threshold

E xcept for a few short, pure speed and/or power events in track racing, cycling is a sport of endurance. And in any endurance sport, what counts is being able to work at a high aerobic level (that is, with oxygen). If, to keep up with the other riders, you frequently have to resort to working anaerobically (without oxygen, as in a sprint), you will accumulate lactic acid in your muscles (see Block 15) that will force you to slow down relatively quickly.

What can you do about this, and how you can increase your endurance and speed? Well, you can actually raise the power output that you generate aerobically. This allows you to ride faster and longer, since you will not need to ride as long in an anaerobic state in order to keep up with your riding group. And all this depends on increasing your lactate threshold (LT).

As you may have read in the preceding block, your LT is the highest level at which you can work aerobically—the point at which your lactate production is at equilibrium with your lactate-clearing activity. The heart rate and power output associated with your LT can both be increased significantly with training, and the best predictor of a rider's racing performance is his or her power output at LT. So, if there is one aspect of your training to work on, this is it.

Training Intensities

There are three training intensities that improve your LT, overdistance, endurance, and lactate threshold. A good training program incorporates all three. Pay close attention to these intensities—inexperienced and uncoached athletes often train consistently at a relatively useless middle-ground intensity. The bulk of your training should be easy to moderate (that means resisting the urge to chase down that guy who just passed you!). And then when you train hard, you train very hard (not medium hard), making sure you are well rested beforehand.

High-Volume, Low-Intensity Training

The first way to raise your LT is with a large volume of training at both "overdistance" and "endurance" intensities (see Table 16.1 on heart rate zones for cycling). Training at these baseline intensity levels is the primary component of any training program, particularly of the base period, during which you develop aerobic capacity and adapt your body to higher training loads. At these training intensities, the body's adaptation and consequent increase in LT happens over a long period—months and years; this is not a quick fix, but it is the most important one. If you stick to these training zones with targeted training, you will accomplish your training goals effectively. LT training incorporates primarily zones 2, 3, and 5.

Overdistance rides (see zone 2) are your longest rides and are done at an easy pace. Start at perhaps an hour, and increase the duration by 10 to 15 percent each week, up to 6 to 8 hours. You should be able to talk easily and maintain the pace for the entire ride. Overdistance rides burn lots of fat, shed weight, train your body to utilize fat for fuel, and improve fitness and your body's ability to resist fatigue. Even though the ride's duration is long, the intensity is low, so recovery is rapid and your body can tolerate a lot of this training.

16.1 Heart Rate Zones for Cycling

	Perceived Effort	Blood Lactate

Zone 1 - Recovery — Very Easy — 2–3 mmol/L below LT

DURATION: 20 minutes–60 minutes

OBJECTIVE: This zone is used for warm-up and cool-down periods and to help assist in recovery from hard efforts and races. Recovery workouts don't necessarily make you faster, but they are crucial in recovering from taxing efforts. If you don't recover, you won't improve.

EXAMPLE: Easy 20-minute spin on Monday following a weekend of racing

Zone 2 - Overdistance — Easy — 1.5–2.5 mmol/L below LT

DURATION: 1–6 hours. Start short, and increase time by about 10–15% per week.

OBJECTIVE: This is the optimum zone to improve base fitness and fatigue resistance. Training in this zone improves your body's ability to use fat as a fuel source. Base training and weekly long rides should be performed at this effort. You should ride slow enough so you can talk and keep the pace for the entire ride.

EXAMPLE: Weekly long ride, progressively getting longer (about 10%) each week, up to 6 hours

Zone 3 - Endurance — Moderate — 0.5–1.5 mmol/L below LT

DURATION: 45 minutes–2.5 hours

OBJECTIVE: Training in this zone improves the ability to deliver more oxygen to the muscle cell and process more energy from aerobic sources. Specific training adaptations include an increase in the size and number of mitochondria (where aerobic metabolism occurs), increased capillarization (carries blood to/from muscles), and an increased number of aerobic enzymes within the mitochondria.

EXAMPLE: Two-hour ride on rolling terrain

Zone 4 - Tempo — Somewhat Hard — 0.5–0 mmol/L below LT

DURATION: 15–50 minute continuous effort, or long intervals (10–15 minutes) for a total of 40–60 min.

OBJECTIVE: Training at this intensity will improve your ability to maintain a high pace for a long time. Speed and power should be slightly slower than 40K TT pace.

EXAMPLE: 10-mile tempo, or 30-minute climb. Always warm up and cool down before and after!

Zone 5 - Lactate Threshold — Very Hard — at LT or 0.5 mmol/L above LT

DURATION: 5–15 minute intervals, for a total of 20–45 minutes. Recovery should be equal to interval time.

OBJECTIVE: Training at this intensity will raise LT as a percentage of VO2 max, increase speed at LT, improve race pace feel and economy, and improve your ability to sustain high levels of lactic acid. For time trial events, your power output at LT closely predicts race performance. For climbing, your power output at LT divided by your body weight (power/weight ratio) accurately predicts performance.

EXAMPLE: 3 x 3 mile at LT, recover 1-mile easy spin or 3 x 5 minutes at LT with 3-minute recovery

Zone 6 - VO2 Max* — Extremely Hard — 2–6 mmol/L above LT

DURATION: 2–5 minute intervals with equal amount of recovery, for a total of 10–20 minutes of effort

OBJECTIVE: This is the optimum zone for improving VO2 max. Training adaptations include an increase in stroke volume (how much blood the heart pumps each beat) and improved lactate tolerance (buffering capacity).

EXAMPLE: 2 x 5-minute steep climb or 5 x 2 minutes at VO2 max with 2-minute recovery

Zone 7 - Speed / Power* — Extremely Hard — 2–15 mmol/L above LT

DURATION: Short: 10–60 seconds with complete recovery; Long: 1–2 minutes with complete recovery

OBJECTIVE: Training at this zone increases anaerobic capacity and buffering capacity. It's easy to overdo it with these workouts. Be sure to be rested before these workouts and recover after them.

EXAMPLE: Hill repeats, sprint intervals, criterium workouts, etc.

* **NOTE:** These workouts are very intense and should only be performed after an adequate aerobic base period of 8-12 weeks. Your recovery time will be much longer with these types of workouts. Be sure to monitor for signs and symptoms of overtraining when you perform these workouts.

SOURCE: BCSM

Certified coach Neal Henderson says, "The key is not 1- to 2-hour rides. The key is getting in those 4- to 6-hour rides. You have significantly more heart and leg muscles contractions than in an interval session of half the length and a much faster recovery." Sometimes it seems like you are going too easy to be doing any good; we are all conditioned to think that from decades of hearing "no pain, no gain." But Henderson notes, "The athletes I have coached who have been the most successful are the ones who did the most volume of easy workouts. Then they are completely recovered for their hard workouts and can really do them hard."

Endurance rides (see zone 3) increase your ability to get oxygen to the muscles and produce more energy through aerobic processes. These rides are done at a moderate intensity ranging from 45 minutes to 2.5 hours and comprise perhaps a quarter of total training hours. Within the cells, endurance training increases the size and number of mitochondria (the site of aerobic metabolism) as well as the number of aerobic enzymes found within the mitochondria. Capillarization also increases—your body increases the number and size of capillaries carrying blood to the muscle cells.

Henderson says, "It is possible to do 5- to 6-hour rides at the endurance level, but the stress hormones released will slow down the recovery process, so it is not optimal."

Low-Volume, High-Intensity Training

The other way to raise your LT is with a low volume of training at, or slightly above, your LT intensity (see zone 5 in sidebar). After establishing an extended base-training period during which you completed high volume of workouts at low intensity, you can do one or two of these more intense workouts per week over a one- to two-month period. The body adapts relatively quickly; the LT increases over days and weeks. While this may be a "quick fix," it requires the prior base-training period to build upon. Low-intensity work helps you produce less lactate; workouts at LT, or just above, improve the body's ability to deal with the lactate.

LT training is hard training. It is "interval" training (yes, the dreaded intervals!), because you cannot just ride at or above your LT for an unlimited period. If you try, you will end up in that relatively useless middle-ground intensity I mentioned before.

These intervals are primarily aerobic, which means they can be longer and more numerous. They should last 3 to 20 minutes at a heart rate that ranges from just below LT to five beats above LT, with a rest period of half the duration of the interval. Rest periods are active rest—pedaling easily. An example of an LT interval would be 6 repetitions of 3 minutes at LT or slightly above, with 90 seconds of rest between. Other intervals are suggested under zone 5. Progressively increase the interval length each week or two.

If you have a power meter, you can measure these intervals even more precisely than with heart rate, since power at LT is more accurate. For instance, if your power output climbs above your power at LT level, you see it immediately on the power meter, but it takes a half minute or more to show up in your heart rate. This is because there is a delay in your heart's reaction, and a further delay from the heart meter, because it averages measurements over a period of 15 seconds or so. By that time, it may be too late—you will have been working anaerobically for perhaps a minute, and the lactic acid buildup will have made it impossible for you to work as hard during subsequent intervals as the workout indicated.

It is useful to get accustomed to what you feel like at your LT. Then, in the absence of a power meter, you can moderate the intensity based on your perceived effort, rather than being a slave to a heart monitor that has a built-in delay.

As you become better trained, your LT increases—specifically your power output at LT increases. The graph in Figure 16.2 shows this movement of the lactate curve "down and to the right" that illustrates the increase in LT. Over time, you must adjust the intensity of your LT workouts to match your new, increased LT, especially if you are using a power meter, since the power at LT will have gone up significantly more than the heart rate at LT. This requires either getting another lactate profile done or estimating your LT yourself as covered in Block 15. To maximize the results from LT training, refer to Block 19 on rest and training periodization. 🚲

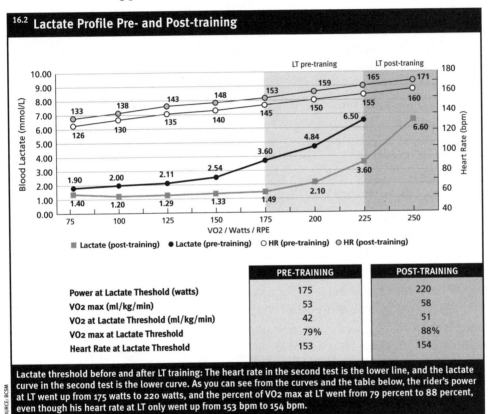

16.2 Lactate Profile Pre- and Post-training

	PRE-TRAINING	POST-TRAINING
Power at Lactate Theshold (watts)	175	220
VO2 max (ml/kg/min)	53	58
VO2 at Lactate Threshold (ml/kg/min)	42	51
VO2 max at Lactate Threshold	79%	88%
Heart Rate at Lactate Threshold	153	154

Lactate threshold before and after LT training: The heart rate in the second test is the lower line, and the lactate curve in the second test is the lower curve. As you can see from the curves and the table below, the rider's power at LT went up from 175 watts to 220 watts, and the percent of VO2 max at LT went from 79 percent to 88 percent, even though his heart rate at LT only went up from 153 bpm to 154 bpm.

SOURCE: BCSM

Neal Henderson, M.S., C.S.C.S., is the coordinator of sport science at the Boulder Center for Sports Medicine (www.bch.org/sportsmedicine).

BLOCK 17

Improving Your Cycling Economy

By improving your cycling economy, I am not talking about buying less expensive bike equipment! I'm talking about improving your body's energy economics—your economy of motion, if you will.

After power at lactate threshold (see Block 16), cycling economy is likely the most important determinant of your cycling performance. Your power at lactate threshold dictates how fast you can go for a sustained period, but your economy is how many miles per gallon you get. Oxygen is the fuel, so you want to get farther down the road with each molecule of oxygen you suck in. There are a number of methods to improve cycling economy. Among them are:

- improving technique and form
- high-volume training at low intensity
- strength training
- speed intervals
- reducing aerodynamic drag and rolling resistance
- reducing weight
- improving comfort

Improve Technique and Form

Your pedaling style is probably not optimally efficient. You can also probably improve your cycling posture and breathing mechanics, to get more air into your lungs with each breath.

When people think about their pedaling style, they generally think only about pulling with each foot through the upstroke. In my opinion, that approach ignores the fact that the vast majority of the power you generate is on the downstroke. I think that the major benefit of focusing on the upstroke is actually in releasing the pressure on the pedal just past the bottom of the stroke. If you do not unweight the pedal before it starts coming back up, then you are working against yourself because your front foot is lifting your back foot, frittering away some of your power.

Another part of this equation is pushing down sooner. If you let your upward foot coast over the top of the stroke and don't start pushing down until you reach the the two- or three-o'clock position, you are leaving some of your potential power unused on a shelf. I like to think of pedaling, whether sitting or standing, as climbing a set of stairs. Focus on stepping up to each successive stair and stepping down onto it as soon as your foot gets on top of it. Doing so, you will naturally lift each foot off the bottom of the stroke and pull up on it, and you will apply power at the top of the stroke sooner. Figures 17.1 and 17.2 show how the feet of two riders differ in the magnitude and direction of force on the pedals at each position in the pedal stroke. Figure 17.1 reveals a more efficient pedaling style than Figure 17.2; in Figure 17.1, the rider's back foot resists the upward movement of the pedal on the upstroke less, and his forward foot begins pushing down at a higher position in the stroke.

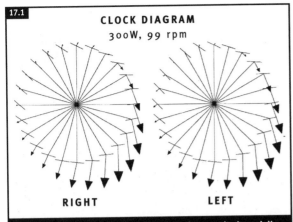

17.1

CLOCK DIAGRAM
300W, 99 rpm

RIGHT   **LEFT**

The size and direction of the arrows show the magnitude and direction of each foot's force on force—measuring pedals at each position in the pedal stroke. You can see that this rider works against himself less on the backstroke and begins the downstroke earlier (higher in the stroke) than the rider in 17.2.

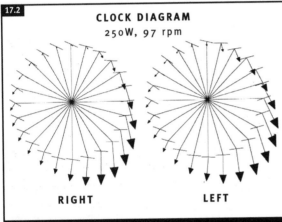

17.2

CLOCK DIAGRAM
250W, 97 rpm

RIGHT   **LEFT**

The size and direction of the arrows in this figure reveal a less efficient pedaling style than that depicted in 17.1. This rider is pushing down with the back foot longer than the other rider, and he begins pushing down with the forward foot later.

JEFF BROKER, USOC

Pedaling while standing up is generally inefficient, since it makes your center of mass move up and down, which requires energy, and it also increases your aerodynamic drag. That said, there are times when standing saves energy in the long run, like when sprinting to reach a group of riders so you can draft among them, or when sprinting to carry your momentum over a steep, short hill. Furthermore, on a long climb, aerodynamic drag has a lesser effect due to the slow speed (air drag increases as the square of the velocity, so at half the speed, the rider has a quarter the drag), so the aerodynamic downside of standing is less. And if being out of the saddle is what it takes to generate enough power to stay with your group over the climb, after which drafting with them will save you energy, then so be it.

When you're standing, again I recommend you use the stair analogy. Put your entire weight on the pedal at the top of the stroke, rather than leaning on the bars or having any weight on the other foot that is coming up. Use your weight to push the pedal down while at the same time forcefully straightening your leg. If you get to the bottom of the stroke with a bent leg, you are again leaving some of your power unused on a shelf. And the act of lifting your downward foot up to the next stair takes your weight off the bottom pedal and pulls it up as well. When standing, use your arms to pull up on the bars, not to rest on them. This will also naturally bring your body into a position of balance over the pedals, so that your force and weight are directed straight down over the pedal, rather than having your butt back, which would require you to transfer power through your arched back.

Pedaling efficiency especially makes a difference when climbing, particularly on dirt, because those pedaling more efficiently and consequently getting better traction will ride away from you. (See the comments of Jeff Broker, sport biomechanist for the U.S. Olympic Committee, on this subject in Block 29, as well as more on the subject in Block 25.) When riding up a steep climb, your cadence is low—an ideal condition in which to learn pedaling technique. Just as you learn a complex piece on the piano by first playing it slowly, pedaling technique is best learned at low rpms. Then work up to higher rpms, keeping the same technique.

You can probably also improve your breathing form. Notice if your chest is open or if your diaphragm and shoulders are impinging on your breathing space. Make a conscious effort to open your chest; you may need to go back and work on some of the fit issues covered in Blocks 2, 3, and 4. Breathing technique is also important, and besides being conscious about it, you can actively pursue disciplines like yoga and Alexander Technique that focus on breathing.

High-Volume Training at Low Intensity

Training a lot at low intensity (see Block 16, Fig. 16.1 for details on overdistance and endurance intensities) conditions the body to work more efficiently. It also burns fat (reducing your weight and hence the amount of power you need to propel yourself) and trains your body to use a more energy-efficient method of fueling your muscles.

Strength Training

The stronger your muscles, the more power they'll deliver to the pedals with the same amount of oxygen taken up. One way to improve strength is by training with weights in a gym.

Speed Intervals

Speed intervals differ from the lactate-threshold intervals described in Block 16, which are extended and incorporate only partial recovery; they are designed to increase your body's aerobic capacity and ability to clear lactate. Speed intervals, on the other hand, are extremely short—lasting perhaps 10 to 20 seconds—and include complete recovery. They are not designed to tax your body. Rather, they are designed to train your muscles to move very fast without exhausting them in the process. This leads to more efficient motion and the ability to turn the pedals faster without increasing oxygen demand. An example of a speed interval is to sprint full out for 10 seconds and then to pedal easily for several minutes before doing it again.

Reduce Aerodynamic Drag and Rolling Resistance

If you can reduce the friction on you and your bike, you will have more of your energy available to actually propel yourself.

The largest frictional force you encounter on a bike is aerodynamic drag, and over two-thirds of the drag on you and the bike is on you. The easiest element to address is clothing. If your shorts are baggy or your jersey, vest, or jacket are flapping, recognize that dressing this way is costing you extra effort to keep up with other riders.

As for your body itself, the first thing to reduce is its width in the wind. Look at your knees as you pedal; if they stick out to the sides, you are paying for that. Consciously pedal with your knees in close to the top tube. If that causes pain or discomfort, look into what might be happening biomechanically and correct it; Blocks 7 and 8 will be beneficial.

Getting your elbows in out of the wind is the next step and can be done with aero handlebars. (Consult Block 5 for more information.) Finally, lowering your shoulders and chin will reduce your drag. (See Blocks 4, 5, and 6.)

As for air drag on your bike, look first for the obvious things. Eliminate handlebar bags, panniers, fenders, racks, etc. If you have a big, wide under-the-seat bag, get rid of some of the stuff in it and use a smaller one. Next, look at the wheels. Wheels with fewer spokes (and flat spokes at that) and taller, airfoil-shaped rims will generally take less energy to propel on most terrain, provided they are reasonably light. Narrower, smoother tires also help. A fork with an aerodynamic shape usually contributes more aerodynamic savings than an aero frame and saves you big bucks in comparison to buying a new frame.

The other frictional forces to deal with are the rolling resistance of the tires and the rotating friction of the bearings in the wheel hubs, pedals, and bottom bracket. Smoother, better-quality tires with higher thread counts generally roll with less energy than tires with fewer, thicker, stiffer casing threads. Also, match your tire pressure to the conditions. The only time you want superhigh pressure is on a supersmooth surface. For instance, on a chip-sealed road, a tire pumped up rock hard cannot absorb the small variations in the road surface and is deflected over each gravel hunk, forcing your entire bike and body up and back and costing energy. But if the tire has less pressure, the individual gravel pieces depress into the tread, and the bike is able to roll more directly, with less deflection.

Also be sure to keep your bearings adjusted and well maintained so they spin smoothly and freely.

Reduce Weight

As with aerodynamics, the greatest contribution to the total weight of you and the bike is you. If you can decrease your weight without decreasing your power output, you will use less energy to ride at the same speed. Blocks 14 through 16 all deal with this at some level.

As for your bike, the only barrier to having a lighter one is usually financial. When choosing where to devote your budget, remember that rotating weight (wheels, tires, shoes, pedals) gives you the most reduction in energy requirements per unit of weight, so concentrate on those areas first. Then, recognize that swapping out large items like frames, forks, and cranks can yield the largest weight reductions, whereas swapping derailleurs, for instance, offers only very slight weight reductions.

Increase Comfort

Finally, if you are uncomfortable on your bike, you will not ride economically. Squirming around to relieve discomfort is neither aerodynamically efficient nor does it allow you to pedal efficiently. Consult Blocks 1 through 13 to address comfort and fit issues.

Training with a Power Meter

What's the best way to tell how hard you're cycling? It's not with a cycling speedometer/odometer. While it may be interesting to see how fast you are going or how far you have come, the information gleaned from a speedometer or odometer is not terribly useful for improving your fitness (other than perhaps by measuring the duration of the ride). A heart rate monitor (HRM) provides much more valuable information, because it gives a clearer picture of how hard your body is working. But the gold standard is an accurate measurement of your power output, since that tells you, definitively and instantaneously, exactly how hard your body is working.

18.1

The SRM measures the deflection of the crank's spider arms to determine power output.

GALEN NATHANSON

While many stationary-bicycle ergometers and trainer stands measure power output, they are not as useful as a bike-mounted power meter with which you can monitor not only all training rides but races as well. The ideal power meter is lightweight, unobtrusive, and accurate, and it also records heart rate, speed, and duration.

The German-made SRM (see Photos 18.1 and 18.2), designed by Ulrich Schoberer, was the first bike-mounted power meter that didn't need to be hooked up via cables to an accompanying computer-laden automobile. The SRM is

18.2

Lance Armstrong racing a time trial with an SRM power meter built into his right crankarm to gauge his effort

COURTESY OF SRM

built into the drive-side crank and measures the deflection of the spider arms onto which the chainrings are mounted. Many Tour de France winners, including Greg LeMond, Bjarne Riis, Jan Ullrich, and Lance Armstrong (Photo 18.2), have depended on the SRM for training and for monitoring themselves in races leading up to the Tour.

An American-invented power meter, the CycleOps Power Tap (see Photo 18.3), measures the torque (that is, the rotational force) on the rear hub shell. The Finnish heart monitor company, Polar, offers a power meter system as an accessory to its fully laden heart-monitor wristwatch (see Photo 18.4). Its sensor mounts on the right chainstay and actually listens to the pitch of the sound coming from the chain to determine chain tension, with which it calculates power output. The German-made Ergomo (see Photo 18.5) is built into the bottom bracket. It measures how much the pedaling forces pry the crankarm away from the bottom bracket spindle; however, it only measures this on one side.

These four systems are all relatively light and unobtrusive and transfer information from moving parts to stationary ones via radio waves. A mechanically aware cyclist willing to read the instructions can install any of them.

The CycleOps Power Tap calculates power output based on its measurement of the torque on the tubular hub shell.

GALEN NATHANSON

Polar's system listens to the musical pitch of the chain to determine its tension, and hence the rider's power output.

GALEN NATHANSON

Ergomo measures the power output from one leg with an sensor looking at how the crankarm is being pried away from the bottom bracket.

GALEN NATHANSON

Why Measure Power Output?

As I mentioned in Block 16, power measurement has an advantage over heart rate monitoring because it responds faster to what your body is actually doing. In a lab, you can find both your heart rate and power output associated with your lactate threshold in order to determine proper training zones (see Block 16). However, on the road, using heart rate as a gauge of intensity is too rough a measure. LeMond, a three-time Tour de France champion, was one of the first to use the SRM, and he gauged both his training and racing with it. He says, "In a time trial, I want to maintain a constant power (determined by lactate threshold tests and power data from actual races) to go my fastest. But if I take on a hill, using only a heart monitor, and try to keep a constant heart rate to gauge my effort, I will go too hard up the hill, because the heart monitor does not immediately reflect increases in power. Then the lactic acid buildup in my legs from going too hard up that hill slows me down for the remainder of the race."

An HRM's delay is partly due to the fact that your heart does not immediately jump up to a higher rate when you start pedaling harder—the heart takes some time to adjust to the higher energy demand. Furthermore, a heart rate monitor does not instantaneously display the measured heart rate. Instead, it displays an average of reading taken over a period of time.

An HRM's time lag can cost you in training as well as in racing. If you are doing specific lactate-threshold training and let your power go too high before you notice it on your HRM, you will have just gone too hard for the training to be optimal.

Another advantage of a power meter over an HRM is its superior accuracy. Your heart rate at the same power output may vary from day to day depending on how you slept, what you ate for breakfast, the temperature, and myriad other reasons. Power, on the other hand, is always power. No matter what the circumstances, the same absolute effort is always required to pedal at 350 watts, for instance. Again, the power meter's greater accuracy allows you (and your coach) to tailor your training very specifically to achieve your goals.

The quality and intensity of training and performance that cycling requires, particularly in special races like mountain climbing and time trialing, can be most easily described in terms of power. Your power is the value you want to increase through training, and if it decreases or does not stabilize, something is off with your body or training. It is much easier to control the quality and progress of the training when you can monitor power.

So, if you want to see optimal improvement in your cycling, get a power meter and slap it on your bike. Then, at the very least, you will want to follow the guidelines in Blocks 15, 16, 17, and 19 to see rapid improvement. Better yet, consult a qualified (and highly recommended) coach who can outline an individualized program based on the information the power meter provides. 🚲

BLOCK 19
Overtraining, Rest, and Periodization

When it comes to training, "no pain, no gain" is a fallacy; so is "more is better." Short-term increases in training stress are necessary to improve your speed and endurance, but following them with recovery periods is necessary for the improvement to take hold. In cycling, as in any endurance sport, your workouts do not make you faster or stronger; you only become faster or stronger when you recover from those workouts!

Muscles develop in response to "overload," or physiological stress. And in general, the greater the overload, the greater the resulting muscular adaptation. However, muscles require recovery to absorb the overload. You have probably had the experience of over-loading your muscles so much that your performance dropped off, you got sick, your muscles felt constantly sore, and/or you generally felt lethargic and unmotivated. These are symptoms of overtraining and must be avoided, or you will not get the training benefit you desire.

When you start riding poorly—your buddies you used to beat are dropping you on the hills—it is easy to think that what you need to do is train more. Actually the opposite is often true; with a little rest, you would be leaving them behind on the climbs again. It is often hard to see this when you are in a slump, and if you train alone and without a coach you must be particularly vigilant about not overtraining. You also need to take into account stresses outside of training, like with your job or family, since those also affect your recovery. Learn to recognize the symptoms of overtraining, and when you see them, back off!

Elite Nordic skier Scott Loomis says, "Certainly, feeling a bit off now and then is normal, and an occasional bad night of sleep is nothing to worry about. However, if you find yourself frequently feeling tired or sleeping poorly, especially if a sustained drop in motivation also accompanies this, then it may mean that you are digging yourself into a hole of overtraining."

> ## Symptoms of Overtraining
> - consistent decrease in training and/or race performance
> - change in resting heart rate (an increase or decrease of 10 percent from normal values)
> - loss of coordination, decreased motor skills
> - significant changes in training heart rate
> - lack of motivation
> - sleep disturbances
> - loss of appetite
> - muscle soreness or feeling of "heaviness"
> - significant decrease in body weight
> - increased susceptibility to colds/flu/allergies
> - decreased libido
> - decreased self-esteem
> - menstrual dysfunction (females)
> - loss of sense of humor
>
> SOURCE: NEAL HENDERSON

There are three main ways to allow your body to absorb training. One is complete rest—taking time off with no training whatsoever. Another is training at "recovery intensity;" recovery rides are easy rides usually of short duration. Finally, "periodization" of training alternates periods of hard and easy training.

Rest

It's simple enough: When you are tired, rest. That is the best way to adapt to the overload. If you don't, you pay for it in the long run. A day or two of rest here and there can save you from weeks of poor performances, misery, and illness later on.

Recovery Rides

Recovery rides, during which you ride at your lowest intensity, promote regeneration and replenishment of the body. Recreational riders often don't do enough easy days or do them easy enough. BCSM's Neal Henderson says, "Recovery is best done actively, pedaling easily. If you push too hard on recovery days, you delay the recovery process."

Periodization

The simplest form of periodization is alternating days of hard training with days of easy training. But on a larger scale, periodization involves several weeks of increasing stress (overload) followed by one or more weeks of recovery.

Over the season, an ideal training program builds the total training load, which is a combination of training volume and training intensity, from one week to the next. But every three or four weeks, there should be a recovery week in which the training load drops before building to a yet higher peak three to four weeks later, followed by another recovery week, and so on. There should also be a taper of one to two weeks before a big event.

Look at Table 19.1, and read it from the bottom up, since it is like a pyramid of decreasing time spent training at each level, with the event you are intending to "peak" for at the pyramid's pinnacle. In aiming for a specific goal of a race or big ride, the terminology is that you have a "base" period

19.1 Approximating Time in Zones for Training Periods

	Recovery	Overdistance	Endurance	Tempo/LT	VO2
Taper 1–2 weeks prior to Race	20%	30%	25%	20–25%	0–5%
Peak 2–4 weeks prior to Taper	20%	35%	20%	25%	2–5%
Build 2–8 weeks prior to Peak	15%	40%	30%	20%	0%
Base 8–16 weeks prior to Build	10%	60%	20%	10%	0%

Example Goal Race Date August 19

Base	**Build**	**Peak**	**Taper**
February–May	June–July	August 1–12	August 13–18

The percentage of the total training in each training zone changes as the training period moves through the Base, Build, Peak and Taper periods. LT = Lactate threshold interval training, and VO2 = maximum-intensity interval training at VO2 max intensity.

SOURCE: BCSM

(two to four months) of steadily increasing volume of training at low overdistance and endurance intensity (of course, interspersed with a recovery week each month). During the following "build" period (one to two months), you keep increasing the total training load, largely by adding more intense workouts, again with a monthly recovery week. The "peak" period of mostly high-intensity, lower-volume training is two to four weeks long, and then the taper period of less volume yet with high-intensity sessions is one to two weeks long. Note that as the intensity increases, you must also increase the supereasy recovery rides between hard days.

Figure 19.2 illustrates this point graphically; each set of three bars (gray, black, and white) stacked front to back represents one week of training. The white bars in back indicate total training load—a combination of training volume and training intensity (explained below). As you can see, total training load steadily builds during the first three weeks of each base month and each build month, with the fourth week of each month having a drastically reduced load. And each new month starts off at the highest load of the preceding month (the week before the recovery week) and builds from there. Then, the loads drop off in the peak and taper periods. The gray bars in front indicate weekly intensity, which steadily grows throughout the training period, with some drop-offs for rest. The black bars in the middle indicate training volume and mimic the total training load (white) bars.

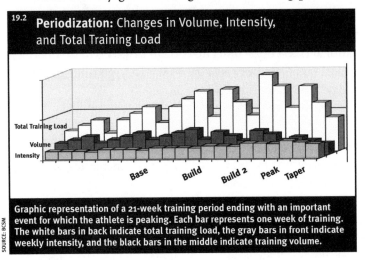

19.2 Periodization: Changes in Volume, Intensity, and Total Training Load

Total Training Load
Volume
Intensity

Base   Build   Build 2   Peak   Taper

Graphic representation of a 21-week training period ending with an important event for which the athlete is peaking. Each bar represents one week of training. The white bars in back indicate total training load, the gray bars in front indicate weekly intensity, and the black bars in the middle indicate training volume.

SOURCE: BCSM

Volume Combined with Intensity

Muscle overload (or total training load) is made up of a combination of training intensity and training volume. When healthy, your body can easily tolerate high-volume training at low intensity or high intensity with low duration and frequency. But when you combine high intensity with high volume, you must be very careful not to overdo it.

One of the best rules of thumb I have ever learned about training is to evaluate every workout on a scale of intensity from 1 to 10, 10 being as hard as you can possibly go. Each day, multiply the subjective rating of intensity by the number of minutes spent at that intensity during your workouts. At the end of each week, add up these products, and if the sum is greater than 4,000, watch out—you are on thin ice! Obviously, a training log is necessary to do this, and most athletes find one beneficial.

Look in your logs from prior years to see where you performed best and worst and what sort of training built up to it. I find that the 4,000 limit works well for me with my training for cross-country ski racing, but I could tolerate more with cycling, since it is not weight bearing and does not involve the upper body. I often found that if I had a number of weekly volume-times-intensity sums in a row greater than 4,000 for skiing or 5,000 for cycling, it was followed by an extended period of poor performance and often illness. However, I was able to work up to races like the Coors Classic or the Tour of Ireland, events over a week long during which my weekly volume-times-intensity was around 10,000—double my 5,000 limit! After those races, though, I had to ride easy for a week or two afterward with only short races on the weekends.

So, make it a habit to frequently ask yourself, "Do I feel rested?" Or, "Have I felt *good* or *great* in the majority of my workouts?" If the answer is no, especially for a number of days in a row, get some rest! 🚲

You can find more information about Scott Loomis at www.dreamofit.com/loomis.htm.

Neal Henderson, M.S., C.S.C.S, is the coordinator of sport science at the Boulder Center for Sports Medicine (www.bch.org/sportsmedicine).

BLOCK 20
Back Pain and Cycling

All cyclists complain about their butts, backs, or shoulders from time to time. In many ways, riding is good for these areas, but in other ways, it is not. If you want to enjoy cycling well into your advanced years, pay attention to what it takes to keep your pelvis, back, and shoulders healthy.

Cycling chiropractor Craig Pearson says, "I am always concerned before riding about how in-line I am. When something is off in the body and you go ride fifty miles on it, you are creating some serious wear and tear."

Pelvis

The pelvis is the body's powerhouse; all of its biggest, most powerful muscles are attached to the pelvis. When you clip into your pedals, you create a closed kinetic chain between the feet and the pelvis. If the pelvis is misaligned, other parts throughout the body's system will have to compensate for it, so you must have absolutely true mechanics to pedal smoothly without bodily damage. Lance Armstrong understands this and even employs a chiropractor at the Tour de France to keep him aligned, particularly after a crash.

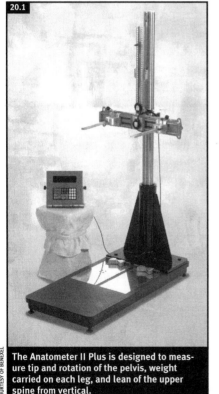

The Anatometer II Plus is designed to measure tip and rotation of the pelvis, weight carried on each leg, and lean of the upper spine from vertical.

COURTESY OF BENEXEL

Cycling, due to its symmetrical motion, tends to keep your pelvis in-line. It develops the muscles so that they work evenly on each leg and point the pelvis straight ahead. Since the center of gravity must be positioned over the longitudinal axis of the bike to ride in a straight line, it requires balancing of the body mass, which is done by shifting the pelvis laterally.

A Florida chiropractor, John Dunn, along with physiologist and cycling coach Ivan Glymph, published a study in the January/February 2000 issue of the *International Chiropractic Review* on the effects of cycling on the lower back. Using an anatometer (see Photo 20.1) on groups of noncyclists and of avid road riders, they accurately measured both the rotation of each participant's pelvis from neutral in the transverse plane and the amount of weight each participant bore on each of their feet. The noncyclists had an average pelvic rotation 4.7 times larger than that of the cyclists, and the percent difference in weight measured under each foot of the noncyclists was 2.9 times greater than that of the cyclists; clearly cycling helps keep the pelvis in alignment. Dunn says, "Patients in general won't do recommended exercises outside of the office to get their backs better. But if I can at least get them to ride a bike, it makes a profound difference."

The pelvis is made up of the triangular sacrum bone and the two hip bones (the ilia), connected at the sacroiliac (SI) joints. The three bones are held together by ligaments. If you have ligament damage in an SI joint—caused by crashing and landing on one hip, for instance—the pelvis will be distorted due to the one SI joint being more open than the other. The pelvic muscles tighten to protect it from further injury, which creates tension in muscles all over the body. These weight-bearing joints are so fundamental that an SI joint injury creates weakness throughout the system. To underline the point, Pearson says, "Pelvic fractures are often fatal (in the elderly). It's *that* critical to maintain a healthy pelvis." Cycling on a misaligned or injured pelvis, while arguably better than running on it, can create chronic problems.

An indication of an uneven pelvis is unilateral (only on one side) pain in the lower back, but an injury to the psoas (hip flexor) muscle in front of the pelvis can also cause unilateral lower-back pain. You can't realign your pelvis yourself, and it is also difficult to stretch your psoas yourself. In either case, you should go to a professional to get the area checked.

Knee pain can also be associated with a whacked-out pelvis. As little as one degree of pelvic tilt can create as much as one centimeter of leg-length difference, and the sit bone

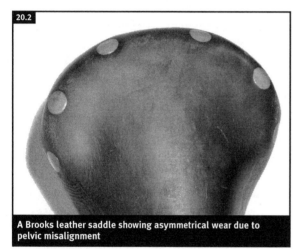

20.2

A Brooks leather saddle showing asymmetrical wear due to pelvic misalignment

will swing forward and down on the side with the shorter leg. Photo 20.2 shows the asymmetrical wear on a leather saddle created by exactly this problem. Note the low, forward depression on the right side of the saddle (left side of Photo 20.2) relative to the smaller, higher, and farther-back depression created by the left sit bone. With such a pelvic tilt, the knee on the longer leg (in this case, the left) will hurt on its medial (inner) side. This is the twisted pelvis pulls up on the sartorius muscle, which in turn yanks on the medial side of the knee. The pain is not caused by a meniscus or ligament; it's a muscle pulling on the bone. If that is the problem and you get adjusted and balance the pelvis, the knee pain goes away.

Chiropractors focus on pelvic alignment, and there are other body workers who address this as well. If for some reason you can't get to a chiropractor or other professional, ask a buddy to help you with a technique I mention in Block 21 that can help free up and line up your pelvis.

Lower Back

I have some flattened discs and an arthritic condition in my lower back. Consequently, I am particularly interested in ways to maintain a high level of activity and fitness without compromising—rather, even improving—the ability of my back to carry me into old age. While I initially assumed that compression of spinal discs (see Photo 20.3) was caused by impact—in my case, from alpine ski racing—I have since learned that it can often be due to sitting on a bike, as well as on a chair, for example in front of a computer. According to Pearson, "Discs stay soft and inflated through imbibition—they imbibe fluids from surrounding tissues. If the back is not moving, they cannot imbibe any fluid, and they deflate. Remember, 'motion is life!'" An important measure required to keep your back healthy is to keep it mobile, and that is also a function of chiropractic care.

Bad posture, sleeping on too hard or soft a surface, dehydration, stress, overuse, fatigue, or trauma also can lead to loss of spinal movement. A chiropractor checks the spine for fixations or locked joints and restores normal joint motion with adjustments. If the problem is uncorrected, the burden of movement falls on the level above and below the area of immobility, forcing those segments of the spine to do more than their fair share. Too much motion on one level, and not any on the fixed one, can result in pain and dysfunction. The long-term result of uncorrected fixations can be arthritis. If your back is getting tight, get it taken care of.

Another issue related to lumbar (lower back) flexibility is the fact that cycling posture tends to reverse the natural lumbar curve. This puts stress on the discs (since adjacent vertebrae are no longer parallel) and on the spinouses (the bony structures projecting off of the back of each vertebra, visible in Photo 20.3). "The cyclists I see generally have enlarged spinouses (also called spinous processes) to prevent them from snapping off when in a reverse curve," states Pearson. "Wolf's Law says that 'a bone develops the structure most suited to resist the forces acting upon it,' which is what the spinouses have done. Then, when standing, there's less space between them, creating 'kissing spinouses,' which hurt a lot." Perhaps you know people who say, "I'm fine when riding, just not when standing." (I have often been one of them!)

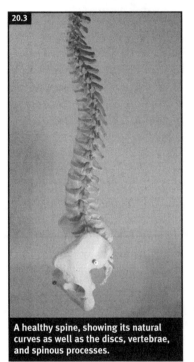

A healthy spine, showing its natural curves as well as the discs, vertebrae, and spinous processes.

Another cycling chiropractor, Richard Cimadoro, says that riders with this condition are most comfortable when on the bike because "being forward flexed reduces the pressure on the back. Most discs bulge posterior/laterally, which forward bending like in cycling will alleviate. More significantly, for most back pain sufferers, and not just the disc-bulging patients, forward bending shortens the pull of the hip flexor muscles on the back, which are a big culprit of back pain in cyclists, along with tight hamstrings and glutes. By the way, sitting for a long time also shortens hip flexors. I'm willing to bet that if more of us cyclists spent more time upright, standing and walking, rather than in a bent forward position, and occasionally doing some stretching with our hands over head, we'd have less achy backs."

The choice of rides can be important, too. While a long, rough ride on a hardtail mountain bike can leave me with sharp pain in my lower spine, road riding or mountain biking with full suspension or on relatively smooth trails leaves my back feeling better than when I got on the bike.

Weak abdominal muscles out of balance with cycling-strengthened lower-back muscles also can create lumbar problems. To improve your lower-back health, take the specific measures detailed in subsequent blocks (21 through 23) on massage, stretching, core strengthening, and crosstraining. Also, see the Upper Cervical Chiropractic Adjustment section below for one chiropractic method I have found to be particularly beneficial.

Shoulders

The only bone connecting the spine to the shoulder is the clavicle (collarbone), which is a small, weak bone. The shoulder blades, which are the platform for the arms, are actually floating structures attached by ligaments, tendons, and muscles. Cycling, particularly on a road bike with low-drop bars or aerobars, tends to roll the shoulders forward, pulling the shoulder blades forward with them while at the same time shortening the pectoral muscles, leading to more imbalance. And if you have a desk job in front of a computer, chances are good that the same thing is happening there as well. When riding with the shoulders rolled forward, the arms are literally falling out, with only tendons and ligaments to hold them in!

As the shoulders roll forward, there is less space between the head of the humerus (the top of the upper-arm bone) and the shoulder blade at the acromion (the bony bump that is the end of the shoulder blade). This can create painful problems, because at the head of the humerus is the point of attachment for not only the biceps tendons but also the tendons and ligaments that make up the rotator cuff. Cycling itself likely won't injure these tendons and ligaments, but it encourages the position and the weakness, which can create the conditions for injury to happen when you're doing something else, like throwing a ball or doing pull-ups. Having suffered from chronic bilateral biceps tendinitis on the bike, and having actually snapped my "longhead" biceps tendon (the most lateral biceps tendon) while simply riding up a mountain, I don't recommend it.

It is important to develop the mid- and lower trapezius muscles to pull the shoulder blades down and back. This is done with exercises like rowing (see Block 23) that create space between the acromion and the head of the humerus, alleviating pressure on the tendon and ligament attachments. This is another step to take if you want to keep riding into your eighties!

Upper Cervical Chiropractic Adjustment

Over the years, I have been worked on by umpteen body workers: chiropractors; massage therapists; practitioners of Rolfing and The Feldenkrais Method; acupuncturists; physical therapists; and ultrasound, electrostimulation, and magnetic-induction technicians. Without question, I have gotten value—sometimes even long-lasting and profound benefits—from of all them.

But one type of chiropractic adjustment, which focuses on the spine's uppermost vertebra, stands out as having consistently made a significant difference for me. This "upper cervical adjustment" has resulted in an immediate and dramatic improvement in my symptoms, and the adjustment holds for a long duration. Since the adjustment is relatively unknown, I will take the opportunity to explain it here.

The C1 cervical vertebra's position at the top of the spine has a profound gravitational and neurological effect. Since the skull sits atop it, C1 (if correctly aligned) balances the head's heavy weight, reducing the need for the muscles to hold it tilted. The brain stem passes through the upper cervical vertebrae, and a badly offset C1 will compress one side of the brain stem and disrupt nerve signals, even to the point of resulting in partial facial paralysis, compromised vision, or even inability to walk. Small misalignment of C1 can also have neurological effects.

Key to alignment of the C1 are the dentate ligaments, which run alongside the spinal cord, stabilize its movement, and prevent the spinal cord from sliding up and down. Upper cervical chiropractor Tom Groover says, "C1 is the only place where these ligaments pass through the dura (the tough, fibrous membrane covering the brain and spinal cord) and connect to the bone, so any misalignment there pulls on the dentate ligament, causing tension on one side of the spinal cord and affecting nerve function." Finally, when alignment somewhere is off, the body's response is to tighten up around that area—that is, to defend it. Thus, a C1 misalignment can cause localized muscle spasms at the base of the head and within the neck and shoulders.

The procedure

The process of an upper cervical adjustment begins with an accurate measurement of the displacement of both the vertebra and of the pelvis. Multiple X rays of the neck taken from different angles are used to precisely determine the angular offset of the C1 vertebra in three dimensions. Furthermore, measurements are taken with the anatometer (Photo 20.1) to accurately determine the rotation of the pelvis in the horizontal plane, the tilt of the pelvis in the vertical plane, the lateral offset of the top of the spine from the centerline of the body, and the weight borne by each foot.

From the X rays, the chiropractor graphically determines a three-dimensional vector along which force will be applied to return the C1 vertebra to its level and untwisted position. The practitioner then applies force along that vector until the vertebra lines up with the rest of the spine.

Afterward, typically all of the pelvis's rotation and tilt is gone, the top of the spine is centered on the body's centerline, and each foot carries the same amount of weight. Unlike the lumbar and thoracic vertebrae we normally associate with chiropractic adjustments, C1 is not connected to any large muscles, so it tends to stay put. Also, since the head is now balanced vertically, muscles do not have carry weight equivalent to a bowling ball on one side, tightening muscles and throwing off alignment.

After undergoing upper cervical adjustment, I have a bit more spring, a bit more energy. However, it is hard to find practitioners who administer it. Also, once you are lined up perfectly, you must find ways (possibly with other, more traditional chiropractors) to keep your spine mobile, your lower back and abdominal muscles in balance (see Block 23), and your shoulders pulled back.

Pain

Pain is inevitable in everyone's life. In fact, one friend who is over 60 years old told me, "If you wake up in the morning and nothing hurts, you're dead!" However, pain also indicates underlying problems and should be listened to. I am alarmed by the number of my friends who take hefty doses of ibuprofen or other anti-inflammatory drugs on a regular basis to deal with pain in tendons, joints, and muscles as well as headaches. As Pearson says, "If your BMW starts making grinding noises, you don't just turn up the stereo and cover the dashboard warning lights, do you? Even though you can get another BMW, it is valuable to you, so you take it to the service center. It is even more important with your body to not mask the pain, since it is the only one you get. Deal with the underlying cause, getting whatever professional help it takes."

People think of the body as a hard skeleton, but it is actually highly movable, including the bones, and it can get out of whack. Muscle, tendon, and joint pain—even headaches—

can be caused by poor body mechanics. You may have to address the problems with body professionals, orthotics (see Block 8), leg-length discrepancy correction (see Block 11), or with any of a number of other bike-fit issues (see Blocks 1 through 13). If you want to ride bikes and be active into your 60s and beyond, you don't want to put unnecessary stress, wear, and tear on the body. Pay attention to the pain messages; don't pile hundreds of miles on misaligned body parts until you create a chronic problem that will greatly curtail your activities. "No pain, no gain" is a fallacy. You can work through pain, if it is global rather than focused on a specific body part. But, except perhaps in the Tour de France, you don't want to do that day after day. The price is much higher than the payoff.

Chiropractors Tom Groover and Craig Pearson practice in Boulder, Colorado; John Dunn practices in Tallahassee, Florida, and Richard Cimadoro practices in Thousand Oaks, California.

BLOCK 21
Massage and Recovery

Massage increases circulation by pushing lactic acid and metabolic waste out of the muscles. This leads to shorter recovery periods after workouts and muscular injury, making it possible to gain a significant improvement in performance; an athlete can train harder using muscles that have recovered faster. Massage also releases endorphins, the body's natural painkillers, into the bloodstream; endorphins help athletes feel better and often give them deeper, more restful sleep.

Regular massage is key for those wanting the utmost performance, but it becomes particularly important as we get on in years. When young, we recover from injuries such as strains and tears without massage, but when we get this type of injury after age 35 or so, we build up scar tissue, fascia restriction, and shortened muscles. We then compensate for these physiological restrictions with distorted body mechanics. Massage can reverse these effects.

However, it may also be true that with middle age comes less time for regular professional massage—heck, most of us are happy if we can just get out riding every day, given our job and family responsibilities. But self-massage and even buddy massage can provide many of the benefits of professional massage, and making some form of it part of your routine only takes a few minutes a day. Massage is part of an overall recovery program that will keep you feeling better and performing at a higher level.

Self-Massage

For a cyclist, self-massage is almost as good as buddy massage, since you can reach your legs. Sports massage therapist Jim Bowen, former soigneur (massage therapist) to the Löwenbräu (men's) and Löwrey (women's) professional cycling teams, has coached cyclists for years in self-massage. His recommendations follow.

Lying down on your back with your feet up on the wall, warm up the quadriceps and hamstrings with friction strokes lubricated with oil or lotion. With the knuckles of one hand, deeply massage the quads and the iliotibial band on the top and outside of the thigh, working back toward the heart. When one hand gets tired, switch hands and work on the other leg. Then, reach behind the leg with both hands together, and use the fingertips to massage the hamstrings from the knee to the sit bones. When you're massaging, bend your thumbs and fingers rather than keeping them straight; this keeps the joints from hyperextending and reduces wear.

To massage the calf, bend the knee and cup the calf while massaging down from the ankle to the knee. When the hands get tired, cross one leg over the other, resting the foot on the opposite knee, and with the thumbs massage the inside of the calf muscle across the muscle fibers.

For the gluteus muscles of the buttocks, lower the feet on the wall and bend the knees, leaning over to one side. Deeply massage the glutes with the knuckles. Obviously, it is better to have someone else, ideally a sports massage therapist, work on hard-to-reach areas like the glutes and the back.

For the back, Styrofoam rollers (see Photo 22.7), back massage tools, or two tennis balls tied up in an old sock (use racquetballs if the back is particularly sore) do the trick. Find the sore spots, lie on your back on the tools, and roll around on them for a few minutes.

Finally, for the neck, Bower recommends that you lie down and reach around to the back of the neck. Make circles with your fingertips and rub the muscles using crossfiber friction.

Massage tools are also great for self-massage. There are many on the market, and I keep a TheraCane, a curved fiberglass cane with massage balls on it, next to my desk to relieve sore areas while writing. My wife, kids, and I also keep some great electrical massagers around the house to work on ourselves and on each other.

At age 60, Bob Anderson, author of the best-selling book *Stretching* (2000), can ride circles around almost anyone. His catalog, Stretching, Inc., offers massage tools, and among them are Pain Erasers, which have a handle affixed with rubber rollers that have massage bumps. Anderson carries a Pain Eraser with him on the bike and uses it whenever he stops. Loosen up tight areas with the tool, then stretch them and continue. You will be faster and feel better than when you stopped.

Buddy Massage

A buddy or spouse can give you a massage using the steps in the self-massage section above—and you won't have to put your feet up on the wall.

Additionally, you can perform the following technique on somebody else, or vice versa, to help free up and align a whacked-out pelvis. This technique is not meant as a substitute for a chiropractic adjustment, but it is a heck of a lot better than not doing anything about the problem!

John Dunn, an upper cervical chiropractor and avid cyclist, came up with this technique. It loosens the tight muscle and ligament that have pulled the pelvis out of alignment. The pelvis is secured in space like a tent pole is by guy wires, which in this case are muscles and ligaments. If any one of them is too tight, the whole thing will be skewed at an angle, just like a tent pole would be.

Have your victim lie on a bed face down with their feet hanging off the end. Pull on and shake their legs and then push back on the bottom of the feet against straight legs, squaring the feet with each other the way a chiropractor does when comparing leg length. The side with the shorter leg usually has the tight pelvic muscles.

Move the patient to the edge of the bed on the side of the body that is tight, still lying face down. Place pillows ramping up under their chest. Stand so you face the bend of their knee. Have your patient guide your elbow to the tight areas.

Rest your left hand on the bed near the left buttock if you are doing the left side of the patient; rest your right hand near the right buttock if you're doing the right side. If you're working on a tight left side, place the right elbow just inboard of the sit bone at the crease of the left buttock (and vice versa for the other side). Pushing down deeply with the elbow, begin sliding your forearm outward at a 45-degree angle, moving the elbow diagonally toward the left hip. Just inboard and up from the sit bone, you will find a ligament with your elbow. This is the sacrotuberous ligament, which Dunn describes as a "speed bump." Go back and forth across this speed bump. You want to loosen up and lengthen the ligament.

Continue sliding the elbow/forearm up and outward around the brim of the pelvis, so your forearm ends up at 90 degrees from the spine. Along the way, you will encounter a broader speed bump, the piriformis muscle, which extends crosswise across the cheek of the buttocks. Don't brutalize either this muscle or the sacrotuberous ligament, but apply firm pressure back and forth over both.

If you went over an area so hard that it hurts, go over it with less and less pressure with the open palm of the hand to take away the pain. Be gentle where you cross over the femur head (the top of the upper leg bone). If the rider complains about pain down the leg or in the foot, you are on the sciatic nerve, so get off of that.

After you're done, recheck the leg length. The legs should be even, because the pelvis should have returned to a neutral position.

Professional Massage

Consistency is important to getting the most benefit from massage. While Tour de France riders get daily massage, that is not practical for most of us, nor does our daily effort on the bike usually warrant it. Getting a massage two to four times per month allows for cumulative benefits to enhance performance.

For avid cyclists, a sports massage therapist will be a better choice than other massage therapists; ask about sports massage certification and experience. The deeper strokes of a sports massage tends to yield greater benefit, since athletes' muscles are more toned than those of the average massage client.

A sports massage therapist also knows which muscles a cyclist uses the most and which muscles to focus on. These include the quadriceps, iliotibial bands, hamstrings, gluteus muscles, calf muscles, hip flexors, lower-back muscles including the quadratus lumborum and mid-back erectors, and posterior cervical (neck) muscles.

Recovery

Recovery during and after a ride certainly improves with massage, but it also depends upon if you've stayed hydrated and nourished during the ride. You can also speed recovery by starting out properly, so your muscles don't tighten up and engorge with lactic acid, and by easing off the last few minutes at the end of a ride. Bowen recommends riders do a 10- to 15-minute warm-up, then stop and stretch gently before continuing. You may find this impractical, but taking time to stretch and do regular massage at all is more important than when you do it. I incorporate stretching and self-massage into my nightly before-bed routine and do an abbreviated version each morning.

As I mentioned in Block 14, eat a balanced meal within a half hour after a hard ride and another after two hours. Ice any muscular or joint injuries immediately for 10 to 15 minutes. Bowen suggests setting aside some time after the ride to do 15 to 20 minutes of self-massage combined with 15 to 20 minutes of gentle stretching before rushing off. With this routine, you will age more gracefully with greater flexibility and fewer injuries. 🚲

Bob Anderson is president of Stretching, Inc. For more information, visit www.stretching.com.

Sports massage therapist Jim Bowen practices in Boulder and Denver, Colorado.

Chiropractor John Dunn practices in Tallahassee, Florida.

BLOCK 22
Stretching

If there is one thing that I think makes a difference in feeling good, performing effectively in athletic endeavors, and aging gracefully with good mobility, it is stretching. As Bob Anderson, author of *Stretching* (2000), says, "Stretching is the important link between the sedentary life and the active life. It keeps the muscles supple, prepares you for movement, and helps you make the daily transition from inactivity to vigorous activity without undue strain." Certainly stretching is key for cycling, but cyclists do not universally embrace it. When I was racing in Europe in the early 1980s, foreign riders used to ridicule me for stretching!

Cycling tends to shorten the muscles and promote inflexibility. For this reason, stretching is particularly important and can help prevent injuries, as well as relax your mind and body. It is easy to do, but if done wrong, it can do more harm than good. It is noncompetitive; you are not doing yourself any favors by trying to stretch farther every day. A cat instinctively knows when and how to stretch and does not try to overdo it. Stretching prepares it for high drops, from windowsills for instance, without tearing muscles or connective tissue.

When to Stretch

If you stretch properly, using pain as a guide (that is, do *not* stretch until it hurts!), you can do it any time lying down, sitting, or standing.

That said, the muscles will stretch more easily when warmed up. Before exercise, you ideally want to start the activity you are going to do at a low intensity for a couple of minutes until you break a light sweat. Then stretch. Near the end of your workout, cool down gradually at a low intensity as well. After exercise, once your pulse has returned to a resting rate, stretching will reduce muscle soreness and stiffness.

Hold for 10 to 15 seconds on each side.

How to Stretch

First off, never bounce! And do not stretch when or until it hurts. Muscles protect themselves with a stretch reflex; to prevent tearing, they tighten up when pulled too far. If you bounce or stretch too far, this reflex is activated, and you tighten the muscles you were trying to stretch! And stretching once the stretch reflex has been activated causes microtears in the muscle fibers, leading scar tissue to form and a consequent loss of elasticity.

Anderson distinguishes between the easy stretch, the developmental stretch, and the drastic stretch. He recommends holding an easy stretch for 10 to 15 seconds until the feeling of mild tension you have applied subsides. You

Hold for 15 to 20 seconds on each side.

Hold for 10 to 20 seconds on each side.

Hold for 15 to 30 seconds on each side.

Hold for 8 to 10 seconds on each side.

Hold for 10 to 20 seconds on each side.

COURTESY OF STRETCHING, INC.

then move slowly into the developmental stretch, extending until you again feel mild tension—you may feel it when you move only a fraction of an inch farther! Hold the stretch again for 10 to 15 seconds, and if the feeling of tension does not diminish over that period, ease off slightly. Breathe slowly and in a relaxed manner. Forget the drastic stretch!

What to Stretch

For cycling, critical areas to stretch are the quadriceps (see Figures 22.1 and 22.6), hamstrings (see Figures 22.2 and 22.3), calves (see Figure 22.4), gluteus muscles (see Figures 22.2 and 22.5), and lower back (see Figures 22.2, 22.3, and 22.5). Including some abdominal crunches (see Block 23) relieves lower-back tension as well.

There are lots of methods of stretching these areas, either lying, standing, or sitting—even using your bike as support or leverage. Find a method that works for you, and follow that. In addition to consulting *Stretching*, you may want to check out Anderson's catalog, Stretching, Inc. In it you can find laminated stretching charts for various sports (like cycling, which includes all of these illustrations and many more) and computer CDs that remind you to stretch while you are working. The important thing is to get to know your body, which stretching greatly encourages, and do what feels good in a routine that works with the rest of your life. I regularly do a number of stretches slightly differently than in the book, and these have worked for me for decades. I do some of my stretches lying down while brushing my teeth (similar to Figure 22.1), for instance! Associating stretching with a daily activity also reminds me to stretch morning and night.

For example, while you are sitting at your desk or at a stoplight while in your car, you can do some neck stretches. Put your right hand under your right buttock, reach your left hand over the top of your head to your right ear, and gently pull the head toward the left shoulder; then switch sides. Or cradle your head with both hands and pull it down to touch your chin to your chest.

Two Critical Areas

I want to specifically mention two areas that are hard to stretch and that tend to get tight on cyclists (both areas have periodically plagued me). One is the iliotibial (IT) band—the wide, fibrous tendon extending from the hip past the outside of the knee. If the IT band is tight, the sharp pain on the side of the knee where it rubs over a bone projection can be unbearable. It is hard to stretch because the body position is so critical during the stretch. Get professional help with this one. Toni Geer, a cycling physical therapist at the Boulder

Center for Sports Medicine, says that "the most effective stretch for the IT band utilizes a 6-inch diameter Styrofoam roll (Photo 22.7). Such a thick, tendinous tissue is hard to stretch, but you can by rolling the tendon up and down on the roll. It's like deep tissue massage, and the pressure hurts like hell, but it stretches it." Also, keep in mind that the IT band is affected by tightness in the quads and hamstrings in particular, and if these muscles are kept limber, the IT band creates less of a problem.

The other specific area I want to mention is the piriformis, a muscle extending crosswise across the butt cheek. Nerves feeding the legs pass through it, and if it is tight, you can get numbness and pain all of the way down the outside of the leg. There are a number of ways to stretch this muscle as well; all that I know of involve bringing the foot up toward the butt and pushing the knee over to the inside to apply tension to the piriformis (see Figure 22.2 for one example). You can also stretch the piriformis at work: while sitting, place your left ankle on top of your right knee and lean forward.

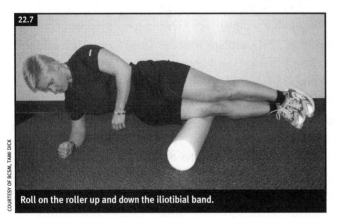

22.7

Roll on the roller up and down the iliotibial band.

Anderson himself is a living testimonial to stretching. At age 59, he can leave young, accomplished mountain bikers in the dust of his backyard playground: Colorado's Pike National Forest. He stretches and uses massage tools (like the Pain Eraser mentioned in Block 21) on his sore muscles before, during (while he is waiting for the latest macho man he's left behind on a steep mountain trail), and after his daily rides. He says, "People doing long rides don't know how to stop and stretch, and when to. They just keep grinding away even though they are slowing down and feeling miserable. You don't need a lot of flexibility to ride a bike, but it helps you feel a lot better. Stretching can bring you back a bit when you are feeling slow."

Anderson relates a stretching story about America's most famous cyclist and (now) stretching advocate, Lance Armstrong. "Ed Burke [the late cycling author and physiologist to U.S. Olympic cycling teams] took me to the Colorado Springs velodrome to meet Lance one time. First thing he [Lance] said to me was, 'I never stretch.' I asked, 'Well, do you yawn?' But Lance now says that the main difference between American and European athletes is that we are more into diet and stretching!"

Bob Anderson of Stretching, Inc., lives in Palmer Lake, Colorado; for more information, visit his Web site, www.stretching.com.

BLOCK 23

Core Strengthening and Injury Prevention

When I was about 22 or 23 years old, it seemed as though I could train 500 miles per week, do week-long stage races, and ride my bike every day year-round without injury—unless I got caught in a crash. Now, at twice that age, I no longer can.

However, since cycling involves no pounding of your joints, injuries are minimized with proper equipment and preparation. That fact, and that you do not need a partner or a team to ride, makes cycling a perfect sport for maintaining health late into life, although it has become clear to me that if I want to be riding my bike reasonable distances at age 80, I must incorporate into my regular routine some strengthening of areas of my body that cycling does not develop. Massage, stretching, chiropractic, etc., (see Blocks 20 through 22) and bike positioning (see Blocks 1 through 13) all are important components of preventing cycling overuse injuries, but strengthening of noncycling muscles, particularly those in the body's core, is critical as well.

There are a number of ways to strengthen noncycling muscles. The two that I have settled on in my own life are crosstraining (participating in other sports that complement cycling by using different muscles) and regularly following an established exercise routine at home or while traveling that requires minimal equipment. Other important ways of accomplishing similar results are with weight training, yoga, Pilates, The Feldenkrais Method, martial arts, and other disciplines. And doing these things can make a huge difference not only for bike riders, but also for anyone who works at a sedentary job.

Abdominal (Core) Strengthening

I think that perhaps the most important thing cyclists can do to prevent overuse injuries is core strengthening. Cyclists probably complain most about lower-back pain, even more than they do about the discomfort of pressure from the saddle. As I discussed in Block 20, if not managed properly lower-back pain can become chronic due to the lower-spine's position and lack of movement while riding. Cycling strengthens the lower-back muscles and does absolutely nothing for the abdominal muscles. When the strong lower-back muscles tighten up and shorten with no muscles opposing them in front, the pelvis is pulled up in back, tipping it forward and arching the lower back to create the "proud butt" posture common to many cyclists.

Maintaining the mobility of the lower spine and strengthening the abdominal muscles are important to keep the lower back healthy. One way to accomplish this is to follow a regular routine of abdominal exercises. If the routine is simple and not time-intensive, you will tend to do it regularly. The more hassle, time, and transportation the routine requires (for instance, if you have to get to a health club to do it), the less likely you will be to maintain it as a regular practice.

One of the best ways to do core strengthening, I am told, is to use a large fit ball that you sit on as well as roll around on with your chest and back. I know many people who swear by fit balls for their back health. On a several occasions, I bought a ball and received an exercise program with it; but I could never stick to it, partly because I kept popping the balls by letting them get too close to a hot heater. Additionally, I travel so much that I need a routine I can do anywhere without bringing a ball along. I have a program that I do on a carpet or floor pad on evenings when I am too tired to think constructively any more. I combine it with my stretching routine and find it to be a relaxing thing to do before going to bed.

A physical therapist can provide you with core strengthening exercises. There are a few that I find to be particularly useful. One is to lie flat on your back and contract your abdominal muscles so that the lower spine is pressed down against the floor. Then "step up and down" with the knees sharply bent. You can also alternately extend one leg while pulling the other up, as if you were pedaling in a prone position. Key to these exercises is keeping the lower spine pressed against the floor throughout the entire movement of the feet.

Another one (the "sit back") is to sit up with the knees bent and slowly lower your rounded torso until your shoulder blades touch the floor, rolling one vertebra into contact with the floor at a time, starting with the sacrum.

Finally, the "pelvic clock" is a great one. While lying flat on your back with the knees bent, start with the tailbone pressed to the floor as your 12 o'clock reference position. Roll the contact point of the back with the floor slowly around from that reference point to one o'clock, two o'clock, etc., all the way around the clock face. You are simply pressing a different portion of your lower back down into contact with the floor to each hour position around this imaginary clock face. Do it clockwise as well as counterclockwise. The Feldenkrais Method would have you do the pelvic clock very slowly, almost imperceptibly slowly, to isolate each tiny muscle movement. This is the way to get the most out of the pelvic clock, but just doing it at all, at any speed, is useful, particularly when your back is so stiff and sore that it is hard to get up in the morning. Doing the pelvic clock before getting out of bed makes all the difference for me. You can also do the pelvic clock sitting in a level chair, where the contact points touching the hour positions around the face of the clock are under your butt and thighs rather than your lower back. Try it while working at your desk; your lower back will feel more mobile within a minute or two.

According to Toni Geer, a cycling physical therapist at the Boulder Center for Sports Medicine, "riders with poor core strength generally have more back problems. The abdominal muscles are hooked to the pelvis, and if the abs are well toned, you have better control over the angle of the pelvis. If you control the position of the pelvis, you control the vertebrae."

Shoulder Exercises

As I mentioned in Block 20, the shoulders can hurt when cycling as they roll forward and pinch the shoulder tendons and ligaments between the acromion (the bony bump that is the end of the shoulder blade) and the top of the humerus. The key to counteracting this tendency, as Geer says, is to "put the scapula (shoulder blade) in your back pocket."

Cycling strengthens and tightens the muscles at the front of the shoulders that hold you up, but it does nothing for the muscles of the mid-back. The trapezius muscles are responsible for pulling down on the shoulder blades, and if they are weak, the shoulder blades will slide upward and impinge on nerves, tendons, and ligaments as the shoulders roll forward to reach the handlebar. The same thing also occurs when sitting at a desk typing or clicking a mouse.

An effective and time-efficient method of getting your shoulder blades to pull back and down is to shrug your shoulders up, back, and down periodically while you sit at your desk. Stretching the shoulder muscles by grabbing the elbow with the opposite hand and pulling it across the chest at shoulder height helps relax the muscles that keep the shoulder blades pulled up tight. I also sit up periodically on the bike while I'm out riding and do both of these exercises (with the hands off the bars). Stretch the pectoral muscles by placing your hands on either side of a door frame and leaning forward; this relieves some pull on the shoulders.

23.1

Rowing exercise with an elastic Thera-Band

At my desk, I keep a 10-foot piece of the wide rubber-band material called Thera-Band that physical therapists chop off of a big roll. It can be hooked on a doorknob, around a desk corner, or through a drawer handle on a file cabinet to do rowing exercises (see Photo 23.1) and lat (lateralis muscle) pull-downs while standing. To do pull-downs, extend the arms straight out in front of you (like Frankenstein) and hold the Thera-Band taut. Then pull your arms down to your sides. While sitting or standing, I do internal rotation (see Photo 23.2) and external rotation (see Photo 23.3) of the shoulders by pulling the band across my abdomen. These exercises encourage me to periodically move and stand up from my desk, which improves my productivity as well as my feeling of well-being.

23.2

Internal rotation with an elastic Thera-Band

If you are experiencing pain in the shoulders at the top of the humerus, you really need to focus on strengthening the lower- and mid-trapezius muscles; the exercises described above will bring the scapulas down and back and create space between the acromion and the head of the humerus, alleviating pressure on the tendon and ligament attachments. Raising your stem or riding a mountain bike, at least temporarily, will help as well, by allowing your shoulders to roll back a bit.

Leg Extensions

Geer says that the second most common cycling injury she sees and works to rehabilitate is patello-femoral pain—irritation between the patella (kneecap) and the femur, usually caused by poor tracking of the kneecap in its groove on the end of the femur. This is often called by the general term "chondromalacia," referring to the irritation and deterioration of articular cartilage, in this case on the back of the kneecap.

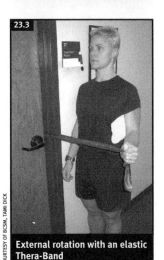

23.3

Cycling tends to overdevelop the large outer thigh muscle of the quadriceps group (the vastus lateralis) relative to the smaller quadriceps muscle to the inside of the knee (the vastus medialis), resulting in the kneecap being pulled to the outside so it does not ride in its smooth groove on the end of the femur. It can get rubbed raw riding against the outer protruding knob on the end of the femur. This hurts—a lot.

External rotation with an elastic Thera-Band

Part of the cure is to develop the vastus medialis to counterbalance the vastus lateralis and pull the kneecap back toward the inside. Leg extensions are a great way to do this.

You can do leg extensions on a leg extension machine at a gym with your foot pointed outward (so that if both legs were straight, heels together, your feet would make a V) to focus the work more on the vastus medialis. Cyclists should just do the last 15 degrees of extension. Geer, an avid cyclist herself, says, "A full extension tends to cause anterior knee pain (patello-femoral pain). Cyclists, being boneheads, will figure more is better and try to do the whole 90-degree extension. I do these very regularly and credit them with fixing my debilitating anterior knee pain. Technique is very important. It is a slow exercise with a *stop* at each end—hold two seconds when extended and then release all tension for two seconds when flexed."

Alternatively, when you are sitting or lying down, you can do leg extensions isometrically. With your leg supported behind the knee on a pillow or the edge of a chair, periodically straighten your leg (foot pointed out) and hold it straight for a number of seconds, contracting the vastus medialis muscle on inner side of the knee as hard as you can. Try to make that muscle rock hard, and then relax it.

Perineal Muscle Toning

As Dr. Robert West, designer of Selle San Marco's Aero line of saddles (the ones with an arrowhead-shaped cutout in the middle), says, "The human anatomy is not designed to straddle a bicycle saddle. A problem develops when the rider's weight compresses the erectile tissues against the top surface of the saddle. While seated on a conventional saddle, the rider incurs a compression injury with each turn of the crank, which is cumulative over time."

By now, most every male cyclist has heard of the possibility of impotency associated with sitting on a bike seat, and women do not need to be told how painful the soft tissue of the perineum (the soft tissue under the crotch) can become when compressed on the nose of a saddle either. However, this conversation always tends to start and end with a discussion of what saddle to buy. At least as important is the rider's fitness and overall position on the bike. The stronger the rider, the harder they pedal and the less weight is carried on the saddle.

But there is an exercise for cyclists, which I have never heard anyone (other than me) talk about, that makes sense as another exercise to balance cycling's compressive effects. That is exercising the muscles of the perineum. Everybody knows that as we age, our tissues become less elastic, and that also applies to the arteries under the crotch. It seems to me that if the muscles surrounding these arteries are flaccid, the artery walls will collapse more easily.

When my wife was pregnant, her midwives had her do Kegel exercises to tone her perineal muscles. To do this exercise, you repeatedly contract the same muscles that you use to shut off your flow of urine. No matter what saddle you use, doing a lot of Kegels on a regular basis has to be good for your circulation, muscle tone, and nerve function. I just do them whenever I think about it—while sitting at my desk, driving, stretching, or reading.

Crosstraining

It is possible to have too much of a good thing. Doing any athletic activity to the exclusion of all others tends to create muscle imbalances as well as a feeling of staleness. To balance muscle tone and keep the body healthy, as well as to stay mentally fresh, do other sports.

To get the most benefit from your overall physical health, select activities that strengthen body parts that cycling does not.

There are myriad sports that complement cycling well. Weight training, yoga, Pilates, The Feldenkrais Method, and other practices can be designed specifically to balance cycling muscles. Rock climbing and swimming build the upper body well. And any movement off a bike saddle that gets your blood pumping helps regenerate tissues damaged by compression from the saddle.

I recommend looking for sports that you love and that work your upper body and core muscles. I break up my cycling with cross-country skiing in the winter and early spring and with white-water kayaking in the late spring, summer, and fall. The poling action of Nordic skiing, particularly the powerful double-poling you constantly use when racing, demands abdominal strength and builds the mid- and lower-trapezius muscles. And after months of skiing, I am really eager to get back on my bike, rather than being burned out from having bundled up daily through the winter and faced the cold on my bike, or, heaven forbid, having ridden on an indoor trainer!

White-water kayaking also obviously works the upper body, but the abdominal workout that comes with it may not be as evident. Proper paddling technique involves using your core strength more than your arms to power the boat forward or backward. But even more important is the abdominal muscle control required to present the proper angulation of the boat to the current to avoid getting flipped over. When you are spinning around in a "hole" (a recirculating hydraulic feature), your abdominal muscles are working hard and fast to tip the boat first onto one edge and then the other. A couple hours of that and you will feel like you have been doing sit-ups all day!

I grew up alpine (downhill) skiing and hiking and still love doing both. Even though, like cycling, they tend to primarily work the quads and lower back, they do offer crosstraining benefits as well as a break from sitting on a bike seat and a healthy change of scenery. Says Geer, "In keeping a training log, I 'discount' the hours and count a full day of alpine skiing or hiking as two hours of training. Depending on how you ski, alpine skiing can be a fantastic core strength exercise. Carving on modern shaped skis requires strong back and abdominal muscles. Furthermore, during a carved turn the quads and hamstrings contract simultaneously and extremely forcefully. The hamstring force actually equals the quad contraction—this provides stability."

To enjoy cycling more and to enjoy the rest of your life, I can't emphasize enough the importance of crosstraining and strengthening of core muscles and other noncycling muscles. 🚲

The Boulder Center for Sports Medicine is online at www.bch.org/sportsmedicine.

PART 3

Road Bike Skills

BLOCK 24
Cornering, Descending, and Countersteering

When you watch the Tour de France, Giro d'Italia, or Vuelta a España on TV, you can learn a lot from the rare occasions that the camera motorcycles get good footage of riders negotiating curving descents at high speeds. You will notice that they always keep their heads level while they lean and tuck. You will also notice that they snap their torsos from vertical to almost instantaneously leaning over into a turn, and that they sit up when they are carrying too much speed when entering tight turns.

All of the components of cornering, as well as of descending, are right there. The riders constantly employ countersteering, the fundamental concept for effective cornering on dry roads (or on slickrock or tacky dirt with a mountain bike). They also brake and air brake at the appropriate times, shift weight, reduce aerodynamic drag, and establish balance with the position of their head and eyes.

Countersteering

Countersteering is the act of turning your front wheel in the opposite direction to the curve. You actually do it all the time when cornering, probably without realizing it. Watching a criterium race, you can see the riders countersteering by noticing two things. When the riders come into a corner, they make a quick swerve to the outside before leaning over into the turn. And when in the turn, their inside arm is straighter than their outside arm (see Photo 24.2), indicating that they are pushing forward harder with the inside arm—counter to the direction of the turn.

Think about how the riders swerve to the outside before the turn. Sure, it increases the radius of the turn, which makes it possible to go through the turn faster. But why not get the largest possible radius, by starting in the opposite gutter, with the wheels right up against the curb, and then lean over and turn? The answer is that riders instinctively know that they cannot do that; the tire has to move a little to the outside, toward the curb, before the bike can lean to the inside. It is the same in skiing or running; you can't turn to the left without getting your feet out to the right to push against. If you don't believe me, ride atop the white line on the road. Now turn sharply to the left. Notice that the bike cannot move quickly off to the left of the line without the front tire first going to the right of the line for at least a fraction of a second.

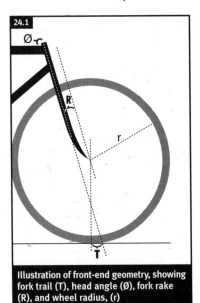

Illustration of front-end geometry, showing fork trail (T), head angle (Ø), fork rake (R), and wheel radius, (r)

If you understand fork trail (read about it in detail in Block 40), then you can see how to use its power while countersteering. Fork trail (represented by T in Figure 24.1) provides the leverage that forces the wheel to get under you when you start to tip over—the greater the fork trail, the greater the force righting the bike. So, if you push the wheel out from under yourself by countersteering, fork trail will cause the bike to lean opposite the direction that you turned the wheel. This will lean the bike over into a curve and generate centrifugal force to prevent you from falling as the bike works to get the wheels back under you.

You can demonstrate this without a rider on the bike, using the method of bicycle researcher Jim Pappadoupolis. Loop two identical rubber bands around the top tube and stretch one around one end of the handlebar, and the other around the other end. If the tension in both rubber bands is balanced, you can roll the bike downhill and it will go straight, without a rider. Now run alongside the bike and cut the left rubber band, which has the identical effect of a rider pushing forward with the left hand. The front wheel will turn to the right, but the bike will not turn right. Rather, it will lean to the left and turn left!

If you have ever seen a motorcycle race on a paved track, you saw the riders leaning way over into sharp corners. Notice that each rider's inside arm is nearly straight and the outside arm is bent. This shows that they are not steering into the turn—rather, they are countersteering, away from the turn, to generate lean.

The gyroscopic effect of the spinning wheels also contributes to countersteering's power. To illustrate, hold a wheel by the ends of the axle and get it spinning quickly. Push forward on the left end of the axle (which steers the hub to the right); the wheel will immediately lean to the left so hard that you cannot resist it! Again, you have set up a lean into a left turn by countersteering to the right.

Even though you countersteer all the time without realizing it, you need to do it consciously to learn how to take advantage of it. Try countersteering first in a parking lot without traffic. Ride along and push forward with your left arm only. Even though this turns your handlebar to the right, you will not turn right. Rather, you will lean sharply left and turn that way! As you get more adept at it, you can even remove your outside hand from the bar while you are leaned over in a turn. Try increasing and decreasing the pressure on the bars with the inside hand—with even just the fingertips—to see how increasing the pressure increases the lean angle and tightens your turn.

Once you get the feel of countersteering, you can tap into its power during situations in which you were previously powerless. Have you ever entered too fast into a switchback on a descent and had to brake in the middle of it to make the turn? Chances are, you found yourself creeping through the turn far slower than you thought necessary, yet you felt powerless to do anything about it. Putting on your brakes stood your bike up, which increased your turning radius. Even though braking slowed you down, your trajectory was still going to take you off the road at the exit of the turn, so you had to slow down more,

24.2

By countersteering, riders attain sharp lean angles. Notice that Dario Frigo's inside arm is straighter than his outside arm.

GRAHAM WATSON

which stood your bike up more, requiring yet more braking. You ended up creeping around the turn with the bike very erect—even a turn that you often ride at a much higher rate of speed when entering it a little slower.

How can you avoid this, if you do misjudge a turn and come into it too hot? By countersteering, you can maintain or increase your lean while you are braking in the corner! Try it. While you are leaned over in a corner, apply the brakes, yet push forward with your inside hand at the same time to hold the bike down into the lean and prevent it from standing up.

As you get used to countersteering, you'll discover more techniques. Former Tour de France rider and 7-Eleven team star Ron Kiefel says, "[Former teammate] Davis Phinney and I teach riders that you can modulate the countersteering even better by pulling back

24.3

Back-and-forth turns in rapid succession require strong countersteering to rapidly go from one sharp lean to the next.

MATT STUART

with the outside arm." Once you have mastered pushing forward with the inside hand, try their method of pulling back with the outside hand.

Countersteering is what causes those Tour de France riders on a fast descent to snap so quickly from vertical to leaned over into a curve. It is also what allows you to quickly turn a stable, slow-turning bike. In order to maneuver quickly, instead of having to get a less stable criterium bike that oversteers due to its supersteep head angle (which reduces fork trail), you can corner a stable, great-descending bike just as fast with forceful countersteering. In the Tour, you would want a stable bike for those screaming fast descents, but you also would want to be able to maneuver it quickly. Countersteering gives you access to that combination.

If you practice countersteering enough, counterintuitive actions that can save your skin will become natural. For instance, if you are leaned over in a turn and suddenly encounter an obstacle (perhaps a fallen rider) in the middle of it, you are screwed if you try to steer farther into the corner, away from the obstacle. You'll only straighten up the bike and skid right into the obstacle, since your momentum is still going straight for it. The same thing will happen if you only apply the brakes. But if you steer *toward* the obstacle—in other words, countersteer—away from the turn, you will increase your lean angle and pass inside of the obstacle.

Braking

There are two ways to apply the brakes when riding at high speed. You can pull the brake levers, or you can sit up to catch the wind. Watch those motorcycle road racers on TV again. Besides countersteering and dropping their inside knee in a curve, they all sit up at the last instant before entering the turn, to slow themselves down by air braking.

As we discussed before, pulling on the brake levers stands the bike up. This is best done before the turn, to avoid braking in the turn and going unnecessarily slowly. When braking hard, push your butt back on the saddle to keep your weight centered over both wheels; if your rear wheel gets too light, it will slide easily.

In contrast to pulling on the brakes, air braking does not stand the bike up or shift your weight to the front wheel. Use it as much as you need to, whenever you need to, and then tuck back down again as soon as you've reduced your speed enough to complete the turn.

Other Cornering Techniques
Shifting your weight

Phinney, a two-time Tour de France stage winner and the winner of more bike races than any other American in history, made his living by winning sprints, which requires cornering at very high speed to stay at the front. He says, "Don't stick out your inside knee when cornering (like a road motorcycle racer); that creates a lot of drag and slows you down. Instead, drop your hip to the inside. It accomplishes the same thing, but you retain more speed."

Reducing aerodynamic drag

Tucking down out of the wind allows you to descend faster. Many riders also grip their bars right next to the stem, so their body assumes an even more aerodynamic shape. However, be prudent with this because you cannot grab the brakes from this position, and a sudden flat tire or impact with a manhole can be disastrous.

Keeping your head level and looking well ahead

It is worth glancing at Block 28 on mountain bike handling, since many of the same principles apply. Keep your head erect so that your inner ear knows which way is up and makes the appropriate balance corrections. Keep your eyes focused on where you want to go. Don't look over the cliff, and don't look at the rock or the rider in front of you. Let your peripheral vision deal with those things, and keep your eyes pointed toward where you want to go, since your body will follow. The best way to crash into that rider falling across your path is to look at him. 🚲

Ron Kiefel now owns Wheatridge Cyclery in Wheatridge, Colorado.

Davis Phinney and his wife, Olympic gold medalist Connie Carpenter, run Carpenter/Phinney Bike Camps, www.bikecamp.com.

BLOCK 25
Climbing

Climbing is one of the ultimate challenges on a bike, which is why it is where most road races break apart and riders get dropped from the group. To get to some of the most beautiful places on earth, and to get the payoff of descending, you have to climb up first. The road rises and beckons. Drafting and aerodynamics are of minor importance; it's just you and the mountain, and sometimes the mountain can be intimidating.

Certainly, to climb well it is critical to have a high ratio of power output relative to the weight of you and the bike. However, there is more to it than that. While all of us can make improvements in power-to-weight ratio, other factors, including adjusting your position, technique, and mental attitude, can often make a bigger difference.

Power-To-Weight Ratio

Since you are climbing against the constant force of gravity, if you become stronger and the weight of you and your bike remains constant, your climbing speed should improve. Similarly, the lighter you and your bike are, the faster you can climb if you put out the same power. Obviously, you or your bike can become too light—that is, too weak to climb effectively without breaking down. Avoid this!

Handlebar Height

Andy Hampsten was one of the greatest climbers of his day and is the only American ever to win the Giro d'Italia (a three-week race around Italy of similar difficulty to the Tour de France). He accomplished the feat in 1988, primarily due to his climbing prowess, as well as to his toughness during a brutal snowstorm on the steep climb and descent of the Passo Gavia. Hampsten also conquered the most storied climb in the Tour de France, winning the infamous l'Alpe d'Huez stage of the 1990 Tour.

25.1

Jonathan Vaughters displays good out-of-the-saddle climbing technique by pulling up his left leg from the bottom of the stroke while forcefully straightening his right leg in the upper half of the downstroke.

GRAHAM WATSON

To climb efficiently, he recommends some adjustments to the bike position. "Often, the first thing I have people do for climbing, particularly those who used to be racers and have maintained the same racing position, is raise their stem," he says. "In the Tour in 1989, we had (7-Eleven team coach) Mike Neel telling all of us constantly to raise our handlebars. Finally, the morning of the Luz Ardiden stage, Dag-Otto Lauritzen, who can be really hardheaded, raised his stem two centimeters. He had a very low handlebar position from the Spring Classics (the major springtime European races, which include Paris-Roubaix, Tour of Flanders, and Liège-Bastogne-Liège). He went on to win the stage! He said afterward that his back had never felt so strong!" Lauritzen had become accustomed to constant back pain due to a parachuting accident years before.

If a higher bar works even for the fittest racers, then certainly those of us who never ride flat out at 40 miles per hour on level ground don't need to be overly concerned about raising ours a bit. Hampsten asks, "If you are picking up a heavy box, would you rather pick it up off of the ground or off of a table?" Notice how often you ride in the drops. If you do it rarely, then why not raise your bar a bit and use the drops more frequently?

Jonathan Vaughters is another of America's best climbers ever (see Photo 25.1). In 1999, in the Dauphine Libere stage race, he set a record that still stands for the fastest time up perhaps the most feared climb in France, Mont Ventoux. Vaughters also believes that position is especially critical when climbing. He recommends that you "be in a position where you can keep an open diaphragm—have your bars a little higher, and have your pelvis tipped forward. You want that pot-belly-hanging-down look, like [five-time Tour winner Miguel] Indurain, or Hampsten."

Pedaling Mechanics

As I mention in Block 17, pedaling mechanics is critical for climbing. Vaughters says, "There is very little momentum in climbing, so pedaling smoothly and perpendicular to your cranks is more important than on the flats or downhills, where you can coast and recover."

GRAHAM WATSON

The late Marco Pantani consistently out-climbed his rivals with an efficient pedaling style, whether in the saddle or standing on the pedals.

The late Marco Pantani, winner of the 1998 Tour de France, was the dominant road climber of the late 1990s, outdueling his adversaries in the mountains in part by pedaling more efficiently (see Photo 25.2). This was apparent when he was climbing in the saddle and particularly apparent when he was out of the saddle accelerating away from the bunch. People focus on the fact that he often rode in the drops to pull harder when climbing out of the saddle, but what he did particularly well was get his body weight up and over the pedal high in the stroke and extend his leg almost completely.

Using the entire weight of his body, and doing it earlier in the stroke (most riders don't apply power until their pedal reaches the 3 o'clock position), gave him extra power at a modest cost. Furthermore, Pantani lifted each foot back to the top of every stroke, so he was not working against himself by making his downward-pushing leg lift an upward-rising foot resting on the pedal (see more on this in Block 17).

Vaughters adds, "In out-of-the-saddle climbing, a lot of the best guys have the descending leg straight by 3 o'clock and use the body weight falling on the pedal to push it the rest of the way down. Pantani's knee was almost locked at 3 o'clock! He was doing most of the pushing with his leg muscles only over the top and through the first half of the downward stroke."

Pantani's swan song was in the 2000 Tour, when Lance Armstrong eclipsed him. Armstrong has also used efficient pedaling to achieve success, riding it to his amazing string of Tour de France wins. He works on his pedaling technique constantly with his coach, Chris Carmichael.

Relax

In Block 29, Ned Overend advises riders to relax when climbing on dirt; the same advice applies equally well when climbing on the road. Notice if your face is relaxed; if it is a mask of pain and suffering, your body gets the message and tightens up as well. Consciously relax your face and breathe deeply and evenly to relax your chest and entire body.

It may help to remember that, even though you may be hurting, it will be over soon. Tomorrow, this climb will be merely a memory, and you have suffered through a lot worse things for a lot more hours than climbing this pass. And remember that a big climb spares nobody. Even though it may look easy for others, everybody hurts when climbing.

Look around—chances are it is very beautiful where you are climbing, and appreciating that may take your mind off your discomfort.

Cadence

Vaughters advises using your energy wisely on long climbs. "Short climbs are different, but on long climbs, you always want to descend your rpms—that is, use a higher cadence at the bottom of the hill than at the top," he says. "It's easier to go from a little too small a gear at the bottom up to a bigger gear than it is to go from a big gear down to the right gear. Physiologically, your body cannot adjust from pushing a big gear at a low rpm to a lower gear and a higher rpm in the middle of the climb. It's better to be undergeared at the bottom and in the right gear in the middle of the climb, so that at the top you might be able to dip into an anaerobic energy system for three minutes or so and push a big gear to make it over the top with the group."

Vaughters continues, "Lots of people make a big deal about Lance's high rpm, but that just comes straight from Michele Ferrari (the famous Italian cycling doctor). Ferrari's studies say that if you keep the muscle contraction force below a certain level by pedaling at a higher rpm—perhaps over 70rpm on a climb for most people—you keep the capillaries from collapsing under the pressure, and you get deeper oxygenation in the muscles. But Lance's 90 to 100rpm when climbing is extreme and unnecessary for most riders, since very few people are putting out 500 watts during a half-hour climb like he is. Consequently they don't have as high a muscle contraction force collapsing the capillaries. You don't necessarily need as high an rpm as Lance, but the theory is the same."

Find Your Pace

U.S. National Team coach Edward Borysewicz (also known as Eddie B.) used to recommend that we start long climbs at the front of the peloton, take the lead, and set the pace. His reasoning was that you could set a pace comfortable for you, and stronger climbers, who otherwise might ride faster and make it harder for you, would be content to let you set the pace. By doing so, you delayed as long as possible the moment when they finally passed you and went faster than you could. He suggested acting as if you were not hurting so that they would question how well they felt and further delay their attack. And when they did come by, he recommended passing them again and slowing back down to your pace when once again in the lead.

In 1980 I won the Durango-to-Silverton "Iron Horse Classic" road race (Colorado) and set the course record by using this technique. My breakaway companion, Tom Sain, was a faster climber, but I set the pace on the two big climbs. Whenever he passed me, I immediately passed him again and re-established my pace at the front. That way, I stayed with him over the passes and beat him on the descent into Silverton.

If you finally did get passed and a gap opened up, Eddie B. told us not to close it right away, unless we were almost at the top and had a descent on which to recover. Instead, he said to just ride steadily at our own pace, and maybe we would catch back up.

The point of all of this is that there exists a pace that you can maintain up a long climb, and it will be efficient for you to go that speed and dictate it to others, rather than the other way around. One mile per hour faster, and you would be fried. Whether you are in a race, climbing with buddies, or riding alone, it still makes sense to find a pace you can maintain and stick to it.

Vaughters says, "If you blow up, you have no momentum when climbing to coast and recover." You don't want to go past your red line, or you will get to the top a lot later. On the other hand, Vaughters, who races and trains with an SRM power meter, says, "A rider's power output is always highest at the bottom. Usually at the top of the climb, the power of most riders is way off from what it was at the bottom, so you can pick off lots of riders (if you have been riding at a steadier speed)."

Canadian Steve Bauer, who had taken the overall lead in the early, flatter stages of both the 1988 and 1990 Tour de France, used these principles in defending the yellow jersey in the high mountains, surprising pundits with his climbing prowess. By no means a pure climber, Bauer rode the long climbs with good form and steady speed. Vaughters, a boy at the time, was impressed. He now says, "At the bottom he would get dropped. But by the top he was passing lots of better climbers. It comes back to the 'no momentum' factor." The riders Bauer passed might have been stronger climbers, but they had burned their candles too early by starting at a pace that was much too fast for them to maintain. By the top, they had slowed way down.

Climbing is something every cyclist can love. It is always a challenge you can rise to and derive satisfaction in having done so. And climbing almost always takes place in a beautiful setting to boot! ⚲

Andy Hampsten now markets Hampsten bicycles and puts on bike tours in California and Italy; for more information see his Web sites, www.hampsten.com and www.cinghiale.com.

Jonathan Vaughters directs Team TIAA-CREF presented by *5280* magazine , an under-23 developmental cycling team (www.tiaacrefcycling.com), and is a realtor in Denver.

Edward Borysewicz is the author (with Ed Pavelka) of *Bicycle Road Racing: The Complete Program for Training and Competition* (1985).

BLOCK 26
Dressing for Mountain Riding and Changing Weather

When the mountains beckon, you want to answer. Going up hills is perhaps a problem for your legs, but you'll have no problem staying warm, as you are going slowly and working hard. However, coming down is where you can get into trouble if you don't dress warmly and get so chilled that you weaken your immune system. You'll pay the high price of a week in bed for only hours of freedom in the high mountains. The same applies to heading out on the plains in changing weather. The key to having a great ride without the downside is dressing properly.

The Spring, Fall, and Altitude Collection

Most people know how to bundle up for cold or wet rides, but for mountain riding in nice weather, you don't want to be bundled up during the climb, since you can get so sweaty that when you come down you'll freeze as badly as if you were wearing only shorts. On the other hand, dressing too lightly is an obvious bummer when you hit the fast descent in the cold air at altitude, or when the arctic wind in the plains hits you far from home.

Bring lightweight, compact items that fit in your pockets and still leave room for food (see Photo 26.1). Keep these clothes by your helmet or shoes so that you don't have to scrounge around for them or remember what to bring. These light, compact items should include the following.

Arm warmers: It is amazing how much warmth arm warmers (Photo 26.1) can provide, especially medium-weight, tightly knit ones like DeFeet Armskins. Get them in black to absorb the sun's heat.

Lightweight vest: I am not talking about fleece vests or insulating vests with a shell front (Photo 26.1). Those are good for cooler conditions but are too bulky to stuff in your pocket easily. A lightweight, unlined nylon shell vest that cuts the wind and folds to the size of a fist is perfect.

Knee warmers: Tights are too big to stick in your pocket, but knee warmers that cover the legs from thighs to upper calves (Photo 26.1) can keep you quite warm. For cooler days, full-length leg warmers (which cover the legs from thighs to ankles) work best and only take a bit more room in your pocket.

Headband, thin cap, or Buff: Unlike a bulky cap, a thermal headband doesn't require that you readjust your

26.1

These lightweight and compact items—a shell vest, arm warmers, knee warmers, and a couple of sheets of newspaper—are easy to carry and put on and off, open or close, or slide up or down to regulate your body surface temperature.

GALEN NATHANSON

helmet strap and will keep you almost as warm. So will a thin, microfiber skullcap. I also recommend a Buff, which is just a seamless tube of thin microfiber knit fabric. On the ascent, keep the Buff in your pocket or wear it under your helmet to keep sweat from dripping down your sunglass lenses and to shade your neck with its long tail. For the descent, pull it down over your ears. If the weather is really cold, pull the whole tube down around your neck and then pull the back of it up over the top of your head so your face sticks out of the hole, forming a balaclava. If you keep your head warm, the rest of your body will fare better.

Thin gloves: Bring thin, stretch knit gloves that fit over or under cycling gloves.

Lycra shoe covers: They have little bulk, yet they give your feet another 10 to 15 degrees of comfortable temperature range. In a pinch, socks with a hole cut for the cleat will do the trick.

Newspaper: Two folded sheets take up minimal room or can be found along the way and can be quickly slid under the front of your jersey to make an incredible difference in a cold wind or on a fast descent. If you are caught out in cold air, sometimes a newspaper you find in a trash can or on the side of the road can prevent misery.

If rain threatens . . .

Thin rain jacket: If this won't fit in your jersey, strap it to your spare tire bag with a toe strap (remember those?), or tie it around your waist.

Helmet cover: Popping on a rainproof helmet cover will keep your head a lot warmer in the rain and even in the wind. A hotel shower cap will suffice.

Quick-Change Operation

Riding up into the mountains means coming down fast through air that can easily be 10 degrees colder at the top than at the bottom. The windchill factor created by moving fast through this cold air is a recipe for hypothermia. Even on the flats, a cool wind can kick up and present similar conditions. Either way, you don't want to be sweat-soaked when the cool air hits your skin,

Being prepared for sudden weather changes or long descents in cool temperatures is something you should not take lightly (though the extra clothes are light to take along).

and you want enough wind protection and insulation to keep warm.

Say the temperature is around 55 to 65 degrees when you leave home. Start off in shorts with a technical-fabric undershirt, a short-sleeved jersey with a full-length zipper and pockets, arm warmers, and knee warmers. As it warms up or as you start climbing, you can push the arm warmers down around your wrists and open the jersey. You can pull the knee warmers (or leg warmers) off over your shoes while you are rolling along.

If the temperature drops or you get to the top of a climb, you can easily add items. Before a long descent (three miles or more), I recommend putting everything on. Slap on the vest; arm warmers; headband, Buff or cap; knee warmers; and shoe covers. Unfold the newspaper and slip it under your jersey to cover your chest. If your undershirt (don't wear cotton—choose a microfiber wicking fabric or wool instead) is dry, put the paper between the layers of clothing. Otherwise, put the newspaper against your skin to protect it from the chilled air coming through wet fabric and to absorb moisture from your skin (and to decorate it with ink!). You can pull the stretch gloves over your cycling gloves so you can pull them off quickly at the bottom, or put them underneath to allow you to wipe glass off your tires with your cycling gloves. If you have a rain jacket and helmet cover and have stopped anyway, you might as well put them on—being too hot is rarely a problem on a long, fast descent.

On a group ride, these items allow you to regulate your temperature without asking others to wait while you change. Just sliding your arm warmers up or down can make a big difference in comfort. It is also a good practice to go to the back of the group to put on or remove a vest, knee warmers, or newspaper while rolling along.

While you are digging around in your jersey pockets, remember to eat something. Keeping yourself warm takes extra energy, and you can set yourself way back by bonking and freezing at the same time!

If you have the right clothing, you can take glorious, long rides in the mountains or in changing weather. You can gleefully pedal hard in light clothing when warm, and you can protect yourself from the cold when that hits too. All this without having to carry a big backpack, either!

BLOCK 27

Racing!

They say that racing improves the breed—at least when it comes to horses. I won't claim that your family bloodline will improve if you participate in some races, but I can promise that you will become a faster, more accomplished cyclist. I can also promise you experiences and friendships that you would not have had otherwise and that you will treasure your entire life.

Becoming Faster and Stronger

I have always been drawn to competing at any sport in which I developed an interest. Being on junior high school track teams morphed into racing slalom and giant slalom on skis and white-water slalom in kayaks. Bike racing was a natural outgrowth of the cycling I did to rehabilitate ski injuries.

While all of my motivations for racing are not apparent, the desire to push myself beyond my present limits is definitely among them. In a race, you hit physical barriers that very few people encounter in training, because it takes such intention to make yourself suffer. You find your maximum heart rate right away, and you also discover a level of intensity that you never thought you could maintain for an hour or so. And, as we discussed in Blocks 15 and 16, training adapts the body to stress, and racing produces a higher level of stress.

All it takes is one race to see how strong you really are relative to others. If you continue to participate in races, you'll naturally begin to focus on becoming stronger and faster. Your weaknesses become apparent, and, without anyone telling you to do it, you begin to turn those weaknesses into strengths. You find yourself absorbing information about training and racing, as well as pushing yourself while training to go beyond your previous capacities. And in the process, you find some nice, new rides!

Developing Skills

I think it is nothing short of miraculous how fast your technical skills improve by doing a few races. I had been riding mountain bikes for over a decade before I did my first cross-country race. Thanks to long road-racing experience, I was strong at climbing, but I was not at all adept at pedaling up steep climbs littered with roots and rocks, and I was poor at technical descents. I even made up a story about how it was physically impossible with my high center of gravity (I'm 6'6") to be good at riding drop-offs because I was just teetering too high above them. That all changed after doing just a couple of races.

On a mountain bike, once you have invested a certain amount of effort to carve out your position ahead of other riders on a hard, singletrack climb in a race, you are loathe to give it up. Your heart may be racing at 180 beats per minute, but if somebody starts to pass you, you will often find new resources to fend them off. Physically, you dig deep, but you also will ride sections you never dreamed possible only a half hour before when you were warming up on the course!

Somehow, to keep your speed up and stay ahead of those behind you and/or catch those ahead, you manage to lift your front wheel up and over that ledge you had to run up before. Or you blast through a section of slippery roots that you had walked or cautiously picked your way through.

On a descent winding steeply down through the trees at some western ski area, the trail will have become a narrow groove interspersed with large, excavated roots and chatter marks (also known as braking bars) before each curve or root-tangled drop-off. You tried to ride it the day before, and there was no way; you felt that the groove was too narrow to ride in without losing your balance and tipping over or hitting a tree. But now, in the race, you are trying to catch up with riders ahead and stay in front of riders you have already passed. This section of trail is more deeply dug out by the riders in front of you, revealing even larger roots, and there is so much dust kicked up that you can't see anything. However, rather than repeating or magnifying your experience of the day before, you instead find yourself riding through it, staying in the trench and going over obstacles you did not think yourself capable of, following the vague outline through the dust cloud of the rider in front, and doing your utmost to stay ahead of the rider clattering up on you from behind.

And it is not just in a mountain bike race that you learn new skills; you will develop new abilities in road races as well. Where you had been nervous to ride close to other riders, you will find yourself staying in the thick of a big pack, having tasted how much harder it is to ride at the back. In a criterium, you will find yourself cornering like you never had before in order to keep your hard-earned place near the front and avoid falling victim to the brutal accordion effect toward the back of the pack. Each rider in a pack going into a curve slows down slightly more than the rider in front, so the pack compresses into the turn and expands out of it like an accordion. This makes the riders in back crawl into each corner and sprint like mad out of it, a situation that nobody can maintain for long.

While you might not race in front of crowds like this (at the 2001 World Mountain Bike Championships in Vail, Colorado), there are many other reasons to do some racing.

Camaraderie

When you have suffered along with another person, you develop a bond with them, whether or not you share the same language, culture, or politics. And you always find abundant opportunities to suffer along with others in racing! Some of my best friends are people with whom I have comiserated through challenging road, mountain bike, or cross-country ski races in horrendous conditions. Racing is also a great way to meet people, and particularly to find training companions.

Seeing the World

One cool thing about bike races is that they are usually held in interesting places off the beaten path. I first developed my love of traveling from bike racing, in this country and abroad. As a young man with no money, to be sent to the Tour of Ireland as a member of the U.S. National Team, for instance, was an unbelievable opportunity to broaden my horizons.

Simply because somebody is putting on a race that has inspired your dreams or those of your friends or teammates, you find yourself going new places and learning new things. I have been all over the United States and Europe to compete in road and mountain bike races and cross-country ski races. I consequently have close friends all over the world, by virtue of having suffered alongside them in races or having stayed in their homes. Those are experiences I would not trade for anything.

Winning: A Minor Motivation

One recent winter morning, I was talking with other guests at breakfast in a small hotel near Winter Park, Colorado. They were going downhill skiing, and were asking me and a friend what we were doing that day. We explained that we were competing in a two-day cross-country ski race that had a similar format to a bicycle stage race, with a classic (kick and glide) technique stage the first day and a skate technique stage the second. One woman asked, "What do you get?" It took us awhile to figure out what she was asking, and then it became clear that she meant, "What prize do you get if you win?" We both laughed—we had no idea what was on the prize list and it hadn't occurred to us to ask. We were racing for the fun, the challenge, the camaraderie, and the satisfaction of completing something difficult and of seeing improvement in our fitness and skills, but certainly not for anything material.

It may seem nonsensical to spend the time training and traveling to the race; to pay entry fees, license fees, high equipment costs, and travel and lodging expenses; and to spend hours beforehand fine-tuning the bike or skis in order to race for "nothing." But those who have experienced racing see no contradiction. There is a raw, pure joy to the whole experience of racing that gives many rewards, even though it may look like pure suffering! Of course, winning can be especially sweet when it happens. . . .

Choosing and Entering a Race

Think about what kind of racing you wish to do. On the road, there are mass-start road races, criteriums, time trials, and stage races.

Racing: Something for Everyone

Road Racing

Road Race: Point-to-point or long loop and circuit race with a mass start

Criterium: Mass-start multi-lap race around a short circuit

Time trial: Individual race against the clock

Stage race: Multi-day races that may contain all three types of road races

Mountain Bike Racing

Cross-country: An up-and-down race through the woods, plains, or desert

Short-track: Criterium-style mountain bike racing on dirt

Dual slalom: Two riders at a time on a downhill, gated course

Mountain-cross: Four to six riders at a time on course

Downhill: All-out racing down a long, steep technical course

Other Races

Cyclo-cross: Off-road events on road bikes with knobby tires

Velodrome: Held on banked track, riding bikes with a single fixed gear and no brakes

BMX: Mass-start racing on short, closed dirt loops over manmade trails on single-speed bikes with small, knobby tires

In mountain bike racing, the vast majority of events, particularly ones that you can enter without a racing license, are cross-country races. One enormously popular cross-country format is the twenty-four-hour race, in which an individual or a team races around a closed circuit from noon on Saturday until noon on Sunday. Short-track racing is the equivalent of a mountain bike criterium. There are also gravity-driven events like downhill, dual slalom, and mountain-cross races. Cyclo-cross, velodrome racing, and BMX also offer competitive opportunities.

Some races require riders to have a license from an organizing body. USA Cycling (USAC) is the national licensing body for amateur and professional road, track, and mountain bike racing. The National Bicycle League, or NBL, offers BMX licenses. There are also a number of regional racing organizations that put on events and charge a license fee as an alternative to a USAC license. If you only want to try a single event, you can often buy a one-day license for a nominal fee at the race.

USAC focuses on elite programs, but it also works hard on membership. According to Dean Crandall, a longtime cycling official for road and mountain bike events, "Local associations still offer the best bang for the buck as far as grassroots racing goes. You will never get on the Olympic team competing with a local association license, but you will have fun. Every cyclist should belong to a cycling association of some sort, even if it is just for supporting those who help you have a place to race."

Crandall says, "The fear of being in a mass-start competition keeps more cyclists away from racing than any other factor. Case in point: the American Cycling Association in Colorado puts on a time trial series every year. The start list fills up months before the first race. More citizen-riders compete in this event than in any other licensed event all year, because it's just them against the clock. The fear of racing elbow to elbow at high speed scares the hell out of some people, regardless of age or ability."

If this is your concern, you might also consider cross-country mountain bike racing. Once the big group thins out after the start, cross-country races usually become individual events, yet you see in real time how you are doing relative to other riders. While you are highly likely to crash in a mountain bike race, the ground is usually more forgiving than pavement, there is no possibility of being hit by an automobile, and any crash is usually your fault—you are unlikely to get caught up in a mass pileup.

How Can You Learn to Race?

Cycling camps offer an opportunity to learn skills and training techniques. Organized group rides and local training-race series also offer the chance to get comfortable riding in a group. You may want to seek out a coach to assist you in more rapidly and effectively improving your technical abilities and your fitness (to work on all of those things in Blocks 14–19!). Crandall says, "Join a club. Clubs are the best way to learn group riding skills through their training rides."

For more information about USA Cycling, visit its Web site, www.usacycling.org.

PART 4

Mountain Bike Skills

BLOCK 28
Basic Mountain Bike Skills

I teach a mountain biking class at a local middle school, and I periodically lead a trip of 100 middle school students to Moab, Utah. It has become apparent to me in riding with kids, and especially with their parents, that you cannot take any of a rider's basic mountain bike skills for granted. You could neglect mentioning the one skill that ends up making the difference for them. And when you do address that issue, all of a sudden the lights come on, and they ride at a higher level.

None of the following basic mountain bike skills are hard to master, but some are not obvious. Furthermore, some may be counterintuitive, or may go against practices you have learned and in which you've trained yourself for years. It is only for these reasons that any of these skills are difficult to learn. An open mind is a useful tool to start with.

By following these simple steps, you'll learn to ride over obstacles that seemed insurmountable before.

Coasting: Stand up with Feet Level

I know that keeping the cranks horizontal when standing (see Photo 28.1) is obvious and totally natural to many of you. But to some, who may even be quite strong riders on the road, it's not. This became clear to me once when riding down a mile-long slickrock slab in Moab with a group of kids and adults. One woman was having all kinds of trouble, because she was riding with one foot down, alternately sitting on the saddle and standing with all of her weight on the down foot. While on the seat, she was being bounced around, and while off of it, she was constantly on the verge of losing control because her bike was so unbalanced to one side and her stance was so weak.

Once she understood the concept of standing up off of her saddle with her feet level with each other, she could cruise down the slab twice as fast, completely in balance. Most importantly, she was happy, confident, and relaxed.

Julien Absalon of France keeps his eyes looking well ahead, his feet level, and his weight balanced while descending narrow, rough, and tightly turning singletrack on his way to winning the 2001 world U23 cross-country title in Vail, Colorado.

GALEN NATHANSON

Steep Descents: Push Your Butt Back

When your bike is tipped downward, your weight shifts toward the front of the bike. To maintain control and avoid flipping over the bar when you hit an obstacle or touch the front brake, you must move your weight back (Photo 28.1). Of course, you must also be standing firmly on the pedals, with your feet level with each other, as we discussed above. This strategy will not work any other way.

If the trail drops off really steeply, you may need to have your butt so far back that your saddle will be up against your chest. It also helps to have your weight as low as possible. This is why dual slalom, downhill (Photo 30.1), and BMX racers use such a low saddle position.

For long, steep descents, it is worthwhile to drop your saddle down. You will be able to go faster with more control and possibly save yourself from an injury that would take much longer to deal with than the time it takes to lower your saddle. If you are in a cross-country race, you cannot realistically take the time to readjust your saddle height. Just make sure that you can slide back and forth off of the saddle without snagging your shorts in the process. Change shorts and/or saddles if you cannot.

Use Your Front Brake

Many mountain bikers are afraid to use their front brake. They learned long ago, possibly the hard way, that they can (or will!) flip over the bars if they pull the front lever. However, if you just think about it for a second, it will be apparent that as soon as you engage the brakes, your weight shifts to the front wheel. Your momentum is going forward, and the bike must tip forward as it slows down relative to your weight moving forward. In the same way, the front of your car goes down and the back of it goes up when you slam on the brakes.

So, since your weight while braking is on the front wheel, if you only use the rear brake, you have very little braking power, because the rear tire has little weight on it and hence little traction. Almost all of your available braking power is on the front wheel. This dynamic is even more apparent on a steep descent, where the slope further unweights the rear wheel.

I recommend putting your brakes on their highest power setting and positioning the levers so that you can only pull them with your forefingers, as described in Block 46. This will prevent you from grabbing a fistful of brake (potentially pitching you over the front) and will give you better modulation. And it leaves you with four other fingers to hold the grip and comfortably control the bike.

Use the front brake judiciously, but by all means use it! When descending a steep slope, let go of the front brake whenever your tire drops over a ledge, to avoid pitching yourself over the bars. But keep your weight back and use the front brake to control your speed.

If your front wheel starts to wash out in a corner, release the front brake and steer into the slide—away from the corner—to regain traction.

Chin up and Eyes ahead

Blair Lombardi, a professional mountain bike coach and the creator of the Lombardi Speed Technique, first told me about keeping the chin up and the eyes looking where the rider wants to go, and it is the single most useful piece of mountain biking advice I have ever received.

The body's inner ear balance system requires that the head be level in order to establish what side is up and how to balance the body. If you ride looking down, the inner ear is unable to maintain your balance.

Lombardi also points out that looking well ahead (as in Photo 28.1) also allows your body to naturally make whatever balance corrections are required to keep you upright and moving in the direction you want to go. Your body tends to follow your eyes, so if you look at the obstacle or the thing you are afraid of, you will tend to go that way. Just let your peripheral vision, and perhaps quick glances down, take care of whatever is right under your wheels.

This dynamic is obvious when you are riding down steep switchbacks. At the bottom of each switchback, there tends to be a dramatic drop off the edge of the trail. If you look over the drop, you not only will tend to get more scared and tense up, but you will also tend to ride right off it. It is not a pretty sight when it happens. But that doesn't have to be you. When you come into a switchback, look around the corner and down (or up) the trail where you intend to go.

In the same way, when you are going up a steep technical climb (actually up any climb, but particularly technical ones), keep your vision trained on the top of the climb and beyond. Let your peripheral vision deal with the rocks, ledges, and roots as you encounter them. If you look down at them, you will surely bobble and tip over or put your foot down. Lombardi teaches that by keeping your head up and looking where you want to go, even when you have very little speed and your front wheel is being deflected this way and that, your natural balance mechanism will keep you steering and shifting your weight as needed to keep you upright.

Finally, looking ahead allows you to anticipate what is coming, rather than having to react suddenly to a series of surprises. If, for example, riders fall in front of you or a deer jumps in your path, it is much better to be looking ahead and giving yourself the maximum possible response time.

Keep Your Weight on the Front Wheel

In order to steer your bike properly, you need to have weight on your front wheel. We are all familiar with the sensation of sitting too far back on a climb so that the front wheel is light and deflects easily, sending you off line and off your bike.

Ideally, your weight should be evenly divided between the wheels. On level ground, this means your center of mass (which is located at approximately your navel) should be over a midpoint between the wheels, or just ahead of the bottom bracket. So, coasting on level, rough terrain requires that you stand up with your cranks horizontal and your butt just above the center of the saddle's nose.

But on a climb, weighting the front wheel requires dropping the chest and sitting on the nose of your saddle or standing with your butt ahead of the saddle. We discuss this in more detail in Block 29 on riding technical climbs.

And on a descent, your navel needs to move back, over the saddle or behind it, as in Photo 28.1. Keeping weight on the front wheel is not a problem on a descent; rather, keeping weight on the back wheel is the trick!

Practice, Practice, Practice

Lombardi points out in her *Mountain Bike Coach Pocket Lesson & Training Guide* (1997) that when you are scared, your survival instincts kick in and bring out three behaviors that are detrimental in mountain biking. She says, "You automatically react by: 1) focusing on the source of danger, 2) leaning or moving back, and 3) freezing in place." We have gone over the downside of looking at what you are afraid of: You will ride right at it. And obviously, trying to back away from the danger removes weight from the front wheel where you most need it to steer with. At best, freezing tenses you up so you cannot respond appropriately; at worst, it leaves you stiff and unable to avoid running right into whatever scared you in the first place.

Lombardi's coaching method is to replace these primitive survival reactions with trained responses that you reinforce every time you ride. This means consciously and constantly performing all of the skills above while riding and reminding yourself of them continuously until they become second nature.

And above all, relax. If you are tense, you cannot control the bike and respond fluidly to the terrain. Check that you are not holding your breath by consciously breathing deeply, particularly on scary descents. 🚲

Blair Lombardi is the author of *The Mountain Bike Coach Pocket Lessons & Training Guide* (1997), and is currently writing a book on her balance training system. Her Web site is mountainbikecoach.com.

BLOCK 29
Climbing Steep Trails

For a decade, 1990 World Champion Ned Overend dominated international cross-country mountain bike racing, a sport that rewards climbing ability above all else. He also was one of the best road climbers in the United States in the 1980s. He outclimbs other riders largely thanks to natural ability and a high power-to-weight ratio; but technique also has a lot to do with his success. Here are some of his tips.

Stand Up

"I don't generate a lot of power in the saddle," Overend says. "I generate some, sure, but not nearly as much as I do when standing. So, for a short, steep climb, I need to stand up. I actually get improved traction standing up. You can understand why if you picture the bike as a lever with the fulcrum at the bottom bracket. When you are pulling up on the bars with your body bent over, you leverage your rear tire into the dirt (see Photo 29.1). Your butt should not be too far forward—maybe right over the saddle nose. Bar ends give you more leverage due to the longer lever to pull on.

29.1

"I definitely get great traction standing up, and I climb some really steep stuff. When it is really steep and technical, I pretty much have got to be standing up.

"You don't want to spend too much time standing up, though, because you're using a lot more energy. But when I need to get over something, I stand up, and then I sit down when the steepness drops a bit. I also stand up in a bigger gear even on gentler grades with good traction to give my butt and my seated-climbing muscles a break."

Relax

"Another important thing for climbing (and for all mountain biking) is to be relaxed," Overend continues. "If riders are grimacing, that indicates that their arms and many of their muscles are tense, and their chest is tense. The tension makes it hard to breathe, and all of those tense muscles are using oxygen. I will make a conscious effort to exhale in a pronounced manner several times, consciously thinking about relaxing and turning my legs over in a smooth circle. In yoga relaxation tech-

Former Olympic champion Bart Brentjens pulls on the bar ends with the bottom bracket as the fulcrum to leverage the rear tire into the dirt.

GALEN NATHANSON

niques, you exhale as you relax certain parts of your body. The pronounced exhale is a cue from relaxation techniques I do to calm my thoughts the night before a race, when my thoughts themselves are racing."

Pedaling Technique

Jeff Broker, sport biomechanist for the U.S. Olympic Committee at the Olympic Training Center in Colorado Springs, Colorado, studies pedaling technique with force plate pedals (see Block 17). He says, "Elite mountain bike cross-country riders generally have the best pedaling mechanics of anyone we test, and John Tomac (during the time he was the top international mountain bike racer) had the best mechanics we had ever seen. I attribute this to the immediate feedback mountain bikers get when climbing on loose dirt. If they do not maintain steady application of power, they lose traction."

Overend's smooth pedaling style is testament to Broker's theory. He recommends that mountain bikers "focus on pedaling in circles. It helps both with traction and relaxation. Practice pedaling with one leg on a gentle climb. The drill forces you to move your foot across the dead spots and gives you a feel for pedaling circles. I don't do this drill a lot, but it is a good one to give you the feel for a round pedal stroke. Another drill that will help you to see the importance of a smooth pedal stroke is to pedal up a steep climb while your feet are not clipped into the pedals.

An experienced rider with the same power output as a less experienced one will go faster by maintaining traction with a smooth pedal stroke. If a guy does not have a good smooth pedal stroke, he will have to sit back to get power, but then the front wheel will get light. He needs to apply power all around the stroke and get more forward for proper fore-aft balance."

Balance

"I love to climb supersteep stuff—almost trials stuff," Overend says with an eager grin. "Supersteep climbing is done at slow speeds so if you are not comfortable balancing, you will have trouble. Track-stand drills are great for mountain bike riding. Doing a track stand (named for the stationary position that track sprinters hold on their bikes for many minutes in order to gain a tactical advantage over their opponent) is not that hard. I once did a twenty-four-hour race in the United Kingdom, and there was a team of guys on unicycles that completed the whole thing! Now that takes good balance! You learn balance quickly if you do it specifically.

"Mountain biking is a front-to-back balancing act as well as a side-to-side balancing act. If your front wheel gets light, then it starts to wander. Sliding forward and back on the saddle and raising and lowering the chest toward the bars allows you to vary the weight distribution between the two wheels."

And, to enhance balance, keep your chin up and eyes focused where you want to go, as we discussed in Block 28. On a technical climb (and on nontechnical ones as well, to make it a habit), focus on the top of the climb and let your peripheral vision deal with the obstacles under your wheels. Your body will follow your eyes, allowing you to make whatever steering and balance adjustments are necessary.

Rhythm

Overend believes that mountain bikers should "start a little more gradually on a long climb and develop a rhythm. Rhythm is very important in a climb. Get into a rhythm at the bottom, rather than sprinting at the bottom. If you blow up on a climb, you lose a lot of time because there is no place to recover. Be more conservative at the base of the climb."

If you have the option, use your suspension lockout devices for extended, smooth uphills. As a rule, if your bike bobs when you stand up and pedal, don't do it for long. For extreme technical uphills you should not lock out your suspension, as the suspension movement increases traction significantly.

Pick the Right Gear

Knowing which gear to ride in takes experience, and Overend can't stress enough the importance of being in the right gear. He says, "It is not always best to be in the lowest gear. Some climbs I can't make it up in too low of a gear. Use a big enough gear to maintain momentum, yet you must downshift while you are pedaling to stay at your ideal cadence. This means actively shifting as you're going up the climb to keep the ideal cadence. As you ride, you've got to be examining and anticipating the terrain based on obstacles, steepness variations, and turns. If you wait until you are about to come off (that is, fall over off the bike or put your feet down), it is too late to shift—you do not have enough momentum.

If you do come off, you are better off pushing to the next gradual place, rather than starting up on a climb. Be in the right gear before you lose all of your momentum. You don't want to have to try and shift gears while you are pushing the bike—that costs you a lot of time!"

Climbing Steep Turns

Negotiating hairpin turns while climbing requires some of the same techniques as rounding any other turn. You want to start the turn wide to the outside of the trail, cut to the inside, and finish back at the outside of the trail. Overend says that "the ideal line takes the least amount of turn of the handlebars; straightening out the turn as much as possible helps. But sometimes it's too steep at the apex (inside of the corner), and there are too many obstacles."

Pedaling around uphill hairpins requires more balance than going around a turn at speed on pavement, because neither your own momentum nor the wheel's gyroscopic action generates enough centripetal force to offer you significant stability. The sharper you have to turn, the slower you must go, and the more balance you require to stay upright. And the balance point shifts both fore-aft and side-to-side as you pedal and encounter obstacles and changes in terrain.

To train for uphill switchbacks, riders should "do small-circle turning drills. See how small a circle you can make on your bike," Overend recommends. "You will discover that you can almost have your wheel turned at 90 degrees and be spinning around in a circle. The sharper you turn, the slower you have to go."

Pedals

"Climbing the supersteep stuff requires having a good pedal and cleat combination that is easy and predictable to get out of," Overend says. "It gives you the confidence to continue balancing when you are about to lose it, if you know that you can get out at the last minute.

"Practice getting out of your cleats at different positions on the pedal stroke. You don't have the time to move your pedal to the ideal position when you're on a steep climb. It takes confidence to get out of the pedals (at a position other than the one you prefer to clip out at). Then you can focus on traction and steering and keeping your front wheel down."

Starting from a Steep Stop

If you do have to get off or stop on a steep climb, you know how hard it can be to get going again, particularly if the traction is loose. Overend says, "Most riders always get off on the same side of the bike—the side they are more comfortable with. I start with my right pedal at two or three o'clock and push it fast to six o'clock. That is all the time you have to get the other pedal over the 12 o'clock position. So you've got to be quick, but you must also be in the right gear. You stand up for at least that one pedal stroke. I generally start with my right foot in the cleat, but it may take a few revolutions before I get my left cleat in."

Overend's suggestion of standing up may not work if you're starting up on a steep, loose climb and the tire spins. If that's the case, try pressing the nose of the saddle down with your butt. You cannot sit on the saddle in the normal way, because all the torque you generate with your first pedal stroke will lift the front wheel right up off the ground. Without any speed to speak of, you will not have enough balance to bring the front wheel back down and continue pedaling straight ahead; you will have to put your feet back down again and start over. I find that if I wedge my right butt cheek squarely against the front of the saddle nose as I start up with my right foot clipped in, I can maintain rear tire traction and keep the front wheel down. This extra weight on the rear tire, as my right foot pushes from two o'clock to six o'clock, is all I need to get my left foot on the pedal and to keep going. But if my butt is not wedged against the saddle, my rear tire spins uselessly.

Teach Others

If you really want to get good at something, teach it! Overend says, "Writing my book helped me be a better rider because I thought about all of these things. If you think about the dynamics that go into climbing, it will be less frustrating." 🚲

Former World Champion Ned Overend wrote (with Ed Pavelka) *Mountain Bike Like a Champion* **(1999) and is a designer of Specialized mountain bikes.**

Zen Hillmeister Alan Hills on Technical Uphills

Technical uphills have crux moves or terrain features that push you to your absolute limit to clear the entire hill. At the bottom, decide where the crux move will be, and save your energy for this spot. As you near the crux, accelerate. Often the only way to clear a very difficult uphill obstacle may be to roll through it for an instant and then resume megapower after clearing the obstacle. This of course is easier said than done when you are at your aerobic, muscular, and pain limit. Bend forward to keep some weight on the front wheel and to generate massive power while maintaining the suppleness to hook the rear wheel up and dance over rocks and roots. You really only need to employ extreme technique for very short power stretches of perhaps 15 feet, so efficiency can go out the window.

Momentum is your best friend in many technical situations. Even if your back wheel spins out and you stop dead momentarily, just keep pedaling and keep your weight balanced over your bike and your vision forward—you can often get through what others don't and what you wouldn't have believed possible.

Also, even if you're a hillmeister, that wheezer in front of you is likely to screw up at the difficult point of the hill. Keep room between the two of you so that when he or she does blow it, you will be able to get by.

The two most common errors on technical uphills are: 1) lack of confidence followed by psyching yourself out, and 2) beginning the hill too fast resulting in running out of gas at the crux obstacle or near the top. Have the confidence to begin the hill at a controlled pace and meter your energy out evenly and appropriately, saving the superhuman efforts for the killer spots in the terrain. Remember that your mind often quits before your body or physics fail you.

BLOCK 30
Descending Technical Trails

Mountain biking's roots lie in technical descending; the annual Marin County Repack race in Marin County, California, was among the first to showcase these skills in the mid 1970s, and riders have been pushing the limits ever since. Mountain bike equipment has improved dramatically since those Repack days, and the level of riding now possible, even for beginners, is astounding when viewed from the perspective of those days of early cruiser bikes. An entire industry has sprouted up around descending, trying to make money off of hauling riders and their bikes up ski lifts in the summertime.

Mastering the Basics

Greg Herbold (also known as HB) has a world downhill championship to show for his descending mastery. His tips for technical descending build on the basics from Block 28 and form a foundation for mastering more advanced descending skills.

"The first and most important thing when you're going downhill fast is to know where you're going," says Herbold. "Scan down the trail (see Photo 30.1), and you can tell by the trees what's coming and what to prepare for." That's harder to do in open areas, but use whatever markers you can to tell where the trail leads.

30.1

"The second critical skill of technical descending is to have your weight positioned properly—back, but not too far back," Herbold continues. "Be back far enough (Photo 30.1), but don't lean back because you're scared. Your control is on the front wheel, so weight your front wheel, but not too much. Lots of people are scared to use the front brake, so you should practice 'endos' on flat ground." Practicing endo entails pulling your front brake hard at a low speed so your bike stands up on the front wheel. Practice shifting your weight back and modulating the front brake to bring the rear wheel back down safely.

Australian Ben Cory on his way to the 2001 junior world downhill title in Vail, Colorado: Cory is looking well ahead, has his weight back and his saddle low, and he has pushed his front wheel out from the ledge he is dropping over.

GALEN NATHANSON

Downhill Switchbacks

Fundamental to riding switchbacks is looking ahead, around the corner, as we discussed in Block 28. HB says, "It's easy for riders to get scared of drop-offs, but lean in, and don't look over. It's better to have your front end planted and your back wheel sliding, and not vice versa (see Photo 30.2). I'm not promoting skidding, but if a tire skids, you want it to be the rear."

"For a lot of switchbacks, especially for slow ones," Herbold continues, "enter in the normal 'attack' position, with your feet positioned at three o'clock and nine o'clock" (as shown in Photos 30.1 and 30.2). Former world cross-country champion Ned Overend describes the attack position as making your "cone of movement" larger, referring to an inverted cone whose vertex is at your feet, allowing conical circular motion about them. To free up this cone of movement, stand on the pedals, knees and elbows flexed, with your butt up off of the saddle.

GT extreme rider Hans "No Way" Rey says, "When not racing, take your time and be patient. Most people try to rush through the turn. Go slowly and safely until you get past the apex of the switchback." Herbold adds that "for faster switchbacks, you can weight your outside pedal. You want a little lean of the bike and of your body (Photo 30.2). If your weight is pressured onto the inside edge of the tires, the bike will turn better than if it is upright, with you just steering the corner (as opposed to countersteering—see Block 24). Initiate leaning as you enter the corner. If you are leaning in and the bike breaks loose, it will slide in the direction you want to go."

This lean is particularly important because of the exposure many switchbacks have on steep mountainsides. Herbold's warning: "You're better to 'low side' than

Former world downhill champion Greg Herbold rails around a bermed switchback. Notice how he is countersteering—his inside (right) arm is straight while his outside (left) arm is sharply bent.

'high side'!" In other words, it is vastly preferable to fall uphill than downhill on a switchback, since going over the high side (and then down the hill) can entail falling for a long time before you stop, with the potential of broken bones.

Weight Transfer

Making linked downhill turns on a mountain bike is similar to making them on skis. Herbold says, "You go from a normal, evenly weighted position, but the crux of the corner is like on skis—to transfer your weight from your downhill ski across to the other ski for the next turn. You experience the same thing on the bike."

Weight transfer takes a leap of faith, whether one is on skis or on a bike, and is difficult to do when one is afraid. Rey points out that "anybody can pedal a bike, but mountain biking is something that most people cannot do. You have to be active on the bike, not like a sack of potatoes. You can't just stand on a pair of skis; you have to work it. It's the same with mountain biking."

Picking Your Line

The lines you can ride depend on the speed you're going. Herbold says, "You have to look ahead enough that you add pieces of the trail together. Otherwise, you concentrate so hard on making it over something, and then you don't know where you're going when you get over it."

Don't think about your line as being the track of your front wheel. Notice mountain bike tracks in snow; the front and rear wheel do not follow the same line. "Think about your rear wheel placement more than your front," says Herbold. "Avoid a big obstacle by six inches, not by two inches, so your back wheel does not hit it. This also is critical for technical singletrack climbing, especially when you are going up in the middle chainring."

Bunny Hopping

Here is where you use the bunny-hopping skill fully described in Block 32. You can use obstacles as small jumps to fly over rough spots. "If you are on a smooth section, and then you have a patch of eight feet of stones, just blip off of a little ramp and bunny hop over them," says Herbold. "You're not airing it out, but it's easier to deal with rough sections by not riding them."

"If you're tired, it's a whole lot easier to hop over the rough sections than it is to absorb them with your arms and legs," he continues. "Bunny hop those ravines and wash-outs across the trail. Find a little lip on the front side—all you need is a couple of inches to load your front suspension and lift a bit."

Dropping off Small Ledges

There is more to riding over shelf-drops a couple of feet high, especially if a number of them are linked together, than just leaning back and keeping your eyes trained well down the trail. Herbold says, "You have to lean back, yes, but it's important to push your front wheel out away from the drop-off (Photo 30.1). If you push out as you come to the edge and your front wheel goes out two feet before dropping down, it makes a two-foot drop-off effectively half as high by decreasing the angle, and the sooner you're ready for the next one. As soon as you land, re-cock your body and push out again, extending your arms while keeping your head up." Rey adds, "Keep your weight back, behind the seat, until your rear tire rolls off the drop. Most riders make the mistake of shifting their weight forward as soon as the front tire rolls over the edge—that's too early."

Equipment

Equipment is critical in any situation, but especially for descending, because speed and trail exposure increase the risk of failure. Herbold says, "You're relying on your sixth sense, so if your bars are straight, if your seat's not too high, and if your tire pressure, suspension balance, and brake setup are okay, all of these things will give you confidence. If something feels weird on your bike, then probably something *is* wrong with it." You will feel more comfortable riding near cliffs if you have confidence in your equipment.

Just Do It

"Just go at your own level and be comfortable with it," says Rey. "Somebody has to be the slowest. Don't be intimidated. Have fun with it. Riding more technical stuff has nothing to do with being ballsy—it has to do with visualizing what you are going to do. If you cannot picture how you are going to do a certain turn or jump, it is not likely to work out, but you might get lucky and pull it off. It comes with experience and trial and error." Herbold says, "Ride your bike in the mountains for twenty years, and you'll get it!"

Greg Herbold spends his life traveling the world riding on trails with friends, beating up the SRAM, RockShox, Scott, Giro, Continental, Ritchey, and Oakley equipment he helps design.

BLOCK 31
Doing a Wheelie

I was not one of those kids who spent countless hours riding wheelies and doing other tricks on my Stingray (BMX bikes did not exist back then), and I wish that I had. I have enormous respect for my riding partners who can do tricks on their bikes. While it is cool just to have those skills for their own sake, they are particularly desirable on gnarly trails.

Wheelies are probably the most useful of those bike tricks I missed out on as a kid. I have since learned how to pull a wheelie, if only for short distances, because on climbs they are incredibly handy for lifting your wheel over ledges. Still, I would like to be able to ride a wheelie all around town, and since I cannot, I will let famous former trials riding world champion, showman, stuntman, and adventure mountain biker Hans "No Way" Rey (see Photo 31.1) tell you how.

31.1

Hans "No Way" Rey wheelie-ing his way through the Alps

"Generally speaking, this is one of the most time-consuming and difficult moves out there," Rey says. "Some guys, even top World Cup riders, cannot ride a good wheelie. But you'll see kids riding them because they put the time into it."

Rey's Way to a Good Wheelie

1. Adjust your seat to a low position. You'll ride the wheelie sitting down, and the low seat position will help maintain your center of gravity and balance. (Note how Rey is sitting in Photo 31.1.)

2. Put the bike into a medium to low gear (but not too low), and begin at rolling speed.

3. Crouch your upper body so your weight is over the handlebars.

4. Turn the cranks to the eleven o'clock position.

5. Pedal down and pull up on the handlebars simultaneously.

6. Immediately lean back, as if you were in a rocking chair, and continue pedaling. You need to trust your rear brake, otherwise you'll flip over backward.

7. Outstretch your arms and sit on the tip of the seat.

8. Keep one finger on the rear brake while the others firmly hold the grip.

9. Feather the rear brake continually. This helps to control speed and can prevent you from falling on your butt.

10. Relax. The front tire should be pretty high in the air.

11. Begin controlling your vertical and side-to-side balance.

12. Adjust the vertical balance with the rear brake (if leaning too far back) or by pedaling (if your front wheel begins to drop).

13. Fight the sideways balance right away; it's impossible to recover if you wait too long.

14. Control the sideways balance by sticking out a foot or knee (Photo 31.1), or by turning the handlebars in the opposite direction. (Just make sure the handlebars are straight before you come down.)

15. Let the front wheel drop to come out of the move.

Rey's Wheelie Tips

"All these intricate and slight movements happen at once, which is why this is a difficult trick," Rey says. You need to practice, practice, practice, to get used to the balance. Fortunately, you can do it anywhere, even in a big city that is otherwise terrible for bike riding. For beginners, Rey says, "try riding slightly uphill. Also, practice hopping off the back for practice—so you'll be able to in a pinch."

As for equipment, Rey has one preference in particular. "I hate riding wheelies clipped into the pedals," he states flatly. "Ride it flat." In other words, switch to flat pedals for this trick so you can take your feet off at any time to get your lateral balance or to catch yourself if you lose your balance.

And remember, you are not seeking perfection and a completely stationary body. "There's no such thing as perfect balance—you will always be plus or minus your balance point. It will slowly become easier to correct," Rey assures us.

No Way's Warnings

First, Rey warns against keeping your weight over the handlebars once the front tire is up in the air. His only other warning is not to try to pedal too fast, or your speed will become uncontrollable. ⊘🚲

Hans Rey is a world leader in extreme mountain biking. He has traveled the world extensively, riding his GT mountain bikes over and through areas previously considered unrideable. See what he is up to and learn more tricks at his Web site, www.hansrey.com.

BLOCK 32
Doing a Bunny Hop

Doing a bunny hop is a simple trick that becomes complicated if you are using flat pedals, rather than clip-in pedals or even toe clips and straps. Bunny hops are just as useful on a road bike as on a mountain bike, for jumping over train tracks and other obstacles on paved roads—even jumping off of curbs. As world-famous extreme mountain biker Hans "No Way" Rey says, "Jumping both wheels off the ground at once will help you out of some tight jams and over many obstacles—whether you're in the forest or the city."

Hopping with Clip-in Pedals

A bunny hop is far easier to do, at least if you are not a trials phenom like "No Way" Rey, if you are clipped into your pedals. It is actually quite a simple motion, which consists of crouching down on the bike with the feet level with each other and jumping upward, pulling the bike up by the handlebars and the pedals. Just this motion is usually sufficient to get across a train track if you are moving fast on a road bike. Just know that a purist like Greg Herbold calls this "credit card air," meaning that you are jumping off of the ground by pulling up clipped into the pedals you bought with your credit card (as opposed to hopping the bike without having your feet clipped in). In any case, whether you are bunny hopping on a road bike or a mountain bike, with or without clip-in pedals, heed Rey's caution, "You gotta be committed! You can not do it half-heartedly!"

Riders who get a lot more height out of a bunny hop don't do it like a roadie (credit card air); that is, they don't just pull up both wheels at the same time. Instead, they yank up on the handlebars first, to bring the front wheel up high, then they push the bar away and roll their wrists over and forward while pulling their feet up as high as they can up toward their butt to pull the rear wheel up high (see Photos 32.2–32.4). If you time this move right, you can get over much larger objects. Perhaps you have seen it done at a bicycle high-jump contest; riders jump incredible heights this way. The timing is critical, just as it is with normal high jumping, since only part of the bike is higher than the bar at any given time.

Hopping with Flat Pedals

If you are going to go for the gusto in the purist way, without being clipped in, I will defer to "No Way" Rey again for precise instructions:

1. Start out by trying to hop over a line on the ground, then move to hopping over a thin stick and progress from there.
2. Keep your cranks horizontal (see Photo 32.1).
3. Angle the toes of your back foot toward the ground and keep your knees bent. This position looks similar to a sprinter crouching in the blocks (which you can see in Photo 32.4).
4. Lean your upper body over the handlebars and keep your weight centered (Photos 32.2–32.4).
5. Roll up to the object at jogging speed and at a perpendicular angle (Photo 32.1).

Approach perpendicular to the object.

Explode up, pulling up on the bar.

Pull back and up with your feet.

Pull up with your feet and push the bar forward.

Land like a cat, like Rey.

Concentrate on the correct footwork for the jump. You actually push your feet down, back, then up in one dynamic motion (Photos 32.1–32.4).

Crouch down on the bike just before reaching the object (Photo 32.1).

Use footwork and the compression of your tires to explode upward (Photo 32.2). You must press the bike down into the ground, compressing the tires and the suspension, and then explosively pull up and jump.

Leaning your upper body over the handlebars with the toes of your back foot angled toward the ground and your knees bent, pull your feet back and up to pull the rear wheel up. Simultaneously pull up and then push forward on the bar (Photos 32.3 and 32.4).

Absorb your landing in your arms and legs. "Land like a cat, not a sack of potatoes," Rey says (see Photo 32.5). As you can see, a low saddle helps with this!

Rey's Bunny-Hopping Tips

The stronger your explosion, the higher the jump. At the jump's highest point, you can try to hold it. Use the rebound of your tires and suspension to your advantage—these will aid the explosive motion.

Find out which is your "chocolate foot"—your favorite foot, which you always keep forward. When bunny hopping (on flat pedals), your chocolate foot is forward, but the other foot (the right foot in these photos) is pointed down and does most of the work.

Rey's Bunny-Hopping Warnings

Ride at medium speed. If you go too slowly, as Hans says, "it takes forever to get over the object. Your airtime should be as short as possible so you retain control of the jump." ⌿

Hans Rey is a world leader in extreme mountain biking. He has traveled the world extensively, riding his GT mountain bikes over and through areas previously considered unrideable. See what he is up to and learn more tricks at his Web site, www.hansrey.com.

BLOCK 33
Planks and High, Skinny Bridges

You've likely seen videos of guys in British Columbia riding over interconnected skinny bridges, ramps, and planks high in the trees above the dark, wet forest floor. It may look nutty and perhaps, at least at first blush, like something you would never consider doing. But the allure of these stunts is strong, not only because the danger and "gee-whiz" factor is high, but also because you know you could follow that same succession of moves if those bridges were just painted on the ground and you'd fall from nothing higher than your bike.

That is the point; these stunts require training your mind as much as your riding abilities. Whether they are easy or sketchy is as much a function of how you construct your mental attitude as of how the bridges are constructed.

Start Low

The key to riding these stunts and impressing your friends is learning them in low-risk situations. Start by riding on small obstacles, like planks you set up around your house, so you can practice close to the ground for a month or so. As you gain confidence, gradually raise the planks. You can put boards across cinder blocks and build a little bridge with a hook onto a ramp landing. You can also practice riding along the edge of curbs. Get good at riding six inches or so off ground without falling off before you try riding on stuff up in the air!

Focus on the end of the plank and practice on lower planks first.

Rules of Thumb

Former world downhill champion Greg "Hairball" Herbold (also known as HB) is a master at riding on things at which onlookers just shake their heads in disbelief, amazement, and most of all, respect. HB says, "First, make sure you are lined up straight and have your balance before you go up on the stunt." If you are trying to get your balance as you get up on a skinny bridge, it is too late. Riding straight down the white line on the road is no problem, but try starting from a stop on the white line without snaking around on either side of it before you get going. It's a lot harder.

HB's second rule of thumb is, "Make sure you are not in too low a gear when you go up on the stunt, so if you need balance, you can push against your leg. Mountain bike riders think they can just spin up it, but really they need to torque it." Being undergeared is a common error on technical climbs as well as on stunts. If your foot just drops away when you push on it, you cannot use it for balance.

The third item of HB's stunt wisdom is, "Visualize your destination. Fixate on the end of the obstacle, not on the middle of it (see Photo 33.1). This is especially tough as you do longer ones, and you may need to focus on a spot out in the middle first and then to the end as you move along." Following your eyes will keep you going straight.

The last piece of HB's advice: "Don't hold your breath. You can ride in a straight line for 15 feet, but because you're up in the air, it's easy to panic. Relax."

Training Your Mind for Stunts

Former bicycle trials world champion Hans "No Way" Rey says that whenever you are doing tricks on your bike, "your mind is the most important part." This becomes particularly pertinent when you are scared and trying to avoid falling, since, as Rey reminds us, "You have to be active on the bike." Just as when you are riding slowly over obstacles on the ground, you must shift your weight forward and backward, or stick out a knee or a foot to gain lateral balance when you are up on something high. Rey recommends to also train your mind—while riding a curb or other safe obstacles, "Imagine in your head that you are up 10 feet in the air—try to put pressure and nervousness on yourself. That way, you learn to ride under pressure and stress and get familiar with the feeling."

Rey continues, "You have to get really familiar with the techniques and with the bike, and hammer it into your brain. It becomes second nature how you are going to lift your wheel over an obstacle, for instance. You have to execute the movements in the proper order. They all happen one after another and go one into the other, but the timing has to be right.

Stunts are a challenge for your mind.

Later, they come naturally. To learn those things, you have to go out and get dirty."

"Some people say, 'This is not my cup of tea.' That is just an excuse. Everything can be learned," Rey asserts. "To do any technical riding, you use muscles and joints that you don't use very much. The movements are very strange. When you break your arm, you can't write with your left hand at first. You can write after six weeks, and after 10 weeks, you don't even think about it. It's like that with cycling movements."

You must start where you are, accept your current skills, and work up from there. Rey states that "even beginner riders set their goals too high too quickly. You've got to get the basics first. It could be doing a track stand. Or riding superslowly without falling over, or doing a figure eight, making the circles tighter and tighter."

Greg Herbold spends his life traveling the world riding on trails with friends, beating up the SRAM, RockShox, Scott, Giro, Continental, Ritchey, and Oakley equipment he helps design.

Hans Rey also travels all over the world, riding his GT mountain bikes over and through areas previously considered unrideable. See what he is up to and learn more tricks at his Web site, www.hansrey.com.

BLOCK 34

Mastering Drop-offs

Most of us cannot imagine getting up high in the air on a mountain bike, but all of us are impressed when we see it. Being able to leap off drop-offs successfully and to tell the difference between the two basic types of drop-offs are very useful skills when riding technical trails. While it might look like you're tempting fate, doing "stunt" drop-offs can actually sometimes save your butt! And these are skills that you can safely learn close the ground, just playing around at your house.

The first thing you must know before hucking yourself off a drop-off is which foot is your "chocolate foot," as Hans "No Way" Rey calls it. Your chocolate foot is your favorite foot, the one you always keep forward when standing up on the pedals. You need to know where that foot is as you approach the lip of the drop-off, or you could be cruisin' for a bruisin'.

The two different kinds of drop-offs are "ladder drops" and "wheelie drops." A ladder drop is level on top or only slightly tilted up or down and has a downward-sloping ramp landing. You approach it with some speed and ride off the end. A wheelie drop refers to the technique you use for a drop with a flat landing. However, if you have very little speed, you can use the wheelie drop technique on a ladder drop.

34.1

GALEN NATHANSON

2003 World Cup overall downhill champion Natahn Rennie executes a ladder jump so that both of his wheels hit the landing simultaneously.

Ladder Drops

1990 world downhill champion Greg "Hairball" Herbold spends a lot of time in the air—on bicycles and motorcycles. He says, "The key to a ladder jump is to have enough speed and lift off the end. Unweight the bike right before you go off and lift the front a bit. In the air, lean forward to let the front end drop, so you land on the ramp with both wheels at the same time" (see Photo 34.1).

Lifting the bars as you go off the lip is a must, because if you just ride off the end and let your front wheel drop, you "endo" when you land. On the other hand, you don't want to pull really hard when you go off the edge and keep your front wheel high in the air either. If you do, your back wheel hits first, and your front wheel slams down right afterward. You can imagine the effect. Your body rotates forward very fast, and all your momentum continues forward downhill at a high rate of speed. Then you endo over the bar. Ouch.

Wheelie Drops

For ledges or cliffs or any other drop-offs that don't have a transition (that is, they have a flat landing), landing with both wheels at the same time is a bad idea. Also, if you are approaching a ladder drop very slowly, the ladder drop technique is harder to do and not necessarily ideal. In these situations, you want to essentially do a wheelie off the edge.

Herbold advises, "Don't use too low a gear. Have a gear that's harder than the speed you're going. Approach slowly, standing on the pedals with the cranks level (of course, your chocolate foot will naturally be forward). As you get closer, rotate the cranks backward a quarter turn, and have your chocolate foot high. The last bike length from the edge, accelerate with one pedal stroke. Push down on your chocolate foot as you are pulling up on the bar and extending your body straight up to absorb the landing. You will land with your back wheel first, then on the front wheel. Use the bike's suspension and your body to absorb the landing."

Former world downhill champion Mike King does a wheelie drop.

This is a great skill that anyone can use on any size of drop. You may have seen a trials rider do it off of a picnic table, for example. Wheelie drops are easy to practice on low-standing objects. You can do them off of curbs, or off of a ramp you make with a board and some cinder blocks.

Check out the Drop-off

"I come to a stop sometimes before a drop-off to make sure I'm in the right spot," says Herbold. "These things can be hairy and you could die if you go off it wrong." "Hairball" has lived a long life doing hairy things by taking appropriate precautions.

Before you do a big drop-off, Herbold advises that you get off your bike and inspect the stunt site. Walk around on the top of it, and jump up and down on it. Make sure it's stable, and that there are no nails sticking out of it. Look down at where you will be landing. Walk around on the landing, too. See if the dirt is hard or soft, and if there is anything else you need to anticipate.

Equipment

The kind of drop-offs you can ride depends a lot on the bike you have. If you have no suspension, or if your seat's high and your bars are low, you want to stay pretty close to the ground.

When doing ladder drops, wheelie drops, and other stunts, it's a good idea to have a thrasher bike you can bang up a bit. It should have bigger tires, a higher stem and bar, and a seat you can push way down—even a hardtail will work. You don't have to spend much money on the thrasher. The drivetrain can be cheaper, because you won't be going far on it. The bike should have strong wheels and good brakes, though!

Inspect your equipment often. Check the frame welds, fork, pedals, cranks, and bars for bends or cracks. Your confidence is partly based on the reliability of your equipment.

Former world downhill champion Greg Herbold spends his life traveling the world riding on trails with friends, beating up the SRAM, RockShox, Scott, Giro, Continental, Ritchey, and Oakley equipment that he helps design.

PART 5

Road Bike Maintenance and Tuning

BLOCK 35

Small Chainrings: Road Triples and Compact-Drive Doubles

If your road bike is equipped with a double chainring, you may find the gearing insufficient for your region's topography, your riding preferences, or your current strength and fitness. If that is the case, you have three options for modifying your bike: Install larger rear cogs, usually with a longer rear derailleur and chain (bottom, in Photo 35.1), install a triple crankset (and a longer rear derailleur and chain, Photo 35.2) so you have a granny gear (small inner chainring), or install a compact-drive double crankset that has smaller chainrings than your standard double crank (top, in Photo 35.1). A triple crankset can offer you the widest gear range, while a compact-drive double crankset will add the least amount of weight to your bike while still giving you a wide range.

35.1

Top: FSA compact-drive double road right crankarm, which has a 110mm bolt circle diameter (BCD), with 50–34 chainrings, along with a short-cage Campagnolo rear derailleur and 12–25 10-speed cogset; *Bottom:* Campagnolo standard double road right crankarm, which has a 135mm BCD, with 53–39 chainrings, along with a medium-cage Campagnolo rear derailleur and 13–29 10-speed cogset.

Benefits of Lower Gears

Obviously, you can ride up hills more comfortably with lower gears, since they reduce the load on each pedal stroke. In July 2003, much of the cycling world watched transfixed as Tyler Hamilton persevered for three weeks with a broken collarbone to finish fourth overall in the Tour de France. He even won the final mountain stage on a long, solo breakaway. Hamilton had an unusual team sponsorship that allowed him to ride with an FSA compact-drive crankset (top, in Photo 35.1) that gave him lower gears and reduced the strain on his collarbone in the mountains. And on stages with several mountains, after the domestiques (support riders) on Hamilton's Team CSC did hard pulls and

35.2

COURTESY OF CAMPAGNOLO

Campagnolo Record road triple drivetrain, showing both medium- and long-cage rear derailleur options

35.3

Campagnolo's short-, medium-, and long-cage Record rear derailleur options

hauled water and food for him, and ultimately were dropped from the lead groups, they could make it to the finish over the final mountain passes with less strain thanks to their lower gearing. They could recover faster to haul Hamilton's water the next day!

With a compact-drive double like Hamilton's, you can have a very light bike with a close-ratio cogset for lots of gearing options, but you will have a lower range when you hit a steep hill and can avoid going into oxygen debt. For many riders with 700C wheels, this will be a no-brainer, but compact-drive gearing is too low to give a reasonably high gear for a bike with 650C (26-inch) or smaller road wheels.

Another option, and the one requiring the least hassle and expense, is to replace your rear cogset with one that has a wider range. Unless you are making only a small change in cog size, you will need a longer rear derailleur and chain to handle it. A great option is Campagnolo's 10-speed 13–29 (13 teeth on the smallest cog, 29 teeth on the largest cog) cogset and medium-cage racing rear derailleur (bottom, in Photo 35.1). Or, if you want to have even bigger cogs or do not have a Campagnolo drivetrain, use a mountain bike cogset with a triple rear derailleur. For example, if you have a Shimano 9-speed drivetrain, you can replace your cogset with an 11–34 or 12–34 9-speed one, and replace your rear derailleur with a Shimano road or mountain triple rear derailleur. If you want even lower gears yet but want to avoid a triple crankset, you could combine a triple rear derailleur and mountain bike cogs with a compact-drive double crank.

Finally, a triple road crank generally comes with a 30-tooth inner chainring (although you could install a small chainring with as few as 24 teeth), with outer chainrings of roughly the same size as a standard road double. A mountain bike triple crank has shorter spider arms that can hold even smaller chainrings, with as few as 20 teeth. When coupled with cogs ranging anywhere from 11 to 34 teeth, you can have as much range as you could possibly ever want on a road bike!

A Little History

Small road double chainrings are not new; doubles with similar gearing to modern compact-drive doubles existed in the 1960s. However, credit for reincarnating this idea on modern superlight bicycles goes to Fausto Pinarello, a bicycle company owner who continues to ride big miles. Like the rest of us trying to coax speed out of a body not as young and fit as it once was, Pinarello wanted lower gearing for steep climbs, like those in the Dolomites near his home in Treviso, Italy. He wanted neither the weight, the increased complexity, nor the stigma of riding a triple, and "50–34 chainrings give me all the gearing I need," he says (50–34 denotes 50 teeth on the large chainring, and 34 teeth on the small chainring).

FSA and Pinarello road double cranksets were the first to accept chainrings smaller than standard doubles that also fit on modern, splined bottom-bracket spindles, namely on Shimano Octalink 109.5mm-long bottom brackets as well as on ISIS splined 108mm spindles. Whereas Shimano offers no smaller than 39-tooth inner road-double chainrings, FSA, Campagnolo, Truvativ, and Pinarello compact-drive double cranksets accept 34-tooth inner chainrings.

The Lowdown

The bolt circle diameter (BCD) of current compact-drive double cranks is 110mm; if you have been mountain biking for long, you may recognize this diameter, as early mountain bike triple cranks had 110/74mm bolt circles (74mm BCD for the inner chainring, 110mm BCD for the two outer rings). These "standard" mountain cranks still exist, but, as they fit no smaller than a 24-tooth ring, they have largely been abandoned in favor of the 94/58mm bolt pattern (which takes a 20-tooth inner chainring) and four-arm (as opposed to five-arm) cranks.

In road cranks, the 110mm bolt circle is far shorter than Shimano's 130mm and Campagnolo's standard 135mm BCD. Campagnolo's old bolt circle was 144mm (remember 42-tooth inner chainrings?), and this continues to be the standard for track bikes. When it became clear by the early 1980s that road riders favored Shimano's 39-tooth inner ring, Campagnolo did not simply reproduce Shimano's 130mm bolt circle. Instead, it went with 135mm, which will fit a 39-tooth ring but not a 38-tooth, as a Shimano will (although Shimano doesn't offer it). Fortunately for us, when both companies followed the recent road triple resurgence, they both chose the "standard" 74mm for the diameter of the granny gear bolt circle. With Shimano's 130/74mm and Campagnolo's 135/74mm triple circles, you can go with as few as 24 teeth, but road triples from both companies come with a 30-tooth inner chainring.

Gearing

To best see how these various options will affect you, consult the gear chart in Appendix 1. If you are considering a compact-drive double, you will see that a 50 x 11 gear (meaning 50 teeth on the largest front chainring and 11 teeth on the smallest rear cog) is bigger than a 53 x 12 (or even a 54 x 12!), and a 48 x 11 is between a 52 x 12 and a 53 x 12. If you want a 53 x 11 or larger, forget about the compact-drive double.

On the low end, a compact-drive double's 34 x 23 (meaning 34 teeth on the smallest front chainring and 23 teeth on the largest rear cog) is lower than a 39 x 26, and a 34 x 25 is lower than a 39 x 29! These are low gears, yet the cogs, rear derailleur, and crank are lighter than a standard double with the same range. And this setup is far lighter, as well as shifts faster, than a triple.

On the other hand, a 39 x 29, or especially a 39 x 34, is very low, and you minimize the cost by simply replacing the cogs, chain, and rear derailleur. If you want a double as well as a one-to-one gear ratio (a 26-inch gear), you can get it by using a compact-drive 34-tooth inner double chainring and a 34-tooth rear cog.

If you want lower than this yet, or more intermediate gear options, your only option is a triple (or a 26-inch or smaller rear wheel diameter). 🚲

BLOCK 36
Tubular Tires and Wheels

Tubular tires (also known as "sew-ups") may be expensive and hard to install and repair, but they do offer significant advantages over clincher tires. First off, tubular wheel sets are generally lighter than clincher wheel sets, because tubular rims have a simple box cross section and do not require additional flanges to hold the tire bead as clincher rims do.

A clincher and a tubular tire have similar casings, but a clincher (see Photo 36.1) has a bead folded into each edge of the casing, while a tubular casing is sewed together around the tube (see Photo 36.2). Because the tire has no bead, and because the tube can be very thin since it does not need to be handled and installed separately, a tubular tire can be significantly lighter than a clincher tire and tube. It also does not require the weight of a rim strip (or a heavier clincher rim).

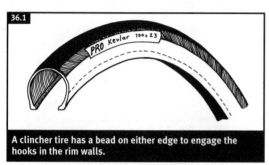

A clincher tire has a bead on either edge to engage the hooks in the rim walls.

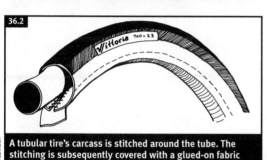

A tubular tire's carcass is stitched around the tube. The stitching is subsequently covered with a glued-on fabric base tape, which the user then glues to the rim.

TODD TELANDER

Clincher tires are generally manufactured by heat-vulcanization under pressure in a mold into a single unit. There are very few hand-made, high-thread-count clinchers (called "open tubulars"), and they are the only tires that can compete with handmade, high-thread-count tubulars in terms of rolling resistance, ride quality, and cornering traction. This is because the finer, more numerous threads in a hand-made tubular or open tubular are not built up and adhered together with so much vulcanized rubber to surrounding threads. These fine threads bend more easily than thicker ones and can move independently to absorb small road imperfections without deflecting the entire tire, thus allowing it to roll faster over the surface. Racing tubulars have all of these advantages, plus they have the additional advantage over clinchers and open tubulars of being round (Photo 36.2), rather than oval, in the cross section when inflated, so that as the tire rolls on edge into a corner, the size of the contact patch does not vary, increasing cornering grip.

Perhaps the main reason to consider tubulars, however, is their inherent safety (provided you glued them on well, that is!). Being sewn together, they can handle higher pressures, and there is no danger of the pressure blowing the tire off the rim. And, in the event of a blowout, they remain glued on the rim. Clincher tires, when flat, can fall into the rim well or pop off of the rim. And if you can't stop quickly enough, you may find yourself trying to ride on the slippery metal rim, rather than on rubber. Tubulars, when punctured, also usually deflate more slowly than clinchers, since the air can only escape through the puncture hole, rather than all around the rim as with a clincher.

If these advantages appeal to you—and you're willing to spend the money and put up with the hassle of gluing them on—switching to high-end tubular wheels and tires will give you a lighter, faster-rolling bike that will corner better than if it had clinchers.

Gluing on Tubular Tires

To get the advantages of tubulars, you will have to learn to glue them on. Your life, or at least your skin, depends on you gluing the tires properly to the rims. Believe me, you do not want your tire to roll off the rim! But follow the steps below and your tire will stay on there. Pay particular attention to Step 2, since all the rim cement in the world will not keep your tire on if the cement does not adhere to the tire.

1. Before gluing on a new tubular, first stretch it over the rim (see Photo 36.3). To do this, install the tire without any glue on it using the method described in Step 6.

2. The base tape on most high-end tubulars is made of cotton with a coating of latex over it, to which the rim cement will not bond well. The tire can roll right off of a thick layer of cement on the rim if the base tape has not been properly prepared. I recommend scraping the base tape's latex to produce a good gluing surface. (This step does not apply to most Continental tires, which usually have no latex over the base tape.) Start by pumping the tire (not on the

Stretching a tubular tire onto a rim: Push down with all of your weight on the heels of your hands, while pulling the remainder of the tire away from the rim with your fingers and working it onto the rim as you progress toward the opposite side of the rim.

GALEN NATHANSON

rim) until it turns inside out and the base tape faces outward. Using the serrations of a table knife or the rough side of a metal file, scrape the base tape back and forth until the latex coating balls up into little sticky hunks (see Photo 36.4). Instead of scraping, Vittoria recommends working the glue into the base tape with a toothbrush.

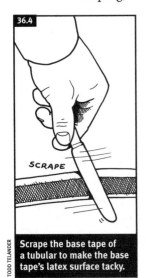

SCRAPE

Scrape the base tape of a tubular to make the base tape's latex surface tacky.

TODD TELANDER

I have also heard of people brushing rubbing alcohol on the base tape to make the surface tacky. I haven't tried that, but I know scraping works. I generally discourage the use of solvents on the base tape for fear the solvent will penetrate the tape and dissolve the glue holding the tape onto the tire. I have seen many a tire roll right off of the base tape, even though the tape was well-adhered to the rim.

3. Prepare the rim for glue. When working with a new rim, clean off any oil with rubbing alcohol and rough up the gluing surface with sandpaper. A power die grinder with a sandpaper roll on it, if you have access to one, works great for roughing up the hard surface of a new rim. When working with a rim that has been glued before, you can just apply a uniform layer of glue, unless there is really thick, lumpy old glue on the rim. In that case, scrape the big lumps off and make the surface as uniform as possible.

4. Put a thin layer of glue on the rim, edge to edge, and on the tire's base tape (the tire should still be inflated so the base tape is outward), edge to edge as well. I recommend squeezing a bead out of the tube and then putting a plastic bag over your finger and smoothing it out uniformly with your finger (or do Vittoria's toothbrush scrubbing). Let it dry for a couple of hours. Repeat.

5. I recommend using red rim glue made specifically for tubulars, of which there are several brands, rather than clear glues, although some of the newer mastics work well, too. Some clear glues stay tacky and do not harden up. With these, I always have the concern that solvent in the glue can break down the glue holding the base tape onto the tire. The disadvantage to the red glues is that they harden up; if you leave them on for years, they get so dried out that they don't hold the tire well and must be reapplied. Pro track riders repeat this gluing procedure at least six times, as the more thin layers you have, the better the bond. Tandem track sprinters need even more layers. More than two layers is not usually necessary for road use. Let the second layer dry overnight, or at least for several hours in the warm sun. When using red glue, the rim and the tire should feel dry to the touch and the glue will not get all over your hands and legs when you stretch the tire. If you are in a hurry and need to use the wheel within a few hours, you can use 3M Fast Tack automotive trim adhesive as a rim cement. Many riders swear by it. In my experience, it dries faster but does not seem to bond as strongly as red rim glue. Also, I think that sometimes its solvent, which evaporates in order for the glue to harden, can cause softening of the base tape glue. After the glue on the rim and tire has dried overnight (or a couple of hours with 3M Fast Tack), smear another thin layer of glue on the rim. Let this set for 15 minutes.

6. Deflate and mount the tire as follows. Stand the wheel up with the valve hole facing up, and put the valve stem through the hole. If you have a deep, aerodynamic rim, you will need to screw a valve extender onto the tire valve, leaving the valve's nut unscrewed so air can get in. (Or, better yet, you have a superlong valve on your tire!) Leaning over the wheel, grab the tire and stretch outward as you lay it into the top of the rim. Keep stretching down on the tire with both hands, using your body weight, as you push the tire down around the rim (Photo 36.3). I like to lean hard enough on the tire that my feet lift repeatedly off the ground. The farther you can stretch the tire at this point, the easier it will be to get the last bit of tire onto the rim. Lifting the rim up to horizontal with the valve side against your belly, roll the last bit of the tire onto the opposite side of the rim. If you can't get the tire to pop over the rim, peel the tire back and start over from the valve stem. You want to avoid the temptation of prying a stubborn tire onto the rim with screwdrivers or other tools, as you will likely tear cords in the base tape and tire casing, leading to a bulge in the tire in this area.

7. By pulling the tire this way and that (see Photo 36.5), align the edge of the base tape with the rim. You want to see the same amount of tape sticking out from the rim all the way around on both sides of the wheel.

Line up the tire so it does not wobble by centering the base tape along the rim.

GALEN NATHANSON

Use a strap miter clamp (or Pony clamp) to tighten a tubular against the rim and improve gluing adhesion.

8. Pump the tire to 100psi and spin the wheel, looking for wobbles in the tire. If you find that the tread snakes back and forth as you spin the wheel, deflate the tire and push it over to straighten it where required. Reinflate and check again, repeating the process until the tire is as straight as you are willing to get it. The final process will depend somewhat on how accurately the tubular was made; you'll find that some brands glue on straighter than others.

9. Pump the tire up to between 120psi and 130psi and leave it overnight to bond firmly. You can get an even better bond by using a woodworker's band (miter) clamp (also-known as a Pony clamp) around the entire inflated tire (see Photo 36.6). The miter clamp is a piece of nylon webbing with a cam-lock buckle on it. Depress the tab on the buckle to let out enough strap to surround the inflated tire and wheel. Pull the end of the strap to tighten the loop around the tire. Use a wrench on the clamp's bolt to tighten the clamp. The strap will put extra pressure on the tire all the way around so that its bottom surface conforms and bonds tightly to the rim.

The next day you can release the miter clamp (using its thumb release tab) and ride or race on this wheel. And you will be fast! 🚲

BLOCK 37

Upgrading Campagnolo Ergopower Levers

One of the coolest things about Campagnolo Ergopower brake/shift levers is that you can disassemble and overhaul them and replace or interchange their internal parts. So, if you have a 9-speed Campy-equipped bike and would prefer 10 speeds (or you have 8 and want 9), you can simply interchange a few parts without replacing the entire, very expensive lever. You still have to get a new cogset and chain for the new number of speeds, but if your cogs and chain are already worn, the additional cost is negligible.

By 8-speed levers, I am referring to 1992–1997 Ergopower levers, right and left. Both the lever body and the rubber hood come to a point (see Figure 37.1 and Photos 37.4–37.8), and

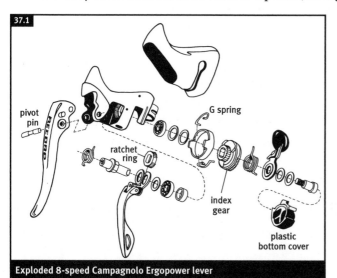

Exploded 8-speed Campagnolo Ergopower lever

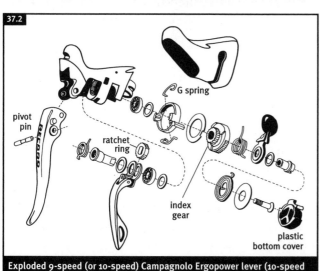

Exploded 9-speed (or 10-speed) Campagnolo Ergopower lever (10-speed varies slightly in bottom bushing and washer)

the lever body allows a brake cable to be installed "old-style," straight into the top of the lever, as well as "aero style," under the handlebar tape. The reference to 9- and 10-speed levers applies to 1998 and later levers (both sides) whose lever bodies (and rubber hoods) are rounded on top (see Figure 37.2) and only allow the brake cable to be routed under the tape to the base of the lever. The exploded dia-grams, Figure 37.1 (8-speed lever) and Figure 37.2 (9- or 10-speed lever) label the parts that are critical to this upgrade. You can find the part identification numbers for your lever's particular year and model on Campagnolo's Web site, www.campagnolo.com, or at a bike shop.

Increasing the Number of Speeds

You can only upgrade an 8-speed lever to a 9-speed, and you only need to buy a 9-speed index gear (see Photo 37.3). Make sure that the gear is intended for an 8-speed lever (in Figure 37.1). If you are upgrading a 9-speed lever to a 10-speed (Figure 37.2), you want to buy both the

37.3

Two index gears, or ratchets: The top one is a 9-speed to replace the bottom one, which is an 8-speed (the 9-speed has the number of speeds printed on it; you can always count the upraised teeth halfway around to find the number of speeds). Note that a 9-speed index gear from a 9-speed lever is slightly different and not interchangeable with an 8-speed lever. The protruding tab (where the "9" is stamped on the 9-speed ratchet) is the cable hook into which the end of the shift cable seats.

index gear and the ratchet ring for a 10-speed. It will work with the old ratchet ring, although not quite as well.

Now for a bit of bad news: You can only upgrade 1999 and later 9-speed levers to 10-speed. 1998 9-speed levers are not upgradeable and are distinguishable in a couple of ways. First, they lack the little oval hole in the inboard side of the lever body for the ErgoBrain computer control button. Another tip-off is if a Record 9-speed Ergopower (shaped like the one in Figure 37.2) brake lever is aluminum, rather than carbon fiber, it is most likely a 1998 model. Upgrading of 1998 9-speed levers can't be done without substituting the entire internals of a 1999 or later lever, which would cost more than a new lever.

When upgrading the gear range of your levers, buy the new index gear ahead of time and, if necessary, the ratchet ring too. Every Ergopower lever has two little G-shaped springs (Figs. 37.1 and 37.2) that click into teeth in the index gear, giving you the indexing steps. These springs can get worn, flattened, or broken, and if they do, shifting performance will drop off or cease to exist. They are the same for every model and year, so go ahead and buy a pair of new G-springs as well; your shifting will improve with new ones.

Here are the steps to upgrade the gear range of your levers.

1. Remove the rubber hood. It's easier to pull it off of the base of the lever, but it will come off over the top as well. On composite lever bodies, pull off the plastic piece that covers the bottom of the shift mechanism. Use pliers if necessary.

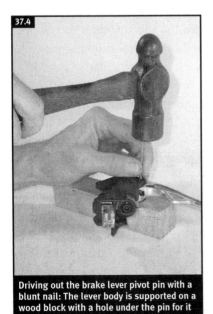

37.4

Driving out the brake lever pivot pin with a blunt nail: The lever body is supported on a wood block with a hole under the pin for it to exit into.

2. Push out the brake lever pivot pin by tapping it out with a blunt nail and a hammer. Support the lever body near the pin so that it does not flex outward as you tap. Holding the lever body flat on a block of wood with a hole drilled in it lined up under the pin does the trick (see Photo 37.4). Pull off the brake lever.

3. Clamp the lever body onto the end of a handlebar held in a vise so that the bar-clamp strap is at the end of the bar and the lower part of the lever body is hanging off the end of the bar; you want to be able to get at the lever's mechanism from the bottom (see Photo 37.5). Hold the bar in the vise so that the lever is upside down. With a 9- or 10-speed lever, shift to the lowest gear position with the finger lever to release tension on the flat coil spring at the bottom of the lever; you can see it

stick out around the large flat washer when you get to the low-gear position. With an 8-speed lever, you do the opposite; shift the thumb lever to the highest-gear position.

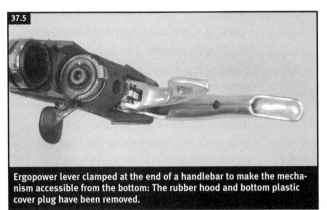

37.5

Ergopower lever clamped at the end of a handlebar to make the mechanism accessible from the bottom: The rubber hood and bottom plastic cover plug have been removed.

4. Hold the top nut with one hex key while you unscrew and remove the bottom bolt with another hex key (see Photo 37.6). On a 9- or 10-speed lever, the top nut takes a 5mm hex key, and the lower bolt takes a 3mm. On an 8-speed lever, the nut and bolt both accept 4mm hex keys (as in Photo 37.6). Watch for washers on the bolt.

*IMPORTANT NOTE: *The bolt on an 8-speed lever is left-hand threaded, so it unscrews in a **clockwise** direction! Also note that 1998 9-speed levers are configured like 8-speed in this way—another tip-off that you might have one that is not upgradeable to 10-speed.*

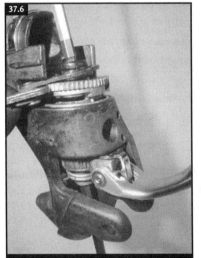

37.6

Unscrewing (or screwing back in) the bottom bolt on an 8-speed lever: The top and bottom bolts on an 8-speed both take 4mm hex keys and are left-hand threaded.

5. If you're working with an 8-speed lever, skip to Step 7. With a 9- or 10-speed lever, remove the bottom washer, pop the compensation spring (a flat coil) out with a thin screwdriver, and take out the thin play-removing washer, if there is one.

6. Hold the (9- or 10-speed) assembly together with your thumb while shifting to the high-gear position with the thumb lever. Hold the thumb lever in place and, with needle-nose pliers, pull out the next part: the bushing in the center of the coil spring.

7. Pop out the thumb lever, the ratchet spring (see Photo 37.7), the index gear, shown in Photo 37.3, and, on a 9- or 10-speed lever, the notched washer. The two G-shaped index springs, the most common replacement item in Ergopower levers, are now visible. One or two washers that sit on top of the cartridge bearing underneath may come out with the ratchet. If not, you can pop the washer(s) out, if installed, after Step 8 and clean, grease, and replace it/them at that time.

37.7

Removing (and installing) the ratchet spring: The index gear's outer teeth are visible below the spring.

8. Pop the G-spring carrier out (see Photo 37.8) and pull the G-springs out of it. Clean and grease all parts.

37.8

The G-spring carrier, with the G-springs still installed (and facing away from the viewer)

9. With an 8-speed lever, unless you want to replace the top ratchet ring, skip to Step 11. To upgrade from a 9- to a 10-speed, pull out the finger-lever assembly as is, with the pins and bearings intact. Flip the lever over so it is clamped upright on the bar. It is hard to get the top spring out; grab it with thin needle-nose pliers and twist it upward with the other end still hooked into the loop atop the finger lever. Pull the finger-lever assembly out. Push the center pivot out. Now slip the ratchet ring out and replace it with a 10-speed one.

10. Orient the ratchet ring with the number (9 or 10) up (i.e., pointed forward when the lever is on the bike). Push the pivot nut and washer into the ratchet ring (line up the flats). Hook the top spring's short hook onto the hook atop the finger lever. Push the assembly back in place, hooking the long spring end into the notch in the lever body with needle-nose pliers. Flip the lever over to get at its underside again.

11. Put the new (or clean and greased) G-springs on the underside of the G-spring carrier (Photo 37.8), and coat them with grease to hold them in place. Push the G-spring carrier back into place in the lever body.

12. On a 9- or 10-speed lever, replace the notched washer on top of the G-spring carrier with the washer's tab facing down. The notch fits around the vertical post on the G-spring carrier. (This washer and the vertical carrier post do not exist in 8-speed levers).

13. Drop the new (greased) index gear (Photo 37.3) down onto the pivot post so that the flats in both parts interlock. Make sure that the cable hook tab on the index gear butts against the outboard side of the lever body. Slip the long end of the (greased) return spring down into the index gear (Photo 37.7), out through its slot, and into the hole in the lever body, dropping the spring down into the index gear with the short end of the spring sticking up.

14. Push the hole in the thumb-lever ring onto the upward-pointing end of the return spring, with the convex side of the ring facing the spring. Push back on the thumb-lever ring to align it over the index gear, so that the spring end sticks up out of the hole like in Photo 37.5.

15. On 9- or 10-speed levers, while holding down the thumb-lever ring, push the central bushing down through the ring. Push down and turn the bushing (on 1999 9-speed and all 10-speed levers use a large screwdriver in the larger set of slots) until the flats on the end of the bushing engage the flats on the end of the top bolt protruding into the index gear. If there were washers on the bushing, make sure you have installed them. On 1999 and later 9-speed and on all 10-speed levers, the bushing is larger in diameter and has flats that engage over the flats on the top bolt, rather than inserting into them. An unfortunate consequence is that the larger bushing is harder to push into place without disengaging the return spring from the thumb lever. Keep at it until you get it. On 8-speed levers, insert the bolt, with any washers it had on it, down through the thumb-lever ring until it engages the nut. While holding the nut with a 4mm hex key inserted into the top of the lever, tighten the bolt with another 4mm hex key (Photo 37.6). Remember that the bolt is reverse-threaded! Now skip to Step 20.

16. Steps 16 through 19 only apply to 9- and 10-speed levers. While holding the bushing in place (it will turn), shift the finger lever all the way to the lowest-gear position.

17. Lay the flat compensation spring on top of the thumb-lever ring. The inner end of the spring hooks into a notch in the end of the bushing, and the outer spring end hooks around the post on the G-spring carrier.

18. Holding the flat spring down, tip the bushing back and forth until you feel the flats in the end of the bushing disengage from the flats on the top bolt (do this with a large screwdriver on 1999 and later 9-speed and on 10-speed levers). Still holding the spring down, turn the bushing about a quarter to a half turn counterclockwise to wind the spring and jiggle the bushing back and forth with the 5mm hex key or large screwdriver until its flats re-engage the top bolt. (Campagnolo suggests an alternative method for Steps 17 and 18, which I find to be more of a hassle but you may prefer it. It goes like this: When laying the flat spring in place, hook the inner spring end into a more advanced bushing slot; the outer end of the spring will be squished up against the back wall of the lever body. While holding the bushing with the 5mm hex key or a large screwdriver, pull the outer spring end to the post, using a hooked awl or small crochet hook.)

19. Holding the flat spring down with your finger, slide the large washer under your finger and on top of the flat spring so it snaps over the end of the bushing. The 1999 and later 9-speed and 10-speed washer has two notches to fit the larger slots in the bushing. Start the 3mm Allen bolt while holding the other end of the pivot shaft with a 5mm hex key. Snug the bolt down as in Photo 37.6.

20. Check the mechanism. If it works smoothly, reinstall the brake lever, the bottom cap, and the rubber hood (engaging all of the hood's nubs into holes, slots, and protrusions in the lever body). It's easier to pull the hood on over the levers from the front than from the base of the lever body.

Congratulations! You are done! Slap that new chain and cogset on your bike, readjust your rear derailleur, and you will have another gear! 🚲

BLOCK 38
Aerodynamic Equipment

If you want to be competitive in individual events on the road, like time trials and draft-prohibited triathlons, you must take steps to reduce your aerodynamic drag by modifying your body positioning and equipment. And if you just want to ride faster on flat or rolling rides, or expend less energy to ride at the same speed, aerodynamic positioning and equipment can make a big difference.

Handlebars

Boone Lennon, a former U.S. Ski Team coach for the downhillers, designed the aero handlebar so a rider could mimic downhill skiing's aerodynamic tuck in cycling. The body position made possible by an aerobar makes a more significant difference than any other piece

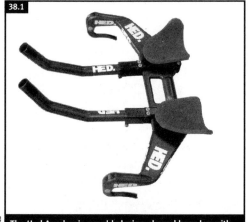

The Hed Aerobar is a molded wing-shaped base bar with integrated brake levers and internal cable routing. The aero extensions and elbow pads are adjustable.

of equipment, since the body accounts for up to 80 percent of the aerodynamic drag of the bike and rider. (Aerodynamic positioning is covered in detail in Blocks 5 and 6.)

The biggest functional improvements in the design of aerobars in the past twenty years are the number of adjustments available for length and elbow placement, and features like wing shape, brake and shifter lever integration, and internal cable runs (see Photo 38.1). Aerodynamic shaping of the bars themselves makes only a minor difference in aerodynamic drag—less than 20 seconds in a one-hour time trial at 50kph—but a top competitor cannot afford to ignore any strategy that shaves a few seconds off of his or her time. And the current possibilities of adjusting a rider's position to idealize aerodynamics and ergonomics can take minutes off 40km time trial times.

According to aerobar maker Morgan Nicol of Oval Concepts, "The biggest change, from when Boone Lennon, Steve Hed, and John Cobb worked with Greg LeMond and Mark Allen in the late 1980s, until now, when they are working with Lance Armstrong, is the realization that the function of the aerobar is really optimizing the drag, cardiovascular, and power (DCP) equation to maximize speed over distance. Boone used to say he would put you in the best aero position and you had to learn to breathe and pedal in that position. Now, aero positioning on the bike is a bit more nuanced."

If you can't breathe or power the pedals in your aerodynamic position, you will not go very fast. You want to minimize the drag and cardiovascular load while maximizing the power output. In an attempt to find the DCP optimum, researchers are adding heart rate monitors and power meters to wind tunnel sessions. However, Cobb says, "[Assistant professors in exercise physiology] Jim Martin [University of Utah] and Andy Coggan

[University of Texas], a couple of other smart guys, and myself have been working for a few years on a way to determine immediate power gains versus aero' changes. It really hasn't proven to work out, once the rider gets on the road. We have been using SRM power meters in the tunnels for six to seven years, combining this with heart rate info and trying to build repeatable baselines. For triathletes, some basic positioning, while taking into account their run speeds, seems to help, but for world-class riders, Boone's theory of learning to ride in the most aerodynamic position might still be the best choice."

Triathletes often move the position of their body on the bike forward, resulting in bikes with steep seat-tube angles, partly to save running muscles during the cycling leg. This is accomplished by moving the saddle and aerobars farther forward.

Road racers don't have to worry about running. They also ride year-round on a road bike with a traditional 72- to 74-degree seat angle. This means the optimum position for a pure cyclist is going to be closer to a standard road bike position than to a forward "triathlete" position, and Cobb's Slam Position described in Block 6 is even farther back than that.

There is still plenty of controversy over aerobar position. A rider may choose one position for longer, straighter, flatter courses where aerodynamics and comfort are a bigger factor, and he or she may choose another for shorter, hillier courses where power is more of a factor. Many question if the optimal position of the extension bar ends should be low to minimize drag, or high to maximize power and cardiovascular capabilities. An aerobar with great adjustability is the tool that will provide you with the best fit.

Wheels

After the aerobar (which reduces drag more with the rider's position than with the aerodynamic qualities of the bar itself), the wheels are the most important piece of aerodynamic equipment. They can make on the order of a half-minute difference over 40km.

A rear disc wheel makes for the fastest bike on a high-speed course (Photos 5.1 and 18.2), but it is not allowed in many triathlons and only in time trials in road racing. Due to instability in crosswinds (and to rules), you cannot use a disc wheel on the front.

On the front, and on the rear when not using a disc, the best choice is an aerodynamic, deep-section composite wheel, which smooths airflow over the deep, wing-shaped rim and

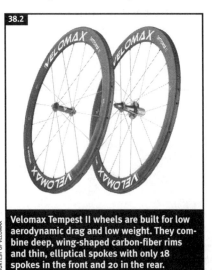

Velomax Tempest II wheels are built for low aerodynamic drag and low weight. They combine deep, wing-shaped carbon-fiber rims and thin, elliptical spokes with only 18 spokes in the front and 20 in the rear.

COURTESY OF VELOMAX

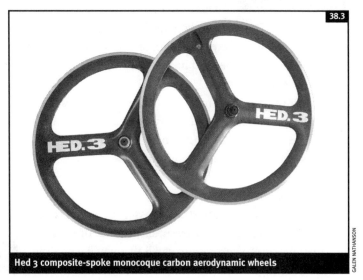

Hed 3 composite-spoke monocoque carbon aerodynamic wheels

GALEN NATHANSON

has few spokes to stir up the air. Similar aerodynamic improvements can be obtained with either wire-spoked (see Photo 38.2) or composite-spoked deep-section wheels (as in Photo 38.3). Aluminum deep-section rims are not generally as effective, because either the rims are not as deep, or they weigh more in order to attain rim depth.

Wheel size does not appear to affect a bike's aerodynamics. Smaller wheels may create a smaller wind shadow, but their higher rotational speed churning up the air and higher rolling resistance on the road balance that effect.

Clothing

Tight-fitting aerodynamic clothing (Photos 5.1 and 18.2) makes a huge improvement over any clothing that flaps in the wind. New fabrics and suit designs, most notably those used in Nike's Swift suit worn by the U.S. Postal Service Team (different from the older suit in Photo 18.2), further reduce aerodynamic drag. The Swift suit's seam placement behind the rider, and the location and shape of fabric panels for optimal aerodynamics or rider cooling, are designed to significantly reduce the drag of a standard Lycra skin-suit. Lycra shoe covers and an aerodynamic helmet also may offer a significant advantage (both are shown in Photo 18.2).

38.4

The Oval Concepts R900 Jetstream road fork has tapered, curved blades for road comfort. It draws air through the thin gap in each fork leg to form a smooth, laminar airflow over the front wheel.

The Fork

After the rider's arms and the front wheel, the first thing the wind hits is the bike's fork. An aerodynamic fork can make a measurable speed improvement and is a must for someone who wants to be competitive. There are a number of forks with wing-shaped blades available; riders should note that the International Cycling Union (UCI) limits the width-to-depth ratio permitted in racing. True Temper offers an aero fork with a lower-drag surface coating, and Oval Concepts offers two fork models that have split fork blades designed to suck air through the gap and create streamlined airflow over the front wheel (see Photo 38.4).

The Frame

The frame is the biggest bike part and the next biggest opportunity for aerodynamic improvement. The first thing the wind hits on the frame is the head tube, so reducing its length or smoothing its shape is a bonus. After that, any aerodynamic shaping of the tubes and hiding of components like brakes can provide an advantage (Photos 5.1 and 18.2).

Eliminating frame tubes, like seat tubes and seatstays, offers obvious advantages, but the UCI outlaws these designs for bike racing. Triathletes, however, can use frames without these parts.

Other Components

An aerodynamic seatpost and an aerodynamic water bottle (or no bottle) can measurably reduce drag. After that, most bike parts are so small that you'll gain little by spending money on aerodynamic versions. 🚲

38.5

A Team Lampre full-carbon time trial bike with an aerodynamic frame made by Wilier Triesting.

PART 6

Road and Mountain Bike Maintenance and Tuning

BLOCK 39
Using Shims to Fix What Ails Your Bike

A can of beer often makes problems seem less important, but sometimes it can actually fix bike problems! Aluminum beverage cans are 0.1mm thick and easy to cut with a knife or a pair of scissors, so they're extremely useful for making minor spacing adjustments on a bike. Here are a few examples of the types of spacing problems you might be experiencing, and how to make beer-can adjustments to fix them.

Slipping Seatpost

A seatpost that gradually slips downward as you ride can be caused by an ovalized seat tube, a sizing difference between the seatpost and seat tube, or a tolerance buildup among a number of parts. The latter problem is particularly rampant with suspension seatposts positioned in oversized seat tubes. The suspension post is normally a standard size, like 27.2 or 27.0mm outside diameter (OD). If the seat tube's inside diameter (ID) is, say, 31.6mm, the seatpost requires a cylindrical sleeve to size its OD up to the ID of the seat tube, and between the seat tube, the post, and the shim, there is more room for slop and slippage.

What can you do to improve the fit between the various parts and stop the seatpost from slipping down?

A common fix is to smear grease mixed with sand or valve-grinding compound on the seatpost. This often does not work and it mars the finish of the post. And if you have a car-bon seatpost you want to avoid both grease and grit (although lightly sanding the slick finish of a carbon post can help). A more elegant and effective solution is to cut a small shim out of a beer can and put it in between the seatpost and seat tube (or seat-tube sleeve).

Cut out a 1 x 3–inch piece of beer can with a pair of scissors, rounding the corners as shown in Photo 39.1. Hold the shim lengthwise down along the inner wall of the seat tube with about half of its length sticking out of the top. Do not put the shim against the slot

Shims cut from beer cans: Clockwise from upper left, they are for shimming seatposts, disc-brake rotors, handlebar clamps or seatpost clamps, other seatposts, and cogs.

in the seat tube, because it will get torn up when you tighten the binder bolt; place it against the opposite wall from the slot. Stick in the (greased) seatpost. If the post won't go in, make the shim narrower. If it fits sloppily, try cutting a wider strip of beer can. Insert the post, assuring that the shim stays in place.

What if you're doing a late-night bike assembly for a big ride the next morning, and you find that the seatpost you were going to use is one size (0.2mm) too small? Help is once again available in the form of a beer! Since a beer can is 0.1mm thick, one full wrap of a long, wide beer-can shim adds the 0.2mm you need. Make the shim just long enough that the ends don't quite meet when wrapped around the post.

Most suspension posts come in only one or two diameters. If you have a 27.2mm suspension post, and your bike takes, for instance, a 30.2mm seatpost, then you need to purchase a 1.5mm-thick shim sleeve that has a 30.2mm OD and a 27.2mm ID. It looks like a short aluminum tube with a lip around one end and longitudinal slit down one side. You may find, though, that there is enough slop in the fit between the seat tube and the sleeve, and/or between the sleeve and the seatpost, that the post slowly inches down as you ride. A small beer-can shim between the sleeve and the post can prevent it from sliding down.

Also, if your saddle is slipping back in the seatpost clamp, a beer-can shim may help. Sometimes the head of the seatpost with a two-bolt clamp won't clamp the saddle rails well if the top piece has become bent. On some seatposts, the top of the clamp wraps over a pair of clamshell-type clamping pieces that resemble a tube sliced lengthwise and notched for the seat rails. If the top of the clamp is stretched or bent, it cannot hold these clamshell pieces tightly, and the saddle can slip straight back or rotate nose-up or nose-down. A beer-can shim or two around the clamshell pieces can fix that. Sometimes it even takes wrapping some narrow beer-can shims around the saddle rails themselves where they are clamped in the post.

Dragging Disc-Brake Rotors

If you have a number of wheels you like to use on your disc-brake bike(s), you want to be able to interchange wheels without any of your rotors dragging on the brake pads. Since the spacing between the pad and rotor in a disc brake is on the order of between 0.01 and 0.015 inches (0.25 and 0.4 mm), a minor rotor offset will make it drag loudly. This problem is exacerbated by any back-and-forth wobble of the rotor (see Block 49 for how to true bent rotors).

How can you put any pair of wheels on your bike without the rotors rubbing on the pads? Crack open a can of beer, of course! Since your rotor shims must be quite precise, use a template to cut them out accurately with a knife. I use a bolt-on disc hub adapter as a template, and I screw it down to a block of wood through one or two layers of aluminum cut from a can. Then I cut around the inner and outer edges of the adapter. I mark the bolt-hole locations with a scribe and pop them out with a hole punch. You can see how nicely it turns out—look at the center shim in Photo 39.1.

These rotor shims work great! Once you go to the initial trouble of making them, you save yourself lots of time in the long run. When you switch wheels, you don't have to adjust the caliper position whatsoever. Incidentally, once I got my rotors all in the same spot this way, I found that I could switch wheels mounted with 160mm Hayes, Formula, Shimano, or Avid rotors back and forth between bikes that have calipers of any of these makes, and all of them stop great and run without any rotor drag!

Noisy Disc Brakes

If you are a stickler for quiet brakes, you can also cut out shim washers for spacing the brake caliper from International Standard brake mounts on the frame or fork. The thinnest spacers you will find packed with a disc brake are 0.2mm, but if inserting one moves the brake in too far and removing it moves it out too far, a beer-can washer between each flange and mount tab will move in the caliper half as much. Punch the hole in the shim with a hole punch.

Skipping Cogset

If you have a cogset with which your rear derailleur works well on some of the cogs but doesn't shift perfectly on every one, a little help from a beer can could do the trick. The spacing between 9-speed and 10-speed cogs is so close that the derailleur has to move very precisely under each cog or the chain will try to climb to the next one. A thin spacer (bottom, in Photo 39.1), judiciously placed between a pair of cogs can completely fix the skipping, automatic shifting, and noise that any amount of cable-tension adjustment cannot eliminate.

I have, for instance, an early SRAM 9-speed 11–34-tooth cogset that I measure to be 0.3mm narrower overall than a Shimano cogset of the same ratio. Similarly, I have a 0.2mm under-width Shimano Dura-Ace cogset from the first round of 9-speed production that frustrates proper derailleur adjustment over the full range. If I get the cable tension right on the small cogs with either of these cogsets, when the chain is on the second- or third-largest cog it will try to hop up to the next larger cog. This is a bummer when you are trying to get up a hill.

The fix is to cut out spacers from an aluminum can and place them between some of the cogs in the center of the cogset. With a knife, cut into the aluminum sheet along the inside profile of a cog, and cut the outer circumference 3mm to 4mm bigger. On that finicky Dura-Ace cogset, two beer-can spacers between the 15- and 16-tooth cogs completely fix the problem. On the problematic SRAM cogset, I put in three beer-can spacers between the 14- and 16-tooth cogs; that makes the stack of the cogset as thick as that of a Shimano, and the chain no longer hops around when I am pedaling hard up steep hills.

Slipping Handlebars

If your handlebars slip in the stem clamp, it can be very dangerous, particularly on a road or cyclo-cross bike. When you slam on your brakes, the bar can twist downward, greatly compromising your ability to control the bike. A beer-can shim between the bar and the stem clamp will prevent the bar from twisting.

It is not a great idea to mess around too much with worn stems and bars, though, especially superlight ones. If either the bar or the stem has become so misshapen that the clamp no longer works well, use the shims only as a temporary fix, and get another stem and bar right away.

A can of beer can't solve big problems, but cracking one open can make many small bike problems go away! ᘔ

Frame Geometry and Bike Stability

I find that when trying to master bike handling, it really helps to understand how frame geometry affects bike stability. As I am a framebuilder with a background in physics, this is a favorite subject of mine, but I think you will be able to understand it, take advantage of it when riding, and impress your friends with some demonstrations.

Unlike many other vehicles with stability challenges, a bicycle is not complex. Armed with this brief discussion of the subject, you should be able to corner and descend with more control, as well as choose equipment better and see through the hyperbole of misleading advertising claims. It can also assist you in understanding some of the bike problems encountered by odd-sized riders, particularly short ones.

Defining Terms

In order that we share a common language to describe and understand frame geometry and bike stability, we must define a few terms. You may find it helpful to refer to the Glossary for definition of bike-part terms. Referring to Figure 40.1, note that fork rake, R, is the perpendicular distance (offset) of the center of the front hub from the steering axis. Fork trail, T, is the horizontal distance between the center of the tire contact patch (with the ground) and the intersection of the steering axis with the ground. Head angle, Ø, is the acute angle between the steering axis and the horizontal. The wheel radius is r.

I will begin simply by telling you that the way to increase the stability of a bicycle is to increase T (fork trail). "Wait a second," you say, "there must be more to it than that! What

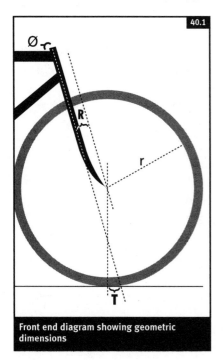

40.1

Front end diagram showing geometric dimensions

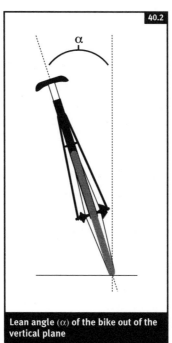

40.2

Lean angle (α) of the bike out of the vertical plane

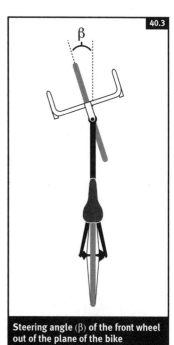

40.3

Steering angle (β) of the front wheel out of the plane of the bike about tire width, rider skill, and gyroscopic effect?" While all three of these variables do affect handling, they cannot account for all of the handling characteristics observed when riding a bike, which the fork trail theory can. These other three criteria can work in conjunction with fork trail to increase stability, but they are not indispensable like fork trail is.

Tire Width

If we think that a bike is stable merely because it is a skinny steamroller, we might be in for a shock. I would say that if you made the tires as wide and flat as those on a steamroller, clearly it would be very stable. But in the real world, if you use a wide mountain bike tire with a very square tread profile, you will find that it will still easily tip over onto those knobs' sharp corners, and some other force is required to stabilize the bike. Conversely, you can certainly reduce tire grip by using extremely skinny tires, but you cannot destroy the bicycle's stability that way.

Rider Skill

In their 1948 book, *Advanced Dynamics*, Stephen Timoshenko and D.H. Young theorize that a bike is balanced strictly by the rider, who constantly steers in the direction the bike is falling by a turning radius small enough to generate enough centrifugal force to counteract the fall. Certainly this can explain some of the story, such as how greater speed increases the bicycle's stability and requires less steering correction, since at higher speeds it takes smaller steering corrections to generate enough centrifugal force. It does not, however, explain how a bicycle can stay upright without a rider. We know that a stopped bicycle will fall right over; many of us have marks on our walls and piano to prove it. We also know that if we give a bike a push, it will roll for a while before crashing, and rolling it down a smooth hill will increase the distance it rolls even farther. We also have the sensation that our bicycle is incredibly stable when we're riding fast—a far cry from the feeling we experience when we steer out of a fall.

Gyroscopic Wheels

The gyroscopic effect of the spinning wheels certainly adds to a bike's stability. Hold a wheel in your hand by the axle ends. Tip it from side to side when it is not spinning. Easy, eh? Now try tipping the wheel while it is spinning fast. It is a lot harder to do.

The gyroscopic effect also contributes to what we observe when countersteering (see Block 24). If you push forward on the left end of a spinning wheel's axle, the wheel will tip to the left, as the "right hand rule" of rotational mechanics predicts. Try it!

David E.H. Jones, Ph.D., in his efforts to produce an unrideable bicycle (*Physics Today*, April 1970), mounted on a bicycle a second front wheel parallel to the normal one, but the second wheel did not touch the ground. He could spin it the opposite direction of the normal wheel to cancel the gyroscopic force, or spin it in the same direction to double it. He found that he was able to ride the bike hands-free either way. Rolling along without a rider, the bike remained upright much longer after being pushed with both wheels spinning in the same direction than it did when they were spinning in opposite directions, as one would predict.

Fork Trail

Jones was never able to build a completely unrideable bicycle, which, he said, "by canceling the forces of stability would baffle the most experienced rider." He did, however, produce some bikes that crashed immediately without a rider as well as some that went on and on alone before finally tipping over. We can learn a lot from his experiments.

If you look at the casters of a shopping cart, you will notice that they are held by little forks that have a rake (offset of the hub from the steering axis). The forks flip around backward when you push the cart, and the wheels "trail" the cart. This would seem to be the opposite situation of what you see in a bicycle, where the fork points forward and stays that way when you push the bike forward. Closer inspection reveals something else, though.

The steering-axis angle of the shopping cart casters is vertical (90 degrees), and for the tire contact patch to be behind (to "trail") the steering-axis intersection with the floor, the fork must turn around backward. On a bike, though, you can see from Figure 40.1 that the wheel contact patch trails the steering-axis/ground intercept with the fork pointed forward by virtue of a steering angle quite a bit less than 90 degrees—generally less than 75 degrees.

Thus, the front wheel indeed trails the bicycle, as does the rear wheel. Have any doubts? Try wheeling a bicycle backward by pulling back on the seat. It doesn't work; the front wheel immediately flops to a wide angle. That's because the front wheel is not trailing the bike when the bike is going backward, even though it is behind the bike!

When Jones increased fork trail by turning the fork around backward (by looking at Figure 40.1, notice how a negative fork rake would increase fork trail), the bike became much more stable. Piling weights on the bike's saddle and giving it a push demonstrated this. Even after the bike had slowed down, it wove back and forth, always seeking a position of stability, until it finally ran out of speed and tipped over.

The least-rideable bike that Jones constructed had an enormous amount of fork rake, and it was only a success as "unrideable" in the weighted, riderless configuration, since a rider was always able to counteract its instability and keep it upright. But clearly, the negative fork trail produced by increasing the rake so dramatically (again, refer to Figure 40.1 and envision R as very long to see how trail became negative) eliminated the bicycle's self-righting capabilities with only weights aboard. It crashed immediately when pushed.

Try It Yourself

Any time you have a head angle less than 90 degrees and a finite fork rake, you create an unstable situation where the front wheel and handlebar turn out of the plane of the bike whenever it is leans (Figures 40.2 and 40.3). The handlebar and wheel turn because this allows the frame's height to fall, and the bicycle and rider weight always seek a minimum potential-energy position (see F. R. Whitt and D. G. Wilson's *Bicycling Science*). Notice that the wheel turns into the lean, to get the wheel to roll back under the center of gravity of the bike and rider.

Using simple trigonometry on Figure 40.1, you can see that:

R = r cosØ – T sinØ   or,   T = (r cosØ – R)/sinØ

This second relationship clearly shows what you can see from Figure 40.1, namely that you can increase the trail (and hence the bicycle's stability) by increasing the wheel radius, decreasing the rake, and/or decreasing the head angle.

Using this relationship for the purposes of demonstration, you can increase trail and stability simply by decreasing head angle. You can simulate this with your own bike by stacking cinder blocks and phone books up under the front wheel (see Photo 40.4). Now if you lean the bike, you will see that the front wheel flops over into the turn to a much sharper angle than before, thus enabling the wheel contact patch to get back under the rider's center of gravity more quickly.

Conversely, you can decrease trail and stability simply by increasing head angle. This time, stack cinder blocks and phone books under the rear wheel (see Photo 40.5). Raise the rear of the bike a little at a time, constantly leaning the bike, and see what happens. You will know when your head angle is steep enough (relative to the ground) to make the fork trail negative, because when you lean the bike, the wheel will turn the opposite direction (as in Photo 40.5)—away from the lean! That means whenever you lean over on a bike with negative trail, the front wheel will turn the other way to try to get farther out from under your center of gravity—so you will crash sooner!

40.4

Simulating a very shallow head angle and consequent large fork trail, which imparts great stability: The wheel flops out of the plane of the bike at low lean angles to rapidly get back under the rider's weight and stabilize the rider.

GALEN NATHANSON

Analyzing Bikes for Handling

Today's bike market demands that all road bikes come with carbon forks and all mountain bikes come with suspension forks that all have about the same amount of rake. This does not allow the framebuilder to change the head angle and fork rake together. However, the above equation clearly shows that the framebuilder must change both together in order to achieve sufficient fork trail with a small bike for a short rider to get stability and agility without toe overlap of the front wheel (that is, the rider's foot hitting the front tire in a tight turn). Thus, the small rider will generally have to suffer with one of the following:

1. **long top tube**—in order to avoid toe overlap while using a stock fork and a standard head angle.
2. **super stable bike**—due to a very shallow head angle coupled with short fork rake. This is done to avoid toe overlap with a stock fork while offering the rider a short top tube. The bike becomes so stable that it is hard to get it to turn, and the front wheel snakes out ahead of the rider when standing out of the saddle.
3. **toe overlap**—in order to offer a short top tube, stock fork, and standard head angle.

Any of these situations can be uncomfortable or dangerous. To fit small riders with a stable bike and no toe overlap, either use a custom fork with more rake, or smaller wheels and geometry adjusted to offer large enough fork trail for stability.

It is also clear, once you understand fork trail, why it is so hard for little kids to learn how to ride without training wheels. It should be obvious by now that the stability would be very low (that is, the fork trail—the lever that rights the bike—is very small) of a bike with little wheels and a very curved fork (small wheel r, large R). I am mostly talking about

40.5

Simulating a very steep head angle to the point of creating negative fork trail and consequent very low stability: When the bike is leaned, the front wheel turns away from the direction of lean to get farther out from under the rider and cause him or her to crash sooner.

GALEN NATHANSON

little pink bikes made for girls; the straight forks with low offset on mini-BMX bikes are a big improvement.

On the other hand, it is interesting to see that many of these concepts of trail were also well understood at some level for most of last century. For instance, bikes used on the track in derny (motorcycle)-paced events have a small front wheel (to get closer to the motorcycle) coupled with a bent-back fork (negative rake) to increase trail and stability. This is not done on road bikes, because they become too stable to be steered—you want to push the bike toward instability for it to be maneuverable. But on a track at 60mph behind a motorcycle, the banking does the cornering for you and you want the stability! 🚲

BLOCK 41
Changing a Flat Tire Quickly

For many people, one of the biggest deterrents to getting on their bike and riding, particularly alone, is the fear of getting a flat tire. But I know that a cyclist is reassured after changing a flat tire once, particularly with this simple method.

The best way to learn is to watch someone do it in front of you (you'll be amazed at how easy it looks) and then try it yourself. Reading and looking at the pictures is not quite as effective. But if you pick up a wheel and do it now, that fear of a flat, if you have it, will be gone forever.

Fixing a Flat on the Roadside

When you head out on a ride, it is critical to bring the materials and tools you need, namely a good inner tube and either a pump or a cartridge inflater with at least one new CO_2 cartridge. Even if you have already mastered this hands-only tire change method with the particular tires and rims you are riding, bring two or three plastic tire levers as well.

These instructions apply equally to road and mountain bike tires. Bigger bike tires are usually easier to change than skinny ones, but I almost never encounter a tire that I can't change quickly, completely by hand, without tire levers. It is not hand strength that is key; it is technique!

1. Remove the wheel by opening the quick-release on the brake and on the hub. (If the wheel is on a Cannondale Lefty one-legged fork, you need not even remove the wheel!)

2. If your tire is not already completely flat, deflate it. To deflate a tire that has a Schrader valve (which looks like a car tire valve), push down on the valve pin with something like a pen cap or valve cap (see Figure 41.1). To let air out of a Presta valve, unscrew the little nut on the tip a few turns, and push down on it (see Figure 41.2). To seal, tighten the little nut down again (with your fingers only!).

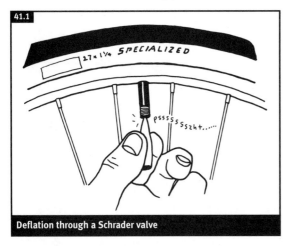

41.1

Deflation through a Schrader valve

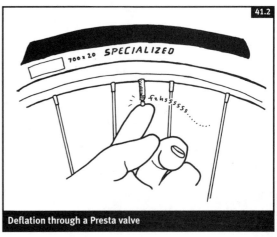

41.2

Deflation through a Presta valve

3. Now here's the most important trick: You can remove the tire most easily by starting near the valve stem. But first squeeze the tire together all the way around the rim, particularly on the side opposite the valve, to release the tire bead from its ledge. That way, the beads can fall into the dropped center (the valley) of the rim on the opposite side of the wheel, so that in effect you are pushing the tire bead off of a smaller-circumference rim. If you try to push the tire bead off of (or onto) the rim on the side opposite the valve stem, the circumference on which the bead is resting is larger, since the valve stem is forcing the beads to stay up on their seating ledges. Refer to Photos 45.1 and 45.2 to see what I mean by the rim ledges and valley; some rims do not have a valley, which makes this process harder, but most rims are somewhat lower in the center. Lift the tire bead above the valve stem with your thumbs and the heels of your hands, while pulling toward you with your fingers to pop a bit of it over the rim (see Photo 41.3). If you can get the bead off without using tire levers, continue around the wheel and skip to Step 8. Using only your hands, rather than tire levers, is not only quicker; there is also less chance of damaging either the tube or the tire. You need only remove the bead on one side.

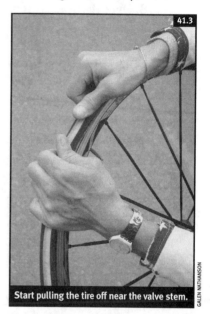

41.3

Start pulling the tire off near the valve stem.

GALEN NATHANSON

4. If you can't get the tire bead off with your hands alone, insert a tire lever, scoop side up, between the rim sidewall and the tire until you catch the edge of the tire bead. Again, this is most easily done adjacent the valve stem.

5. Push down on the lever until it pulls the tire bead out over the rim. If the lever has a hook on the other end, hook it onto the nearest spoke. Otherwise, keep holding it down.

6. Place the next lever a few inches away, and do the same thing with it (see Figure 41.4).

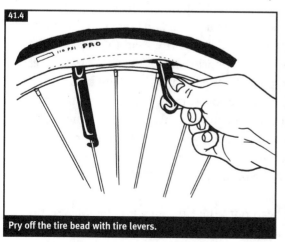

41.4

Pry off the tire bead with tire levers.

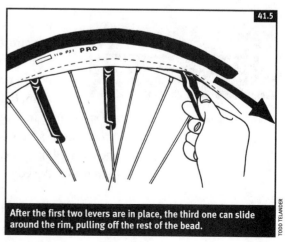

41.5

After the first two levers are in place, the third one can slide around the rim, pulling off the rest of the bead.

TODD TELANDER

7. If needed, place a third lever a few inches farther on, pry more of the tire bead out (see Figure 41.5), and continue sliding this lever around the tire, pulling the bead out as you go. Some people slide their fingers around under the bead, but beware of cutting your fingers on sharp tire beads.

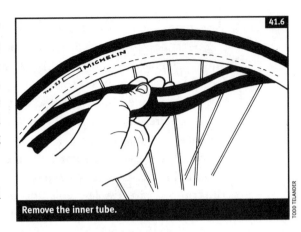

Remove the inner tube.

8. Once the bead is off on one side, pull the tube out (see Figure 41.6).

9. Feel around the inside of the tire to see if there is anything sticking through that can puncture your new tube. This is a critical step! Check that the rim tape is in place and that there are no spokes or anything else sticking up that can puncture the tube.

10. Put a little air in your new tube to give it shape. If your plan is to inflate the tire with a CO_2 cartridge, put air in by mouth at this juncture (only possible with a Presta valve) to avoid exhausting your cartridge before the tube is installed. Close the valve.

Starting opposite the valve stem, push the tire bead on and work back toward the valve stem in both directions.

11. Push the valve through the rim valve hole.

12. Push the tube up inside the tire all of the way around.

13. Starting at the side opposite the valve stem, work around the rim in both directions with your thumbs and the heels of your hands, pushing the tire bead onto the rim (see Photo 41.7). Be sure that the tube doesn't get pinched between the tire bead and the rim.

14. Finish from both sides at the valve (see Figures 41.8 and 41.9). You will usually want to deflate the tube just before you get to this point, for two reasons: so that the inflated tube doesn't bulge out and hinder your mounting efforts, and to allow the tire bead to drop into the rim valley on the opposite side of the rim. That makes it easier to push the tire bead over the rim by the valve stem, thanks to the consequent smaller circumference over which you are stretching it. You will probably be able to install a mountain bike tire without tools, and if you follow these steps, you can install most road tires with only your hands as well. If you cannot, use tire levers, but make sure you don't catch any of the tube under the edge of the bead. Either way, finish at the valve.

15. After you have pushed the last bit of bead onto the rim, suck up any folds of the tube stuck under the tire bead by pushing up on the valve (see Figure 41.10).

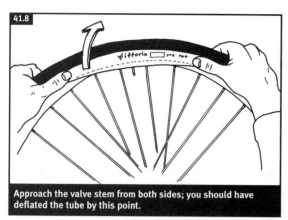

41.8

Approach the valve stem from both sides; you should have deflated the tube by this point.

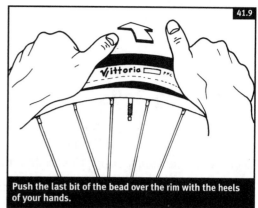

41.9

Push the last bit of the bead over the rim with the heels of your hands.

16. Go around the rim and inspect for any part of the tube that might be protruding from under the edge of the tire bead. If you have a fold of the tube under the edge of the bead, it can blow the tire off of the rim either when you inflate it or while you are riding. It will sound like a gun went off next to you, and the tube will be irreparable.

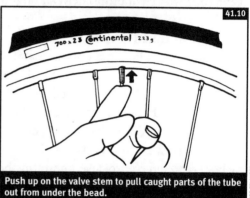

41.10

Push up on the valve stem to pull caught parts of the tube out from under the bead.

TODD TELANDER

17. Inflate the tire with a pump or with a CO_2 cartridge (see Photo 41.11). Make it tight enough that you don't run the risk of a pinch flat (also known as a "snake bite," which occurs when an underinflated tire is compressed down to the rim upon impacting an obstacle, pinching the tube between the obstacle and the rim and making two small holes in it, like a snake bite). A road tire is difficult to overinflate with a hand pump, but you can pump a mountain bike tire to such a high pressure that the ride becomes harsh.

There! Now wasn't that easier than you thought? (Changing the flat, I mean. Reading directions without the wheel in your hand is always tough.) 🚲

41.11

GALEN NATHANSON

Inflate the tire with a CO2 cartridge.

BLOCK 42
Tightening Bolts

It is an unpleasant situation when a critical part on your bike loosens up while you are out riding. This is particularly true when you are in the backcountry on a mountain bike. Bolts can loosen due to insufficient tightening, improper bolt preparation, stripping of the bolt, or breakage. All of these potentially dangerous situations can be avoided by following proper bolt tightening procedures. That includes correctly preparing the bolt threads, using your wrench appropriately, and tightening the bolt to the proper torque.

Prepare All Bolt Threads

Depending on the bolt in question, coat its threads with lubricant, thread-lock compound, or an antiseize compound. Clean off the excess lube or thread-prepping compound so dirt won't adhere to it. Here are a list of thread types and how to prepare each of them.

Lubricated threads. Most threads should be lubricated with grease or oil. If a bolt is already installed, you can back it out, drip a little chain lube on it, and tighten it back down. Lube items such as crank bolts, pedal axles, cleat bolts on shoes, derailleur- and brake-cable anchor bolts, and control lever mounting bolts. You can also smear grease or drip oil down into the female threads that the bolt will engage.

Locked threads. Some threads need to be locked in order to prevent them from vibrating loose; you'll find these types of threads on bolts that need to stay in place and often are not supposed to be tightened down fully for some reason or other, usually to avoid seizing a moving part or stripping threads in a soft material. Examples of bolts of this type are derailleur limit screws, jockey wheel center bolts, brake mounting bolts, rear-suspension pivot bolts, shock mounting bolts, and spokes.

Some untightened bolts that must hold their positions, like shift cable barrel adjusters, derailleur limit screws, and brake-lever reach adjustment bolts, have a spring on their shafts that maintains pressure between the bolt head and the part so the bolt won't loosen up. Make sure that you replace the spring if you remove one of these bolts or if one falls out on its own. Since the bolt is designed to turn relatively easily to fine-tune its adjustment and yet hold that adjustment, using thread-lock compound on the threads will not work; you must have that spring!

Use Loctite or another brand of thread-lock compound on bolts such as the center bolt holding on a rear derailleur jockey wheel. This bolt is small, and if you tighten it too much to keep it from unscrewing, you can strip the threads in the aluminum jockey wheel cage as well as pinch the jockey wheel so tightly that it won't turn. Thread-lock compound will keep the bolt from unscrewing when it is cinched down to the correct torque.

When building wheels, use Wheelsmith, Mavic, DT, or another brand of spoke-prep fluid on the spoke threads. The nipple seat in the rim can be lubricated with linseed oil. Really tight spokes can be greased so the nipple will turn smoothly without twisting the spoke, and the spoke tension will hold it firmly enough against the nipple seat in the rim.

Antiseize threads. Some threads tend to bind up and gall, making full tightening as well as extraction problematic. They require antiseize compound to prevent galling. Examples of this type of bolt are any steel or aluminum bolt threaded into a titanium part (this includes any parts mounted to titanium frames, like bottom bracket cups), and any titanium bolt threaded into a steel or aluminum part. Use Finish Line Ti-Prep or the equivalent.

Caution: *Never tighten a titanium bolt into a titanium part; even with antiseize compound, it will almost certainly gall and rip apart when you try to remove it.*

Wrenches and Screwdrivers

Engage wrenches and screwdrivers (some types are shown in Photo 42.1) fully before tightening or loosening a fastener, and make sure you are using the correct size for the fastener.

42.1

Various types of wrenches and screwdrivers useful on bicycles

LAUREN DUNDON

Allen wrenches (also known as hex keys) must be fully inserted into the bolt head, or the wrench and/or bolt hex hole will round off. A good example of a bolt that requires an Allen wrench is a shoe cleat bolt; clean dirt and rocks out of the bolt's hex hole and tap the hex key fully into it.

Open-end, box-end, and socket wrenches must be properly seated around a hex bolt, or it will round off. Other than on suspension parts, hex-head bolts are rare on modern bicycles. However the aluminum headset nuts and tiny derailleur mounting bolts from bikes made in the 1980s round off easily. Always use the smallest wrench that will fit; you can ruin a thin cone wrench or the cone on a hub axle by using a cone wrench that is too big.

Splined wrenches must be fully engaged or the splines will be damaged or the tool will snap. If you strip the splines in a cog lockring or in a bottom bracket cup, you will not be able to unscrew it.

Toothed lockring spanners need to stay lined up on the toothed lockring; if they slide off, they will not only tear up the lockring, they will also damage the frame paint. Toothed lockrings can be found on older bottom-bracket adjustable cups.

Pin spanners need to be fully seated in the holes to prevent slipping out and damaging the holes in the part. You can find pin holes to accept pin spanners in some bottom-bracket adjustable cups, crank bolt collars, and cartridge bearing hubs.

Tightening Torque

The best way to assure that a bolt is tightened properly is to tighten it to the torque specified by the manufacturer. This requires reading the owner's manual as well as having a torque wrench of the appropriate size. For big bolts, you need a long wrench with lots of leverage that goes to high torque; for small bolts, you need a short one that is accurate at low torques (see Photo 42.2).

An important thing to recognize is that the torque setting in an owner's manual is often the maximum torque the bolt can handle; you do not necessarily need to tighten it to that point. However, that maximum varies from manufacturer to manufacturer, and some list the ideal torque and *do* want you to tighten to exactly the number in the manual, while others list the maximum torque the fastener will take, so that you will stay below it.

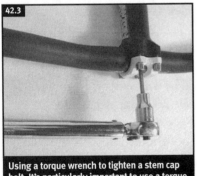

Torque wrenches of various sizes: The torque setting is adjusted by turning the knob at the bottom of the handle and reading the torque on the scale on the handle. The head of the wrench clicks off to the side when the torque setting is reached.

Note that on a four-bolt stem cap, the bolts need to be tightened to the same torque (see Photo 42.3) or they will not pull with even tension, like a sheet that is not pulled with equal force at all four bed corners. However, the bolts generally only need to be tight enough to prevent the handlebar from twisting; they do not necessarily need to be as tight as the maximum torque listed in the owner's manual.

Generally, the degree of tightness can be classified in four levels:

Snug (10 to 30 inch-pounds): small set screws (like Gripshift mounting screws), bearing preload bolts (such as a top cap bolt for a threadless headset), small screws in aluminum threads, and screws threaded into plastic parts all need to be snug.

Firmly Tightened (30 to 80 inch-pounds): cable anchor bolts, shoe cleat bolts, and brake mounting bolts need to be firmly tightened.

Quite Tight (80 to 300 inch-pounds): stem bolts (usually), seatpost clamp bolts (usually), and disc brake caliper mounting bolts (often) need to be quite tight.

Really Tight (300 to 600 inch-pounds): crankarm bolts, cassette lockring bolts, and bottom bracket cups are large parts that need to be really tight.

Using a torque wrench to tighten a stem cap bolt. It's particularly important to use a torque wrench on bolts like these on a four-bolt stem cap, because the clamp does not function properly if all four bolts are not tightened to the same torque. Also, the bolts are small and can be easily overtightened, stripping the threads in the soft aluminum of the stem.

Test Ride Your Bike

After installing or adjusting parts, always test ride your bike before riding far from home, since the parts will behave differently under load. And bring tools along with you when you ride.

BLOCK 43

Making Your Drivetrain Last Longer

While a bike chain is an efficient way to transmit power, it does have some downsides. It is exposed to the elements, takes continual shifting side loads, and is covered with lubricant that attracts abrasive grit which can grind it down. It wears out, and then doesn't shift smoothly and engage the cogs properly.

Frequent lubrication of your chain is paramount to its long life and good performance, but that won't make it last forever. Replacing your chain frequently is one way to ensure proper drivetrain function. While frequent replacement, warranted or not, is the method many professional racing teams use, unlike them most of us do not get crates of free chains each year. And chains keep getting increasingly expensive as they get narrower and more precise to accommodate more cogs on the rear. The financial incentive to getting longer life out of your chain may be substantial, so keep that chain lubed!

Is Your Chain Really Shot?

My opinion is that you should replace any part on your bike once it gets out of spec, and I recommend buying and using a chain wear indicator to periodically check to see if your chain is in spec. I find the Rohloff Caliber 2 indicator, which is a simple go/no-go gauge, to be quick and easy to use (see Photo 43.1). You just flop it into the chain, and if it lays flat on the chain, the wear is excessive and you should chuck the chain. The Park CC-3 works similarly (see Photo 43.2). Both tools are two-sided, and with both of them, I recommend replacement as soon as the side with the tighter specification lays flat on the chain. I find that waiting until the looser specification is reached will result in cogs that are so worn that a new chain will skip on them.

LAUREN DUNDON

Inserting the Rohloff Caliber 2 go/no-go chain wear indicator

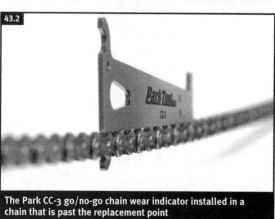

COURTESY OF PARK TOOLS

The Park CC-3 go/no-go chain wear indicator installed in a chain that is past the replacement point

Park and Wippermann make other chain wear indicators as well (see Photo 43.3). The Wippermann one works similarly to the Rohloff and the CC-3, while the Park CC-2 has a window you look through to determine the level of wear (see Photo 43.4). I recommend replacement when 0.50 shows up in the window. Don't wait until it says 0.75 or 1.0; you will have already fried your cogs.

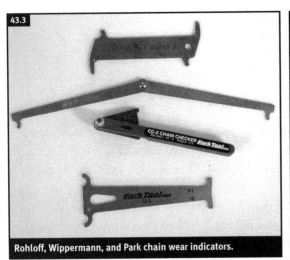

43.3	43.4
Rohloff, Wippermann, and Park chain wear indicators.	Using the Park CC-2 chain wear indicator

If you don't have one of these indicators, you can measure your chain against a foot-long ruler. I recommend replacing the chain if the edge of the link rivet at one end of the ruler is 12-1/16 inch or more from the identical edge of the rivet 24 segments away.

My opinion about chain replacement is based on disastrous races long ago, in which my chain and cogs did not mesh because one was worn more than the other. Whenever I pedaled hard, the chain skipped, ruining my race and endangering me to boot.

As a racer, I had several bikes, a number of different wheels, and yet more sets of cogs. I interchanged all of them. I discovered the hard way that, in a single race of an hour or two, I could ruin brand-new cogs by using a worn chain. This was disheartening, because not only was a new cogset (actually, an entire freewheel in those days) very expensive for a poor bike racer, but so were the entry fee, transportation to get to the race, months of training, and dashed hopes.

Even if you race with a worn chain but make sure to only use cogs that have worn in with it and do not skip, disasters can still happen. For instance, I had four flat tires in a single stage of the Tour of Ireland in 1981, and if I had been chasing back to the pack with an old chain that had skipped on the cogs of the spare wheels I had received, I would have been even more pissed off than I already was!

The costs of using a worn chain were way too high for me, and they may be for you, too. Now, as soon as I see any indication that my chain is worn, I make sure that I replace it. I have 10 bikes and at least 20 cogsets that I interchange, and it is too expensive to have one bike with a worn chain going around and wrecking a bunch of cogsets.

Things were admittedly different in the early 1980s, when you could get a Sedis Sport chain for four bucks or so. These days, a 10-speed chain can cost a pretty penny. But if you have more than one cogset, I see no way around it. A chain is still cheaper than a good cogset, particularly a titanium one!

The "Let It All Wear Out" Approach

There is another perspective, however. If you only have a single cogset that you use exclusively on the bike, you can just let both the cogset and chain wear out until they give you problems. This perspective is elucidated in the following e-mail I received from a reader of my question-and-answer column on the *VeloNews* Web site, www.velonews.com:

I train through the winters here on the roads of New Jersey, which are a good, grimy mix of New England winter and mid-Atlantic drizzle. This involves riding through endless miles of grit. It doesn't matter how much I clean my bike, at the end of every day it's a total mess. With all the melting snow, there are no dry days in the winter here. Even when I spend an inordinate amount of time meticulously cleaning my chain (as opposed to riding) I'm hard-pressed to get a whole month out of a chain before it wears to the point that my cogset would be incompatible with a new chain. I find that most of my friends who replace their chains according to conventional wisdom are inside on the trainer when I'm out commuting to work. Instead, I just leave the same old chain on, wipe it from time to time with a rag, and add oil when it squeaks (frequently). My chain stretches farther than my trusty bike shop mechanic has EVER seen, but, because it's continually running along the same cogset, it lasts for an entire year, at which point it begins to shift off the big ring when it's cross-chained and I pedal hard—out of the corners in a criterium, for instance. So, instead of buying 12 new chains per year, roughly $400, I buy a single chain and cogset once per year, roughly $125.

If you are committed enough to saving the money, you can get around replacing your chain when it is worn beyond what I would use. But don't borrow anybody else's rear wheel unless you want to lose a friend!

Lubrication

Keeping your chain clean and well-lubricated is always the first and most important method of extending your chain's life, as well as of maximizing its performance. If you simply wipe and lubricate your chain before every ride, you will have won the majority of the battle.

You will have to pick one of the many chain lubricants on the market. Any lube is better than none, but not all lubes are created equal, nor will all of them work well in your neck of the woods.

Here in Colorado, I have gotten longer life from my chain with daily application of ProGold as well as with a number of wet lubes of various brands, and quite a bit shorter life with wax-based lubricants. Every lube manufacturer thinks it's the best, and I have to think that each lube probably has good performance under some set of circumstances. I also have been around long enough to know that someone, somewhere, has had problems with every product. Find a lube that works for you by keeping track of how long your chains last with it.

Inverting Your Chain

This tip on extending chain life comes from Wayne Stetina, Shimano's research and development manager. "If you remove the chain when it is only halfway worn out and flip it over," he says, "you will double your chain life. In other words, your chain will now be turned inside out. The *other* side of the rollers will now contact the gears, and the derailleurs will now be laterally bending the chain the opposite direction." Stetina says that Shimano engineers discovered this phenomenon quite by accident, but that you should not attempt it with Shimano 10-speed chains.

Today's narrow chains do not allow you to push out any rivet you want to accomplish this sort of thing; even with 7-, 8-, and 9-speed chains, you must use a special link assembly pin rather than the original rivet for reassembly. Campagnolo chains come with only one assembly pin, and it is supposed to be inserted through the "virgin" hole in the open link at the end of the chain. Similarly, Shimano's 10-speed chains are very specific for the optimum connection procedure. So, unless you have a master link, don't remove the chain, even for cleaning, until it is time to dispose of it. Remove and replace rivets, and you could find yourself flat on your face! When you stomp down, the chain link plate could peel off the end of the rivet. SRAM and Wippermann chains have a master link, which allows you to easily remove the chain for cleaning or flipping over. ☉⚡☉

BLOCK 44

Keeping Your Chain On

N othing slows your uphill progress like a thrown or jammed chain, be it on a road or a mountain bike. Proper front derailleur adjustment, as well as a favorable chain line, is critical to avoiding this problem. These are discussed in Chapter 5 of both my road and mountain bike maintenance books, *Zinn and the Art of Mountain Bike Maintenance* (VeloPress, 2001) and *Zinn and the Art of Road Bike Maintenance* (VeloPress, 2000).

However, having these two adjustments dialed in does not guarantee that you will never throw or jam your chain. Given the right set of circumstances—including but not limited to front shifting under a heavy load, hitting a big bump while you shift, stiff or worn chain links, or bent chainring teeth—you can lose your chain.

Install an Antichain-Drop Device

A practically foolproof way to prevent your chain from falling off to the inside is to install something that will push it back onto the chainring if it comes off. The Deda Dog Fang (see Photo 44.1) and the similar Third Eye Chain Watcher are two options. These inexpensive plastic gizmos cinch around the seat tube next to the inner chainring. Clamp one on and adjust the position so that the tip (or "fang") nudges the chain back on when it tries to fall

44.1

A Deda Dog Fang

off to the inside. This means setting the fang so that it is right next to, but not quite touching, the chain as it runs past on the inner chainring (see Photo 44.2).

The Dog Fang is available in different clamp sizes to fit different seat tubes. The Third Eye mounts with a standard hose clamp, so it fits many seat tube sizes and shapes.

I can see virtually no reason to not mount one of these devices on any bike it fits. Dropping your chain to the inside is a rare occurrence on a properly adjusted road bike, but if you frantically shift in a race situation, it can still happen. It adds virtually no weight or wind drag and gives you peace of mind, so why not? Some teams in the Tour de France have Dog Fangs mounted on their bikes. If they are willing to pack the weight, so can you!

Unfortunately, the Third Eye and Dog Fang don't fit on a lot of full-suspension bikes. The bike on which I have the most trouble with dropped chains has a shock mount right where the clamp would go.

Some of Shimano's bottom-bracket-mounted front derailleurs offer security

44.2

A properly adjusted Deda Dog Fang just clearing the chain

against the chain jamming between the bottom bracket and the crankarm. These have a plate that extends up from the drive-side BB cup to help secure the front derailleur (see Photo 44.3). The plate, while not quite as effective as an inner guard in preventing the

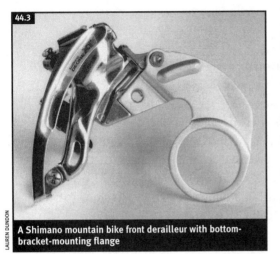

44.3

A Shimano mountain bike front derailleur with bottom-bracket-mounting flange

chain from coming off to the inside, at least prevents the chain from getting in between the crank and bottom bracket and will fit many places a Dog Fang or Third Eye will not.

Front Derailleur Adjustment

Wayne Stetina, Shimano's head of product development, says, "Installing an inner guard is a good idea, and I do that on all my personal bikes. However, there is an easy improvement just by readjusting the front derailleur angle. Turn the rear very slightly inward more than the front of the front derailleur. This decreases the downshift force. More importantly, this allows you to turn in the limit screw farther without rubbing in the small-to-small gear. Then the inside plate of the front derailleur cage functions more as an antichain-drop device."

Chain Suck

Chain suck occurs when the chain does not release from the bottom of the chainring and pulls up rather than runs straight to the lower rear derailleur jockey wheel. The chain will come around and get "sucked up" by the inner or middle chainring until it hits the chainstay. Sometimes, the chain becomes wedged between the chainstay and the chainring.

Generally limited to mountain bikes, chain suck is an unpleasant occurrence that riders often blame on the front derailleur. However, chain suck is often caused by a worn chain. When the shifting initiation point reaches the bottom, if the chain is so laterally flexible that it can still hang onto teeth on the chainring it is leaving, that chainring will just keep carrying the chain up and around, tangling it in the frame, front derailleur, and chain coming into the top of the chainring.

A stiff link can also cause chain suck, as can an extremely dirty or rusty chain. Chain suck can also be caused by a chain that is too narrow to release easily from the chainring teeth. Bent or mangled chainring teeth will create the same problem. And a weak spring in the rear derailleur lower knuckle (also known as the P-spring) may not pull the lower jockey wheel back hard enough to keep sufficient tension on the chain coming off the bottom of the chainring and keep it from being sucked upward.

Reducing chain suck

1. Clean and lube the chain and see if the chain suck improves; a rusty chain will take longer to slide off of the chainring than will a clean, well-lubed chain.

2. Check for tight links by watching the chain move through the derailleur jockey wheels as you slowly turn the crank backward. Loosen tight links by flexing them side to side with your thumbs.

3. If chain suck persists, check for bent or torn teeth on the chainring. Try straightening them with pliers.

4. If your chain still sucks, try another chain with wider spacing between link plates (if it is too narrow, it can pinch the chain ring). You can use a caliper to compare the link spacing of various chains.

5. Another approach is to replace the inner (and perhaps middle) chainring with a thin stainless steel (or shiny chromed) chainring. The thin, slick rings will release the chain more easily.

6. Check that the rear derailleur's jockey wheel cage springs back forcefully. If it does not, increase the P-spring tension; my books *Mountain Bike Performance Handbook* (1998) and *Zinn and the Art of Mountain Bike Maintenance* (VeloPress, 2001) both describe how to do so. Otherwise, replace the P-spring or the entire rear derailleur.

7. If the problem persists, a new chain and chainring, or an antichain-suck device that attaches under the chainstays, may help. Ask at your bike shop about options.

PART 7

Mountain Bike Maintenance and Tuning

BLOCK 45

Setting Up and Maintaining Tubeless Tires

Tubeless mountain bike tires offer some significant advantages over standard tires. You can go faster more comfortably and more reliably, and with better traction, than with a tube system. For these reasons, a majority of World Cup cross-country racers use a tubeless system of some sort, even if their tire sponsors do not make tubeless tires.

Advantages and Disadvantages

The most important advantage of a tubeless tire is reliability. You can never get a pinch flat (there is no tube to get pinched!), and if a thorn pierces the tire, the air comes out very slowly. The thorn fills the hole, and, as long as you don't pull it out, you can ride the tire for quite some time before you lose all air pressure. This is in sharp (pun intended) contrast to a thorn in a tube, as air escapes out of the tube around the thorn. It then can leak out through the tire casing, even if the thorn is sealing the hole in the tread.

Moreover, you can run tubeless tires at low pressure and nevertheless be confident of completing the race or ride (since you cannot get a pinch flat). Your tires grip better on side hills and sharp rocks at low pressure. Furthermore, low tire pressure can reduce your rolling resistance on rough terrain, since the tire will absorb bumps that your bike's suspension or your body otherwise would, thus saving you energy.

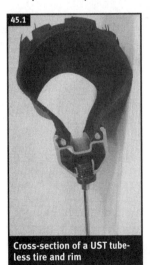

45.1

Cross-section of a UST tubeless tire and rim

Contrary to what you might think, a tubeless tire is not necessarily lighter than a tire and tube. There are a number of tubeless bike tire systems, but the one that predominates is UST (the acronym stands for the French name, *Universal Systeme Tubeless*), pioneered by the Mavic, Michelin, and Hutchinson tire company, largely thanks to its availability, simplicity, and reliability. The UST system offers no significant weight loss or gain, because the rubber coating on the inside of the tire casing, which creates an air seal, is as heavy as a tube. An extra rubber flap along the tire bead seals over an extra hump on the bead ledge of the rim (see Photo 45.1).

A tubeless alternative by Stan's No Tubes uses standard tires (and standard rims) with a sealant solution containing liquid latex. This system does offer a weight advantage over a tire and tube, since the solution only adds a few grams to a standard tire's weight.

You can mount standard tires on UST tubeless rims, and vice versa, because UST tubeless and normal 26-inch mountain bike tires are built to the same standard rim diameter. You can use the same inner tube with either one, and the only difference is that a UST tubeless rim requires no rim strip, since the spoke holes are either nonexistent in the rim bed, or they are sealed over.

The major disadvantage of the UST system is the high cost of the tire. You also pay a premium for the rim, but this generally is not an item you have to replace as often. A tire, however, wears out, and a tubeless tire gets just as ruined from a sidewall cut as a standard tire.

Manufacturers offer tubeless and standard models of their most popular tires, and you pay considerably more for the tubeless version. Stan's No Tubes method of converting a standard tire to a tubeless tire, though, is highly economical.

The other disadvantage of a tubeless system is only a disadvantage in the sense that you gained an advantage and may have to pay a price for it. That is, if you do run low tire pressure, you run a higher risk of denting your rims.

Installing a UST Tubeless Tire

Warning: To prevent damage to the seal, do not use tire levers. If you have mastered Block 41, that will be no problem. You can pre-stretch the tire by mounting it on a standard rim with a tube inside to make it easier to mount. (Follow the tire-mounting instructions in Block 41 and leave the tire inflated overnight to stretch the bead.)

1. Examine the rim to be sure the tire will seal to it. First of all, it must be a UST rim (and tire). Only a rim without spoke holes on the inside and with the hump along the edge of each bead ledge will seal with the tire (see Photo 45.2). Furthermore, the rim edges and hump must not be dented or gouged, or air will escape there.

2. Wet the tire beads with dish soap and water or simply just water to facilitate sealing on initial inflation.

3. Determine the rotation direction of the tire. On the front, you want the scooping edges forward for braking, while on the rear, you want them pointed back for propulsion traction. Some tires have an arrow indicating rotation direction for use on either the front or the rear. If not, hold the tire up above your head and look at the tread as the ground "sees" it. Consider which way the wheel is rotating and what would happen during braking and driving, and orient the tread accordingly.

45.2

Cross-section of a UST rim

45.3

Adding tire sealant to a UST tubeless tire

4. Push one bead of the tire onto the rim with your thumbs and fingers only.

5. Push the other bead onto the rim by hand, starting on the side of the rim opposite the valve stem and finishing at the valve stem (as in Figures 41.7 through 41.9). If you start at the valve stem, rather than on the opposite side, you will have to work harder, because the valve holds the tire bead up on the ledges, forcing the bead to stretch around a larger circle.

6. Consider adding tire sealant (see below). You can eliminate slow leakage by squirting sealant into the tire during initial installation (see Photo 45.3).

7. Pump the tire up with a floor pump, getting air in as fast as possible, until you hear the tire bead seat with a popping noise. As with a tubeless car tire, seating the bead is a lot more effective with an air compressor. Unlike a car tire, however, a UST tire can be seated with a manual pump. Sometimes a UST tire can even be seated with a portable frame pump, but be aware that you have to get a lot of air into the tire in a hurry to force the beads to pop up over the humps and onto the ledges.

8. Pump up (or deflate) the tire to your desired riding pressure. Remember that you can ride a tubeless tire at a pressure much lower than 35psi.

9. Loosen the valve nut, and tighten it by hand, so you can remove it by hand if you puncture on the trail. If you puncture, install a tube to get you home—don't forget to bring one! Tire designer Keith Bontrager recommends that you also carry a tire tool, "The tires (should) come off by hand, but weird things happen out there. Wrap the tire lever with a few inches of duct tape in case you need to boot a tire."

Applying Tire Sealant

UST tires almost always slowly leak air. As a matter of course, I put Slime, Stan's sealant (see below), or another brand of tire sealant in them when I first install them. Then I never have to deal with leaks. There are specific tubeless sealants available now, but I find that any tire sealant meant for bicycle inner tubes works. Simply pop the tire off of one side of the rim (see tire removal, below), shake the bottle, and squirt 2 to 4oz or so of sealant into the tire (Photo 45.3). Push the tire bead back onto the rim (see above), and inflate.

If the tire leaks air, riding it will usually adequately disperse the sealant throughout the tire. The sealant will try to flow out of the holes, but the fibers will jam the holes, plugging the air leaks. As you ride on the wheel, it seals better.

Installing a Standard Tire as a Tubeless Tire

With Stan's No Tubes systems, you can use a standard rim and tire, and even make a 29-inch tire tubeless. Stan's system includes sealant, 1/2-inch strapping tape, and a rubber rim strip with thick edges to seal the tire beads (see Photo 45.4). The rim strips are available for three

45.4

Stan's No Tubes system

different 26-inch rim widths, as well as for 29-inch wheels. You can also just tape over the rim holes and use Stan's sealant (this was the original way Stan offered the system).

I find that Stan's system works well for wheels that you use frequently. Standard tires that you don't ride often are difficult to keep sealed with the sealant solution, because if the wheel just sits, the latex in the solution tends to pool up and harden at the bottom of the tire.

1. Unless you are using a UST rim (Photo 45.2), enlarge the inside valve hole to 3/8-inch (with a drill, and smooth the burred edge). This allows clearance for the rubber sealing section at the base of the valve stem. With a UST rim, skip to the second part of Step 2.

2. Wrap two layers of 1/2-inch-wide fiberglass strapping tape around the rim, completely covering the rim holes. Cut through the tape at the valve hole. Install the rim strip, stretching it evenly around the rim and pushing the edges under the rim hooks; wetting the strip with soapy water makes this easier. If you are using a UST rim (Photo 45.2), install the valve instead of a rim strip. (If you are using Stan's old system—that is, using Stan's sealant without the rim strip—wrap a layer of electrical tape over the strapping tape. This method works better if you first smooth the edges of the rim holes with sandpaper and clean the rim bed with rubbing alcohol before applying the strapping tape. Then install the valve, first dripping a little sealant solution around the rubber base and rubber washer.) Tighten the valve nut down by hand against the rim.

3. Determine the rotation direction of the tire. If the tire does not have an arrow indicating rotation direction for use either on the front or the rear, hold the tire up above your head and look at the tread as the ground "sees" it. Consider which way the wheel is rotating and what would happen during braking and driving, and orient the tread accordingly. You want the front tire's scooping edges forward for braking, and the rear tire's biting edges pointed back for forward traction.

4. Install one bead of the tire on the rim, covering the sidewalls and along the rim beads with a one-to-eight solution of dish soap and water.

5. Shake the sealant bottle well, and turn it upside down when pouring it to keep the particles in solution. Put 60g (1.5 scoops, or 2 to 2.5 scoops for large tires or more sealing protection) of the sealant solution into the tire (see Photo 45.5). Install the other tire bead, as in Step 5 for installing UST tires. If you have Stan's 2-oz. U.S. measure refill bottle, you can install both beads of the tire first. You then unscrew the valve core and squirt in the sealant through the valve stem.

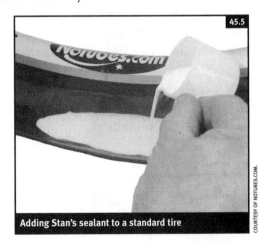

45.5

COURTESY OF NOTUBES.COM.

Adding Stan's sealant to a standard tire

6. Inflate the tire to a maximum of 40psi, preferably with an air compressor. Wear safety glasses. To check if you've got the rim strip on correctly, it is a good idea to inflate the tire first with just soapy water covering it and the rim edge before adding the sealant.

7. Wherever you see soap bubbles, which indicate escaping air, tip the wheel so the latex solution flows to the area and fills the holes. Continue doing this, repeatedly reinflating the tire to 40psi, until the tire seals completely.

When riding, the latex splashing around inside will not seal the tire beads or sidewalls if you did not seal them completely before. If you have leaks, repeat Step 7.

Removing a UST Tubeless Tire

You must remove and install UST tires with your hands only, as tire levers can damage the sealing flap that extends beyond the tire bead (Photo 45.1), and then your tire will not seal.

Note that if you are planning on patching a tubeless tire, you must find the leak before removing it from the rim; see the section below on UST patching.

1. Remove the wheel. If the wheel is on a Cannondale Lefty one-legged fork you can skip this step!

2. If your tire is not already flat, deflate it at the valve. Tubeless tire valves just screw into the rim with rubber seals around them. They can be either Schrader valves (like on a car tire), Presta valves, or both. UST valves are designed to be set up as either Schrader or Presta. To go with the Presta version, unscrew and remove the outer, Schrader-size externally threaded tube of the UST valve to leave only the Presta valve. To use it as a Schrader valve, unscrew the little nut on the end of the inner Presta valve pin until it stays stuck in the position to let air out; then screw on the Schrader outer tube. To deflate a Schrader valve, push down on the valve pin with something thin enough to fit in and not break off, like a pen cap or a paper clip (Figure 41.1). To let air out of a Presta valve, unscrew the little nut a few turns, and push down on the thin rod (Figure 41.2). To seal, tighten the little nut down again (with your fingers only!). Leave it tightened down for riding. Push inward on the beads all the way around to get them to pop off of the rim hump (visible in Photo 45.2) and fall into the dropped center of the rim.

3. Starting adjacent the valve stem, push the tire off of the rim with your thumbs.

Patching UST Tubeless Tires

Patching a UST tubeless tire is the same as patching a tube, except that you patch the inside of the tire rather than the outside of a tube. If you don't want to deal with patching the tire, you can always remove the tubeless valve from the rim and stick a tube inside a tubeless tire. And if you're using a tubeless tire in areas with lots of cactus or thorns, it is arduous and next to impossible to find and patch all the holes that can occur. Rather than throw the (expensive) tire out, fill it with tire sealant (Photos 45.3 and 45.5).

1. Dry the inside of the tire thoroughly around the hole.

2. Rough up and clean the surface of about a 1-inch radius around the hole with a small piece of sandpaper (usually supplied with the patch kit). Do not touch the sanded area.

3. Use a patch kit designed for bicycle tires that has thin (usually orange), gummy edges surrounding the black patches.

4. Apply patch cement in a thin, smooth layer all over an area centered on the hole that is bigger than the size of the patch.

5. Let the glue dry until there are no more shiny, wet spots.

6. Remove the foil backing from the patch (but not the top cellophane cover).

7. Stick the patch over the hole, and press it in place, making sure that all the gummy edges are stuck down.

8. There is no need to do so, but you may remove the cellophane covering. If you do this, be careful not to peel off the edges of the patch. Often, the cellophane atop the patch is scored. If you fold the patch, the cellophane will split at the scored cuts, allowing you to peel outward and avoid pulling the newly adhered patch away from the tube.

9. Install the tire as described above.

A tubeless tire will give you a real performance advantage, with increased traction, greater reliability, and reduced rolling resistance. Stan's No Tubes system also works for more wheel sizes and provides a weight savings at the most important place, the rotating tire weight. Be aware, however, that the sidewalls of nontubeless tires are more flexible than those of UST tubeless tires. This means that they will wear faster and can fold over more easily when the tire experiences high lateral forces, particularly on a large tire.

Experiment with tire pressures with your tubeless tires, and don't be afraid to try even less than 20psi—you might like it. But be careful not to dent your rims at these pressures! 🚲

BLOCK 46
Setting Up Brake Levers

All the riding skills that we discussed in Part 4 require a good brake setup. Proper bike control requires powerful braking, that you can modulate easily with only the application of your fingertips. This applies equally to rim brakes and disc brakes. What you want is complete braking control using only your index finger of each hand. The rest of your fingers should be wrapped around the grip for better steering control and shifting with speed and ease. When you pull the brake lever, it should be positioned and adjusted so that it does not hit any of your other fingers as it comes back toward the grip.

Yet most mountain bikes come from the bike shop, or out of the box, with the brakes set up poorly. This is either because of convention—what consumers expect—or because of the bike assembler's liability concerns and need for simplicity and/or to save time.

If you have your brakes set up like most people do, you have three fingers on the lever, and only your pinky and thumb are surrounding the bar. Obviously, that setup sacrifices control, since you cannot hang onto the bar very well that way on a rough, high-speed descent or over technical drop-offs. Moving your fingers from the grip and onto the lever and back again is also cumbersome.

The brake will most likely be set up for low leverage, so that you need two or three fingers to pull it hard. But it is also easy to panic, grab of fistful of brake with all of those fingers, and pull it too hard, sending you into a skid or over the handlebar—especially as you are being bounced around and trying to hang onto the grip.

Leverage Adjustment

Even though a lot of people want a hard feel to the brakes, you should know that the harder the brakes feel, the less power you have. The hard feel indicates that you have less mechanical advantage. Wayne Lumpkin, president of Avid Brakes says, "It is like climbing a hill in the big chainring; it feels hard because you are doing all of the work!"

A softer feel when pulling the brake lever means that you have more leverage. Your fingers require less force to compress the brake pads against the rim or the brake shoes against the disc. You will more easily stop the bike and moderate its speed.

Leverage adjustments really only came into prominence with the advent of V-brakes, also known as sidepull cantilever brakes. The caliper arms are so long that leverage is a lot higher than with an old-style centerpull cantilever brake. Think for a minute about how, when your friend sits way back on the end of a teeter-totter, she can easily lift you if you are sitting close to the pivot, yet she goes farther up and down relative to your movement. It's the same with a V-brake; the greater leverage means that the brake arm's upper end moves less than the pad.

New bikes come with the V-brake levers set on the lowest leverage, so that the end of the cable is close to the lever pivot, like you on the teeter-totter. At this setting, the lever can pull a lot of cable, just as you do when sitting close to the fulcrum, if you are heavy enough, you can lift your friend a long way when she is far from the fulcrum.

Levers come from the factory on low leverage because the V-brake pads can be adjusted farther from the rims, and the levers can still bring them into contact. Thus bike adjustments require less precision. The wheels can spin without dragging on the brake pads, even if the wheels are less than true and the brake pads are uncentered on either side of the rim. This has obvious cost advantages for a bike assembler. It also means that the consumer can abuse the bike longer and perform less maintenance on it before the brakes rub so much that he or she finds them aggravating.

The second reason levers are set on low leverage is because of bike- and brake-sellers' concerns about liability. If the levers are set with low leverage, bike equipment sellers can sleep easier, because you're less likely to slam on the front brake, flip over, and land on your head.

How to Increase Leverage

Hydraulic disc brakes do not require leverage adjustment, so the following section does not apply to them. That said, you may want to experiment with the little screw on your hydraulic disc brakes that determines how soon the brake engages during the lever stroke.

With a cable-actuated disc brake or any type of rim brake, you want to set up your brake

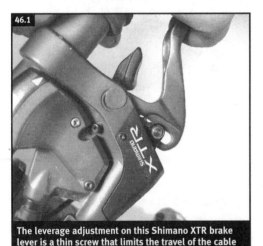

46.1

The leverage adjustment on this Shimano XTR brake lever is a thin screw that limits the travel of the cable hook inward in its slot.

46.2

The leverage adjustment on this Shimano XT brake lever consists of removing inserts from the cable-hook slot that limit the travel of the cable hook inward. All of the inserts have been removed from this particular lever so the cable hook can go inward closest to the lever pivot, thus achieving the highest leverage possible.

levers for high leverage, even though you may lose some pad travel. High-quality brake levers have a leverage adjustment (see Photos 46.1 and 46.2) that moves the cable end (or the cable path) in or out relative to the lever pivot. The closer the cable passes by the pivot, the higher the leverage, but the less cable the lever pulls, and vice versa.

On Shimano XTR (Photo 46.1), Avid, and high-end SRAM cable levers, a long screw performs the leverage adjustment, limiting how far the cable hook can slide inward in the lever slot. On Shimano XT cable levers (Photo 46.2), altering the leverage adjustment requires installing, relocating, or removing a series of inserts that allows the cable hook to slide up and down in the slot. On Shimano LX, DX, and M600 levers, you loosen a small bolt on the upper face of the lever arm with a 3mm Allen key, slide the leverage adjuster up and down, and retighten the bolt. LX, DX, and M600 levers have a hook to hold the cable end far out along the lever (as does SRAM); the cable passes over a trough whose position away from the pivot determines the leverage.

On some levers, a rotating notched eccentric disc adjusts the cable-head position relative to the pivot. Again, remember that leverage is increased (and amount of cable pulled is reduced) if the cable head or cable path is closer to the lever pivot, and vice versa.

Lever Position

Most hydraulic disc brakes (and hydraulic rim brakes) offer tremendous braking power. And if you have V-brakes (sidepull cantilevers) or cable-actuated disc brakes, you have just now maximized their performance and minimized your effort by increasing the leverage. However, with either a hydraulic or a hopped-up cable-actuated brake, you must place the lever so that you can only reach it with your forefinger; otherwise you can grab too much brake and do an endo. With only one finger on the brake lever, and the others hanging onto the grip, you will have better control not only of the brake but also of the steering.

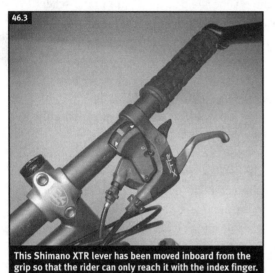

This Shimano XTR lever has been moved inboard from the grip so that the rider can only reach it with the index finger. As a result, when the lever is pulled, it does not hit any of the other fingers when they are wrapped around the grip.

Move your lever inboard on the handlebar (see Photo 46.3) so that the tip of the lever is under your index finger. The lever will bypass your second finger when you pull it to the grip, rather than losing some range by hitting your finger(s). Hold the grip with three fingers and pull with one. Make sure you pull on the end of the lever (Photo 46.1), since that is where leverage is.

You will find that you can grip the bars better, and your arms will stay more relaxed when braking. In addition, it will be comfortable to simply rest your forefingers on the levers, so that you will be ready to brake at any time.

Some Observations on Brake Setup

With Shimano Rapidfire integral brake/shift levers (Photos 46.1 through 46.3), it is generally easy to move the brake lever far enough inboard. The only thing that can really interfere is the bend or bulge of the bar, but these are usually inboard far enough, given that there is only a single band clamp to accommodate.

With twist shifters (such as Gripshift), there is also usually no problem moving the lever inboard as far as you need, since the shifter goes up against the grip, and the brake lever and its thin band clamp can move inward unimpeded. That said, some brake levers have a sharp bend in the middle that can run into the Gripshift body before the lever end comes near to the grip. This is a problem, but experimenting with different grip lengths as well as perhaps a longer shifter body (such as the Halfpipe twist shifter) can alleviate it.

Problems with lever positioning sometimes come up with Shimano Rapidfire or SRAM trigger levers that are mounted on their own, separate band clamps. The shifter's band clamp and gear indicator, which mount inboard of the brake lever (some SRAM 2005 levers will mount on either side of the brake lever), can run into the bend or the bulge of the bar and may prevent the brake lever from moving far enough toward the stem. Riders with large hands (and whose bar ends take up some handlebar real estate) may not be able to brake without hitting their second finger. Furthermore, particularly with fatter hydraulic levers, it may take a lot of readjustment to orient the brake and shift levers until you find a setup comfortable for both braking and shifting. 🚲

BLOCK 47

Keeping Your Grips in Place

It can be disconcerting to have your grips twist around when you are working to control the bike on tricky terrain. Or if you followed my advice in the previous block and moved your brake levers some distance inboard from your grip, you may find your grip sliding inboard as you ride, leaving the outer palm of your hand with nothing to rest on but bare handlebar. How can you keep your grips from twisting or from sliding inward? Here are some ideas.

Rubbing Alcohol

The simplest way to install grips is to pour rubbing alcohol into them and onto the bar. The grip slides on easily, and after the alcohol evaporates, it adheres to the bar with modest force. This is far better than using water in the grip, which evaporates so much slower that the grips constantly slip. If alcohol does not cut it, try one of the following solutions.

Wire

A common method is to twist wire around the grips to hold them in place. Cheaper grips will still slide even while wired, though.

Bonding Agents

Hair spray was the secret grip installation and bonding agent for many years. Then WD-40 became the magical stuff under grips on the BMX circuit. It lubricates the grip so that it slides on easily, and the oil bonds well after evaporating. However, WD-40 neither bonds as well as the following two options nor evaporates as fast.

According to the grip maker ATI, the pro team mechanics in the late 1990s, were using Spray 99, 3M's superstrength spray adhesive. With it, the grips slide on nicely and stay in place once the glue sets up. The problem with the spray is that it is very messy. Your fingers and everything you touch sticks to it!

When Shimano's citrus degreaser (meant for cleaning parts) came out at the end of the millennium, technicians started using it to install grips. It eats into the grip and bonds it tightly to the bar. The grip slides on well, and the degreaser evaporates very quickly.

If you absolutely have to get your grip to keep from slipping even under the rainiest, worst condition, you can superglue it on; this works for everything except really low-quality grips. But you won't be able to remove it without cutting it off!

Better Grips

ProGrip's Vince Marazita says, "If grips slip or not depends on the underneath layer. If a grip is soft throughout, it will twist on the bar no matter if you wire it on, glue it on, or anything else. That is why we introduced a two-part grip that is hard on the inside and soft on the outside. The hard inner surface holds the bar, and the soft outer part feels great in your hand. But the ID (inside diameter) of the grip is also very important. Even with a two-component grip, if the manufacturer gets the ID wrong, it will slip."

Bolt-on Grips

Some really expensive grips come with a built-in clamping collar that locks down onto the bar with a pinch bolt.

Longer Grips

If your problem is not so much twisting as the steady inward advance of the grip because the brake lever or shifter is not butted up against it to stop it, why not just get a longer grip? Going from a 4.5-inch grip to a 5.5-inch grip can make all the difference in preventing the heel of your hand from resting right on the bar itself by the end of a long, hot ride (see Photo 47.1).

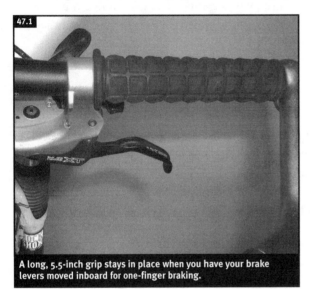

47.1

A long, 5.5-inch grip stays in place when you have your brake levers moved inboard for one-finger braking.

Removing Grips

If you have to get a grip off and have really stuck it on well, first try sticking a screwdriver under the grip and squirting some rubbing alcohol under it (I use an eyedropper). Do it from both ends, and twist the grip off. Instead of rubbing alcohol, you can also try squirting WD-40 underneath. If it is really on there (like with superglue), you may need to slice it lengthwise with a box cutter and peel it off.

BLOCK 48
Upgrading Your Bike to Disc Brakes

Disc brakes offer great stopping power and smooth modulation, no matter what the conditions. The rims and tires do not constantly drag mud, water, snow, and dirt into a disc brake the way they do into rim brakes. In fact, they are throwing detritus away from the disc. Also, the rims do not get hot from braking and explode tires or slip the rims inside them, tearing off the inner tube valve stems. And brake pads are generally far quicker to replace and adjust on disc brakes than on rim brakes, and they usually wear longer to boot.

The only downside to disc brakes is that the wheels and the calipers are heavier than superlight wheels and rim brakes. But the braking is so good that unless you are trying to be competitive in hilly cross-country races on dry ground, where weight is at an absolute premium and bad-weather braking is irrelevant, there is no reason not to use discs.

Disc brakes can be hydraulic or cable-actuated. Hydraulic disc brakes (shown in all photos in this block) offer all of the above-mentioned disc-brake advantages, in addition to the smooth action you are used to in car brakes, because they transfer force to the brake pads via hydraulic fluid, not cables. Cables can stretch and have friction, but hydraulic fluid cannot be compressed and flows with little resistance.

Installing Disc Brakes

Many people are intimidated by working on disc brakes, because they look different and complicated. Once you get over that, installation and adjustment of a disc brake is usually at least as simple and quick as that of a V-brake.

All you have to do is bolt the rotor to the hub, tighten the lever onto the bar, bolt the caliper to the mounts on the frame or fork, and tie down the hose or cable. The trickiest thing is that the space between the pads and rotor is

48.1
Fork IS mounts with a post-mount caliper mounted via an adapter to the fork's IS mounts

48.2
Fork post mounts with a post-mount caliper attached to them

48.3
Hydraulic disc-brake calipers: The center one is a post-mount style, while the outer two are for IS mounts.

small, so mounting the caliper precisely without the pads dragging on the rotor can be frustrating on your first try.

There are two types of built-in disc brake mounts on frames and forks: International Standard (IS) mounts (see Photo 48.1) and post mounts (see Photo 48.2). IS mounts are drilled transversely and not threaded, while post mounts are threaded and the holes are directed into the frame or fork in a plane parallel to the wheels. IS-mount calipers have threaded tabs on them, while post-mount calipers do not (see Photo 48.3)

Rear post mounts are rare on current frames, and Manitou is the only major fork manufacturer building post-mount forks; RockShox, Marzocchi, Fox, and most others use IS mounts.

Installing a Rotor

Avoid touching the rotor's braking surface and getting grease on it. If brake performance ever drops off, clean the rotor and pads with isopropyl alcohol.

Rotor bolt patterns varied widely in the early days of disc brakes, but now the six-bolt pattern originated by Hayes has become the standard (see Photo 48.4). Still, some disc-brake hubs do not have six holes. Instead, they either have an adapter, often with the standard six-bolt pattern to accept the rotor, that bolts or splines onto the hub. Or they have a splined rotor mount. Shimano's latest disc rotors called "Center-Lock" (see Photo 48.5) have splined hub attachments to reduce weight. However, a rotor of the same diameter on a standard six-bolt hub will work fine with the brake.

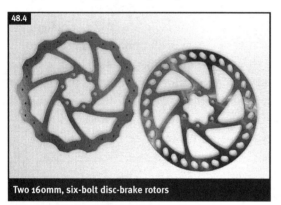

48.4

Two 160mm, six-bolt disc-brake rotors

48.5

COURTESY OF SHIMANO

Shimano's "center-lock" rotor/hub attachment is quick to assemble—simply tighten the lockring. The hub is also much lighter than an equivalent hub with a six-bolt flange.

With any rotor, the logo on the rotor should face outward so that the rotor turns in the proper direction. For bolt-on rotors, loosely bolt the rotor to the hub flange. Gradually snug the bolts, consecutively tightening the opposing rather than the adjacent bolts. A hex key or a Torx wrench (like a hex key, but with a star-shaped end) is required for this; manufacturers using Torx bolts usually supply the Torx T-25 wrench you need. Bolt-tightening torque ranges from 18 inch-pounds for some manufacturers to 55 inch-pounds for others. Shimano's early rotors have spring-steel plates that bend over the corners of the triangular bolt heads, tightened with a 3mm hex key, so they cannot unscrew (Photo 48.2). Torx bolts (Photo 48.1) do not need the triangular heads and bend-over securing plates, because they can generally be tightened to higher torque than hex-key rotor bolts thanks to stronger wrench engagement.

IS Mount Caliper Installation

These instructions are for brake calipers that attach directly to IS mounts. If you are using an adapter to mount a post-mount brake to an IS fork (Photo 48.1) or frame, instead, first bolt the adapter to the IS frame or fork mounts. Then skip to the directions below for installing a caliper onto post mounts, and install the caliper as if the adapter itself were the frame or fork post mounts.

1. Slip the caliper over the rotor (your wheel must be installed) and up against the frame or fork mounts. Never pull a hydraulic brake lever unless there is a rotor or a spacer between the pads to keep the piston(s) from popping out.

2. Loosely install the mounting bolts and pull the brake lever to squeeze the pads against the rotor.

3. While squeezing the lever, measure the gap between the caliper and the mounting tab at each bolt, and make up a stack of the supplied shim washers of that height to put between the caliper and mount on each bolt. Remove the caliper, and slide each stack of shim washers on its bolt between the caliper and mount tab.

4. Tighten the bolts. Torque varies from 53 inch-pounds to 110 inch-pounds, depending on brand. The pads should not rub. If they do, add or remove shims until the rubbing has been eliminated. If the rotor wobbles, you will have to straighten it. See Block 49 on how to do that.

Note: Some brakes have only one moving pad and instead flex the rotor toward the stationary pad. Some Magura, Avid, and Formula models are like this. You adjust the stationary inboard pad independently with a knob until it just barely clears the rotor; details are in the following section.

Also, some older IS brakes use a "floating caliper" in which the entire caliper moves as the pad(s) on the outboard side push against the rotor and pull the stationary pad(s) over to the rotor. It is almost impossible to eliminate brake rub with these, as the rotor is the only thing that pushes the caliper back over. On the old Pro Stop brakes, the caliper is fixed, but the "floating rotor" slides laterally on plastic bushings. These also tend to rub.

Post Mount Caliper Installation

If your frame or fork has post mounts, you can still mount calipers designed for either post mounts or IS mounts. First and simplest, you can install a brake caliper designed to fit post mounts (Photo 48.2). If you have a caliper designed for IS mounts, you can mount it through a different adapter bracket to post mounts. In that case, first tighten the bracket to the caliper, then follow the procedure below.

Another possibility is that you have IS mounts on the frame or fork and a post-mount caliper as mentioned at the beginning of the previous section. You can attach that caliper to the IS mount through an adapter bracket (Photo 48.1). Once the bracket is bolted to the IS mounts, the bracket then behaves like integrated post mounts would, and you can follow these instructions as well.

An advantage to post mounts is that you don't need to slip shim washers between the caliper and the mounts so the brake can be moved laterally, as you need to with IS mounts. This applies even if you are mounting an IS brake via an adapter to a post-mount frame or fork, or vice versa.

Loosely bolt the post-mount caliper to the post mounts on the frame or fork, or to an adapter bolted to IS frame or fork mounts. (Or, if you have an IS brake tightened to a post-mount adapter, loosely bolt its adapter onto the frame or fork post mounts.) The caliper slot will be over the rotor (your wheel must be installed), and the caliper will have some lateral freedom of movement. Again, never pull a hydraulic brake lever unless there is a rotor or a spacer between the pads, to keep the piston(s) from popping out.

1. Slip feeler gauge blades in between the rotor and the pad on either side. Start with about a .015-inch thickness. Two business cards will work as well.

2. Squeeze and hold the brake lever while tightening the mounting bolts.

3. Spin the wheel to check for brake rub. If you hear the sound of rubbing, peer through the gap between the rotor and the pads, using a white background for contrast, noting which pad (or worse, which side of the caliper slot) is rubbing. Loosen the bolts again, and slip a thicker feeler gauge or an extra business card between the rubbing pad and the rotor, and use a thinner one on the other side.

4. Repeat Step 3 until the rotor spins without rubbing. If you're desperate, just loosen the bolts, eyeball the gap, and tighten while holding the caliper; expect some frustration!

A bent rotor will rub or at least reduce pad adjustment range. Block 49 describes how to straighten it.

Some disc brakes that flex the rotor toward a fixed pad require that you turn screws on one or both pads until the pads just barely clear the rotor. On an Avid cable-actuated caliper, turn the large red screw on the wheel side until the fixed pad centers the rotor in the caliper slot. Then turn the red screw on the cable side until the rotor is pinched between the pads and centered in the slot. Tighten the mounting bolts and back off the fixed-pad screw until the rotor spins freely. Now tighten the cable and back off on the red screws on either side a few clicks each to get the desired pad-to-rotor spacing.

Hydraulic brake levers (also known as master cylinders) that have integrated fluid reservoirs

Similarly, the inboard (stationary) pad on Magura hydraulic models and on mechanical Hayes, SRAM, Grimeca, and Formula brakes can be adjusted independently to get ideal pad-rotor spacing. On Hayes mechanical calipers, squeeze the brake lever with the caliper loosely mounted over the rotor, shake the caliper into its favored position, and tighten the mounting bolts. Then turn the fixed pad adjuster counterclockwise a one-eighth turn with a 4mm hex key to attain the specified 0.15-inch pad-rotor spacing. Magura inboard pads are adjusted with a 5mm hex key until the pad just clears the rotor without rub.

Move the entire SRAM, Grimeca, or Formula mechanical caliper laterally by means of its thumbscrew so that the fixed pad just clears the rotor.

Mount the Levers

Bolt the levers (see Photo 48.6) to the bar, paying attention to the torque spec in the owner's manual and to the instructions from Block 46 on lever location.

Tie Down the Hoses

On hydraulic brakes, attach the hoses to the frame and fork with the hoseguides integrated on the frame, zip-ties, tape, or stick-on or screw-on cable clips. If your hoses are too long or short, you have more work to do: cutting the hoses to length and bleeding the system. That process is covered in *Zinn and the Art of Mountain Bike Maintenance* (VeloPress, 2001), as is any other maintenance and adjustment of disc brakes.

Hook up Cable-Actuated Disc Brakes

Route the cable housing to the brake. Zip-tie it down where there are no cable stops. Push the cable through the housing stop on the caliper, and tighten it under the cable anchor bolt. Cable routing and tension adjustment is identical to that for rim brakes. If you are at all unsure about how to do this, refer to *Zinn and the Art of Mountain Bike Maintenance,* which covers that process as well.

Wear in the Rotor and Pads

The brakes will not perform optimally until the rotors have been worn in a bit. Pull the brakes hard on your first ride or two, and you'll be all set. 🚲

BLOCK 49

Truing Wobbly Disc Brake Rotors

If you purchased disc brakes for their performance advantage, perhaps you did not expect to turn heads with the scraping, squealing, and howling noises they can make as you ride! That great disc brake performance can go right down the drain if your rotor gets bent. You may have had the calipers perfectly centered over the rotors (see Block 48), but now they may make all kinds of noise!

The spacing between brake pads and rotor is so tight on a bicycle disc brake that there is almost no room for the rotor to wobble whatsoever. The spacing is around 0.015-inch—that's not much leeway for a bent disc. Even a mildly bent rotor will rub, or at least reduce pad adjustment range.

The thing is, unlike car brake discs, bicycle rotors are thin and relatively unprotected, and they can get bent for all sorts of reasons. Rocks can be thrown up and nick them as you ride. You can crash on them and bend them. When you pack your wheel in a car or a bike bag, the rotor can get tangled up in the bike or in another wheel's spokes or rotor and get bent in transit or when unpacking. And finally, on a long, steep descent on a hot day, the heat generated from braking can warp the rotor.

You can't avoid the bending—and nobody likes riding with that relentless howl—so you need to be able to straighten your rotors.

Note: If a rotor is really potato-chipped, you will first need to remove it from the hub and pound it as flat as you can with a hammer on an anvil. Then you can proceed with any of the methods below.

Straightening a Rotor without Tools

If you are patient enough, you can often do an adequate enough job to at least minimize, if not eliminate, the brake pads from rubbing on the rotor. But be forewarned that it can test your patience!

First, the bike needs to be firmly held in a bike stand with the wheel free to spin. Place a white background (a piece of paper is fine) on the floor or the wall below or level with the caliper so that you can see the space between the rotor and the pads. Notice where the disc rubs on each pad, and mark it with a felt pen. Carefully bend it into alignment with your fingers, rechecking constantly by spinning it again through the brake. A rotor easily bends by hand. When you are done, remove the felt pen marks and the fingerprints with isopropyl alcohol.

Using a Pointer

You can also try attaching a pointer to your frame or fork in such a way that it touches the rotor and can be used like a feeler on a truing stand. Then just bend the rotor away from the points at which it touches the pointer. But unless you really spend some time mounting your pointer securely, this process can also be frustrating. Like sighting on air spaces, you can make mistakes and think it is bent one way when it is actually bent the other, and you can make it worse before you make it better.

Truing with the Morningstar Rotors on Center Tool

If you straighten rotors a lot, eyeballing it or using a rigged-up pointer will soon drive you mad. Fortunately, from the inventive mind of toolmaker Paul Morningstar comes the Morningstar Rotors on Center (ROC) tool (see Photos 49.1 and 49.3). This dial indicator shows the lateral position of the rotor within 0.001-inch, so you can get the rotor as straight as it was when it was brand new.

The ROC indicator includes a base that clamps through the center of the hub. It can be installed in place of the skewer when it is on the bike or in a truing stand. Even cooler is that this tool costs less than $90—a good deal if you have to align your rotors frequently.

To use the ROC tool, all you do is tighten the long mounting screw through the axle and set the dial indicator's foot against the rotor. You rotate the indicator face so that the needle is on zero, and then see where and by how much the rotor is bent to the inside and outside. At the highest deflection points in either direction, you bend the rotor back through center, and keep checking it with the dial indicator. You can bend the rotor back with your thumbs as in Photo 49.1. In this way, I have aligned a lot of very badly bent rotors and was able to return them to supertrue, within a couple of thousandths of an inch.

Now Morningstar makes it even easier with his "rotor tuning forks," dubbed Morningstar Drumstix (see Photo 49.2), that slip onto the rotor and give you a lot of leverage to bend the rotor very precisely. You stabilize the rotor in position with the two symmetrical Drumstix, one on either side of the bent spot. With the third Drumstix, which has an angled slot for the rotor, you precisely bend the rotor and eliminate the warped spot, as in Photo 49.3.

The Drumstix stabilizers, by isolating the bent spot, eliminate the rotor's spring back from the alignment process. When you are bending with your fingers, the entire rotor flexes

49.1

The Morningstar ROC dial indicator is mounted through the hub in place of the skewer while the wheel is still on the bike. The dial indicator's foot rests on the rotor and shows the side-to-side movement of the rotor in thousandths of an inch on the dial face. Knowing exactly where and how much to bend allows you to get the rotor very straight with just your thumb.

GALEN NATHANSON

49.2

The outer two Morningstar Drumstix stabilizes the rotor on either side of the bent spot. The center one with the angled slot works as a bending lever at the bent spot. And yes, the bottle opener on the center tool works great when you are done!

and springs back, and it takes guesswork to figure out how far to bend it so that it springs back to the position you want without going too far.

Other ROC Options

The ROC tool has other optional parts, such as a clamp to hold the tool onto Park's standard workhorse model TS-2 truing stand, or a different clamp for Park's deluxe model TS-3 truing stand. The TS-3 already has two dial indicators—one for lateral wobble and one for the rim's vertical hop. With an ROC clamped to it, you can true disc-brake wheels in assembly-line fashion to great accuracy, from roundness and lateral true of the rim to lateral true of the rotor.

A longer arm and clamp are available to use the ROC dial indicator to true the rim—laterally and vertically—while it is on the bike. ⊘🚲

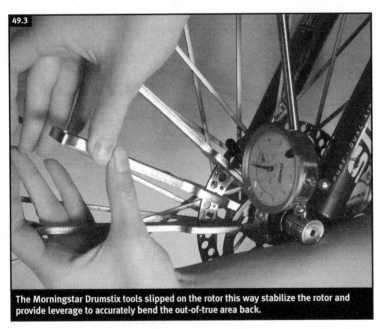

49.3

The Morningstar Drumstix tools slipped on the rotor this way stabilize the rotor and provide leverage to accurately bend the out-of-true area back.

BLOCK 50

Suspension Tuning

While suspension tuning may be the last item in this book of "Lennard's Top 50 List" of ways to ride faster and more efficiently, comfortably, and confidently, as well as enjoy yourself more on your bike, it is certainly not ranked fiftieth in importance. On rough ground, almost any suspension is better than none, but suspension tuned to your weight and riding style, and even to the particular trail you are on, can greatly enhance your control and overall experience of the ride.

This block will guide you to an understanding of suspension tuning adjustments and how to determine which ones you want to make. Suspension systems vary widely, so you will need to refer to your owner's manual to find out exactly how to make the adjustments on your own bike. Yes, that means you will have to hang onto and read the thing!

Suspension Parameters

There are three main parameters of suspension: travel, spring rate, and damping. You may or may not all be able to easily tune any or all of them on your fork and rear shock.

The first suspension parameter, travel, simply refers to how far the suspension allows the wheel to move up and down. Rear shock travel, because of the use of linkages, is always a ratio to the amount of rear wheel travel. For example, 1-inch of shock shaft movement may result in 3-inch of rear wheel travel; this is described as a 1:3 ratio.

The second parameter, spring rate, is the amount of resistance of the suspension element's compression action and is intimately connected to "sag," or "ride height." The stiffer the springs, the less your bike will compress when you sit on it. Spring rate is a function of position in the spring's travel, so it is best expressed by a graph—that is, as a curve of spring compression force versus position along the travel. Terms like "rising rate" and "falling rate" refer to this spring curve, indicating that the spring compression force is increasing or decreasing as it moves through its course of travel.

The third suspension parameter, damping, is control of the action and reaction movement of the spring. An example of damping is the difference in how a screen door slams when it has only a spring pulling it back versus when it has a damper unit that slows the door down before it closes. (Note that we are talking about "damping" and not "dampening." When you dampen something, you make it wet; when you damp something, you control its motion.) When tuning a front or rear shock, you will be interested in both "compression damping" and "rebound damping." Just as their names indicate, these terms refer to how the suspension movement is controlled as it compresses on impact and as it rebounds after impact.

Suspension performance is also a function of cleanliness. If your system is gunked up or worn out, it will neither work well nor respond properly and predictably to tuning adjustments. If you ride a lot, your bike's suspension system needs a lot of service, so either turn your bike over regularly to a suspension mechanic you trust, or get the tools and do it yourself, consulting service manuals in print and on the Web.

To illustrate the importance of frequent suspension maintenance, consider the differences between a car engine's oil and filter system and that of a bike's rear shock. You change the oil in your car every 3,000 miles or so, which equals about 50 hours of driving at an average speed of 60mph. Whereas your car engine has lots of oil volume and an oil filter, the piston in a rear shock, which is going up and down repeatedly whenever you ride on rough ground, only has a teaspoon of lubricant in there and no room for an oil filter. So, believe shock manufacturers when they say, for instance, that after every 40 hours of riding you should service the rear shock air sleeve. (On an air shock, the air sleeve is the outer "can," and the service consists of removing, cleaning, and lubricating the sleeve and checking the seals.) If you do it frequently, you won't have to replace the seals or the entire shock.

Suspension Fork Tuning

Since bikes more often have suspension forks than rear shocks, let's address front suspension first. Forks have either steel or titanium coil springs, urethane elastomer springs, a combination of both, or a compressed air spring (see Photo 50.1). Air springs weigh less than coil or elastomer springs, and air spring forks sometimes also have a coil or elastomer spring inside to supplement the air spring's performance.

It's most important to get the spring rate right first before doing any other tuning. You initially adjust spring rate by installing the proper coil spring/elastomer stack from you local dealer that corresponds to your weight or by pumping up your fork to the manufacturer's recommended pressure. Only after setting the spring rate should you start playing with other settings.

Tuning coil springs and elastomer springs

To adjust your coil or elastomer springs, you first interchange them (that is, change the spring rate), and then you can precompress (preload) them.

Interchanging coil springs and elastomer springs

To change the fork's spring rate, change the springs inside. Manufacturers usually color code the elastomers and coil springs for stiffness, though you can tell the difference between stiff and soft elastomer bumpers by squeezing them between your fingers. (Some manufacturers refer to an elastomer as an MCU—microcellular urethane—referring to small air voids trapped inside it.) Extra springs usually come with the fork, or you can buy them from a dealer.

Fox Float F80X air/oil fork

The fork needs stiffer springs (or more spring preload) if it sags excessively when you sit on it. Set your sag (or "ride height"—that is, the amount the suspension compresses from just sitting on it) at about 20 percent of your fork's total travel, and closer to 10 percent for cross-country racing. Measure sag by tightening a zip-tie around the fork's upper tube—or the rear shock shaft—that stays in place when you get off the bike.

If hard impacts with large bumps do not use the fork's full travel, the fork needs softer springs (or less compression damping—see the damping section that follows).

Setting spring preload

Spring preload is the amount of compression of the spring at rest and should only be used for fine-tuning, not as a way to compensate for a spring that's too soft. The more preload the fork has, the more impact force is required to get it moving, and vice versa. It can be adjusted on mid- to high-end coil spring and elastomer forks by turning the preload adjuster knob(s) on the top of the fork crown, even while you're riding.

Rotating the adjuster knobs clockwise gives a firmer ride by tightening down against (and thus shortening) the spring stack. Rotating the adjuster knobs counterclockwise softens the ride. Make sure the top cap surrounding the knob does not unscrew from the fork crown; you may need to hold it tight with one hand (or a wrench) when you loosen the adjuster knob. Check the top cap occasionally to make sure it is not unscrewed or being forced out due to stripped threads; if the top cap pops off, the spring can shoot up into your face at high velocity.

Preloading the springs only determines the force required for a bump to initially compress the fork but will not change the overall spring rate, meaning a spring rate that's too soft will still be too soft as the fork compresses past its initial travel. Preloading does not limit the full travel for large bumps, but it uses up some of the spring's length. Varying the preload also changes the fork's sag, and it shortens the life of the springs, because they are being compressed even while your bike is hanging in the garage. It is better to change the spring stack to get the ride you want and minimize preload. Use preload only as a way to change the fork quickly during a particular ride.

Tuning air spring forks

The beauty of an air spring, besides being lightweight, is that it is easy to experiment with, since it takes just seconds to change air pressure.

Adjusting air pressure

Higher air pressure makes for a stiffer fork, and vice versa. Do not use a tire pump; its large stroke volume is a poor way to adjust low volumes of air at high pressure. And the gauge won't tell you how much air will be left in the fork, since you will lose most of the air when removing the pump head. You need a shock pump with a no-leak fitting, or a no-leak pump adapter specific to your fork. Otherwise, you will lose air when removing the pump.

The fork needs higher air pressure if it sags excessively when you sit on it. Like when tuning coil springs and elastomer springs, set your sag (which can be measured by tightening a zip-tie around the fork's upper tube—or the rear shock shaft—that stays in place when you get off the bike) at about 20 percent of your fork's total travel—and closer to 10 percent for racing. The fork needs softer springs (or less compression damping) if hard impacts with large bumps do not use the fork's full travel. Remember that the main spring will be partially balanced by the negative spring, if you have one—see the next section on adjusting negative spring.

Check your air pressure periodically, since air springs lose pressure over time.

Adjusting negative spring

The negative spring in an air fork works against the main air ("positive") spring to compress the fork. This makes the fork more compliant over small bumps and makes it behave more like a coil spring throughout its travel. Early air forks did not have negative springs, and riders used to suffer on stutter bumps.

Air springs have a progressive spring rate, meaning that as the spring is compressed, the force it takes to move to the next increment of travel goes up exponentially, rather than linearly. Also, the tight air seals in an air fork usually mean it has more stiction (the coefficient of static friction, or the force it takes to make it move initially) than a coil spring fork. A coil spring, on the other hand, has a linear spring rate through much of its stroke; it takes the same increase in force to move 1mm farther, whether you are at the beginning or middle of the spring's compression.

So, it takes more force to get the air fork to move initially on a little bump, and the force it takes to keep moving farther into the stroke on bigger bumps ramps up. A negative spring, by pulling the fork down, can help the fork react quickly to small bumps. A negative air spring—a separate air chamber—will also start in its fully compressed (hence fully ramped-up) point. As it moves through the stroke, its force ramps down rapidly while the main spring's force is ramping up rapidly, so the net spring rate of the fork is fairly linear. Some air forks instead have a negative coil spring, which is not always adjustable.

Other air spring adjustments

Varying air volume in an air fork is similar to varying preload in coil and elastomer forks. Reducing air volume makes the fork stiffen up faster as it moves (that is, the spring rate ramps up faster), and vice versa. For instance, if you find an air pressure that works well through its initial and intermediate travel, but you bottom the fork too often, you can decrease the air volume to stiffen the fork sooner with the same air pressure. On virtually any air fork, you can decrease the volume in an air cylinder by removing the valve and pouring in some oil, but many air forks also have an adjustable piston to vary the air volume.

Tuning damping

High-end forks have a hydraulic damping cartridge or cylinder inside one or both lower legs, but not all are adjustable. Look for adjuster knobs on the top and bottom of the legs, and read your manual.

Damping—that is, the control of the speed of spring movement—is performed by oil (or by compressed air, in the case of the Englund/Cane Creek/White Bros. TotalAir system) moving through or around a piston that is being forced through the oil chamber. The same process is used in the damping device that slowly closes a screen door. The size of the hole(s) in or around the piston and the viscosity of the oil dictates how easily the piston can move through the oil.

Compression damping

Compression damping controls the speed at which the spring compresses during the fork's downstroke. Excessive compression damping will give you a harsh ride over repeated rocks, but won't allow the fork to dive through all of its travel when you encounter a compression dip (called a G-out) or hit a large obstacle. Too little compression damping will lead your bike to bottom out harshly on big hits and to bob noticeably when climbing, but the bike will feel active over repeated rocks. For riding on smooth surfaces, you can stiffen your fork by increasing your compression damping adjustment to help eliminate suspension bobbing, which robs you of energy.

Some forks have a lockout—controlled either manually by a knob, lever, or button, or automatically by the motion of the bike—which closes off the compression-damping oil port. A manual lockout will not allow the fork to move unless you really slam into something and blow off the emergency shim stack covering the oil hole. An automatic lockout will be released and will allow the fork to move fully when you hit even small bumps.

Rebound damping

Rebound damping controls the speed at which the fork returns to its original position after it has been compressed and released. Rebound damping is too high when you get a harsh ride over repetitive bumps because the fork packs up—that is, it keeps getting shorter with each bump, since it cannot return fully before the next impact. Too little rebound damping will let the fork snap back too fast (called pogoing), which often results in topping out; the fork clunks when it hits the top of its stroke. It is usually best to start with minimal rebound damping, so the fork is very active, and reduce the rebound adjustment if you are pogoing too much.

Suspension fork adjustment guide

The best way to find out how you like your suspension tuned is to experiment. Find a short downhill test course with some sharp turns and an uphill. Make only one adjustment to your suspension at a time. Ride the course after each adjustment to isolate the effect of each change. Keep track of your observations in a notebook immediately after every ride, rather than waiting until you have time to work on your bike and have forgotten what you wanted to change.

Most of the recommendations below were taken (with permission) from a Manitou fork tuning manual.

Before adjusting your fork, there are two important things to keep in mind.

1. A bottoming sensation (even if the fork is not bottoming) may actually be caused by the inability of the bike and rider to overcome an overly stiff spring or excessive damping.
2. A harsh sensation (even if the bike has soft springs) may actually be caused by a spring rate that's too soft for the bike and rider, causing the suspension to ride with much of the travel compressed (that is, packed up).

Spring rate

Too soft: indicated by bottoming of fork; high preload needed; front end too low on downhills.

Too hard: indicated by a fork that rarely or never bottoms (that is, the fork does not use its full potential travel).

Spring preload (coil and elastomer forks)

Remember to adjust spring rate first.

Too little: indicated by excessive static sag; front end too low entering turns; oversteering.

Too much: indicated by not enough static sag; fork feels stiff/harsh; understeering; poor ability to make tight turns at low speeds.

Rebound damping

Too little: indicated by a fork that extends too quickly and a wheel that springs up from the ground after landing from a jump; difficulty in maintaining a straight path through rocks; front end attempts to climb the berm/groove while cornering; high ride height; understeering.

Too much: indicated by a harsh feeling, especially through successive rapid hits; bottoming after several successive large hits; failure to rebound after landing from a jump; low ride height; oversteering; bottoming occurs even though compression damping and spring rate are correct.

Compression damping

Too little: indicated by bottoming; fork dives while braking; oversteering; fork is unstable.

Too much: indicated by harsh feeling; fork rarely or never bottoms; high ride height despite soft spring and/or little preload; understeering.

Here are some common ride symptoms and some fixes for them:

Fork too hard
1. Decrease compression damping
2. Decrease rebound damping
3. Decrease spring rate
4. Decrease oil viscosity
5. Increase spring rate*

Fork too soft
1. Increase spring rate
2. Increase compression damping
3. Increase oil viscosity
4. Replace old damper oil
5. Put oil in (empty) damper

*If you are running a spring rate that is too soft for your weight and ability, you can be misled into thinking that the spring rate is too stiff. This is because you are using up the fork travel before you begin to ride. Furthermore, the fork is working in a stiffer spring-rate range on smaller hits, giving the impression that the fork is harsh and stiff. This is where the ride-height (sag) adjustment is important.

Front end searching/nervous descending
1. Increase rebound damping
2. Increase spring preload
3. Increase spring rate
4. Decrease compression damping

Front end "knifes"/oversteers
1. Decrease rebound damping
2. Increase spring preload
3. Increase spring rate
4. Increase compression damping

Front end pushes or washes out in turns
1. Increase rebound damping
2. Decrease spring preload
3. Decrease spring rate
4. Decrease compression damping

No response to small bumps
1. Decrease compression damping
2. Decrease spring preload
3. Decrease spring rate
4. Increase negative spring rate
5. Decrease rebound damping
6. Overhaul dirty fork

Rear Suspension Tuning

The information above on front suspension explains suspension spring rates, preload, compression damping, rebound damping, and other considerations. The same information applies to rear suspension. You can use the Suspension Fork Adjustment Guide above for rear suspension as well.

The four main types of rear suspension shocks are air/oil, air/air, coil spring (or "coil over"), and elastomer (or "elastomer over").

In both air/oil and air/air shocks, compressed air acts as the spring. Air/oil shocks (see Photo 50.2) rely on the flow of oil through a small opening separating two chambers to slow the suspension movement. Air/air shocks (such as Cane Creek) operate on the same basic principle but rely on the movement of compressed air to damp the suspension. Coil spring shocks (see Photo 50.3) and elastomer shocks use either a coil spring or an elastomer spring surrounding an oil chamber or gas/oil chamber. The oil provides the damping, and the pressurized gas provides an additional spring. Nitrogen is commonly used as the gas, since it is less likely to emulsify with the oil. This type of shock is not to be pumped by the consumer.

50.2

DT SSD 210 air shock with lockout lever

50.3

COURTESY OF MANITOU

Manitou Swinger coil spring shock with a "piggyback" oil chamber

Air/oil and air/air shocks are tuned for spring rate by varying the air pressure, usually via a Schrader valve (which is like a car tire valve, as in Figure 41.1). You must have a shock pump with a no-leak head to pump these shocks or to check the air pressure, since the air volume is so small and the air pressure is so high. Start with the pressure recommended by the bike manufacturer for your weight, and experiment from there. Since the location of the shock and pressure requirements vary from bike to bike, the recommendations will come from the bike manufacturer—not the shock manufacturer.

You can change the spring rate of most coil spring (Photo 50.3) and elastomer shocks by turning a threaded collar surrounding the threaded shock body.

On rear shocks with hydraulic damping systems, adjust damping by varying the size of the orifices through which the oil (or compressed air) flows, or by changing the viscosity of the oil. On many models, the damping orifices are adjusted with knobs, but the adjustment mechanism varies from shock to shock, so read your owner's manual.

The general recommendations below apply to full-suspension cross-country bikes as well as to downhill versions, although I've included more specific downhill considerations farther down.

There are three main variables to take into account when setting up the rear suspension system: sag, compression damping, and rebound damping.

Setting sag

Sag, or ride height—the amount the bike compresses when you sit on it—functions independently of damping, because there is no movement involved; it only depends on spring rate and preload. You can adjust sag by changing your springs and/or your spring preload adjustment. A good rule of thumb is to set your springs so that sag uses up 25 percent of the bike's travel.

You can measure the travel and sag by tying a zip-tie around the shock body of air shocks (or the rubber O-ring that comes on the shaft of many shocks, as in Photo 50.2). Or, as with any shock, you can measure the height of the saddle above the ground at unloaded height, ride height, and full compression (with the shock disconnected or deflated). Adjust the sag in an air/oil shock by adjusting the air pressure.

On a coil or elastomer spring shock, measure the shock shaft when you are off the bike. Have someone else measure it again when you are sitting on it. If less than 75 percent of the shaft length is still showing, increase spring rate or preload. If more than 75 percent of the shaft length is showing, decrease spring rate or preload. The preload is usually set with both of these systems by turning a threaded collar surrounding the shock body that compresses the coil spring or the elastomers. If you have used more than six preload turns of the spring collar to reach a sag of 25 percent of travel, you need a stiffer spring. *Warning:* Excessive preload on a soft spring can cause the spring to fail.

If preload is zero and you get 25 percent sag, you're there! On steep downhill courses, more of your weight will be shifted to the front of the bike, so more sag in the rear is a good idea.

Compression damping

If adjustable, set the compression damping as light as possible without bottoming out the shock on the biggest bump you hit.

Rebound damping

If adjustable, set the rebound damping as light as you can without causing the bike to pogo—that is, bounce repeatedly after a bump.

If you can adjust your rear suspension rebound on the fly, turn it up when you climb. It does not need to toss you up as much when you hit things, as you are going much slower anyway. You will climb faster this way. Some shocks have a lockout lever (which usually greatly increases compression damping) that is also great for this. Remember to reduce the rebound damping or flip the lockout lever open again when you head back down!

Front and Rear Balance

You want the front and rear suspension balanced so they work together. Check suspension balance while standing next to the upright bike on level ground. Lightly apply the front brake, and step straight down on the pedal closest to you while the crank arm is at bottom dead center. If the top tube doesn't tip forward or back as the suspension is compressed, the spring rates are well balanced. Next, sit on the bike in riding position. If one end drops noticeably more than the other, increase the spring preload and/or spring rate on the end that dropped farther (or soften the spring on the end that dropped less).

Shock Mounts

Some shocks have adjustable attachment positions. Usually, these shocks have a number of different mounting holes for one eye of the shock; but some frames mount the body end of the shock via a threaded collar that can be turned to vary the shock's position. Varying the position changes the head angle, bottom-bracket height, and ride height of the bike, and it may also adjust the rear travel length.

Some frames also have adjustable head angles to get similar effects. A shallower head angle makes the bike more stable at high speeds and gets the front wheel farther out ahead for steep drops.

Test Riding

Follow the guidelines in the Suspension Fork Adjustment Guide above to pick a test course and take notes. You want to bottom out a couple of times on the front and rear on a course. If the suspension never bottoms out, the spring is too stiff or the compression damping is too high. Make setting changes in small increments. It is easy to overadjust. Make only one adjustment at a time.

Once you have balanced your front and rear end, any adjustment you make to the front you should also make to the rear, and vice versa. Read your frame manual as well as your shock manual for adjustment methods and recommendations.

Suspension tuning is affected by: 1) rider weight, 2) rider ability, 3) riding speeds, 4) course conditions, 5) rider style, and 6) rider's position on the bike, and 7) temperature. If any or all of these factors change, so should the tuning.

Springs

You want to bottom out occasionally, but not frequently. If you are bottoming out too much, you need to change your compression damping or your spring rate. If the compression is slow, yet you are still bottoming out, your spring is too soft. You will feel beaten up on the intermediate hits, or, when bottoming out on a big hit, it will be harsh through the entire stroke. Stiffen the spring rate and lighten the compression damping. The ride height (again, use up 25 percent of stroke when you sit on the bike) dictates some of your spring rate.

Preload makes the spring rate ramp up faster. If you can use a stiffer spring and back off on preload, you will be happier for it.

Compression damping

Your plush spring won't bottom out harshly, anyway! The compression damping should be set high enough that on big hits you use up all of your travel, but your saddle doesn't smack you in the butt when you hit bottom. Tighten up the compression damping if you blow through the stroke and get bounced too hard.

Rebound damping

You want a lively rebound, since a sluggish return will allow the suspension to pack up (as you go over stutter bumps, water bars, or closely spaced rocks, the bike will ride lower and lower). If you have no damping adjuster, change your oil viscosity.

Increase the rebound damping if the bike springs back too fast

The rebound should not be so quick that you are getting bounced. Increase it for climbs, if you have a quick adjuster and no lockout lever. If you do have a lockout lever (Photo 50.2), use it instead on smooth climbs.

Damping is speed sensitive. Don't worry that settings which feel good at low speeds will be too light for high speeds; the shock will get stiffer as you hit obstacles faster. At all speeds, you want the shock to pop back as quickly as possible without kicking back.

Damping is also temperature sensitive. Oil is thick and sluggish in the cold, but when the outdoor temperature gets hot, oil thins and makes your shock really lively. You will need to adjust accordingly in summer, with stiffer springs and firmer damping adjustments. You can lighten up your springs and damping adjustments even more in the cold of winter. Your overall speeds are slower, the grease and oil in the shock is thicker, and elastomer and coil springs will be stiffer. Lighter weight oil in the shock will help.

If you have no damping adjuster, you can vary the oil viscosity. Find out what oil weight you have from your manual. Rely on manufacturer recommendations to help you decide on your new oil weight. Higher viscosity oil slows the shock; lower viscosity oil speeds it up. Changing the oil in your shock is a good idea, even if you like its performance. Replacing the oil is necessary periodically, since it breaks down with use, and there are little worn bits of your shock floating in it, sometimes even on a new shock. Using a lighter oil in winter and a heavier one in summer is also a good policy.

Downhill Adjustment Recommendations

Everything I said above applies, with a few additions, to downhill adjustments. Again, you are looking for a setup in which, when you're going at race speed, your front and rear shocks bottom out on the biggest bump on the course.

On rougher courses, increasing spring rate will keep you from bottoming out quite so much. Compensate for small bumps by reducing rebound damping to keep the shock from packing in on successive hits. If the bike is bucking, increase damping a bit, but remember that too much damping, as well as too little damping, can sometimes cause bucking. Heavily damped shocks will respond so slowly that they will pack in over repeated bumps, giving you a rigid bike and low ride height.

On smoother courses, try decreasing spring rate (or preload) and increasing damping. Negotiating turns will usually be the major challenge, and the lower ride height (sag) provided by the softer springs will keep you closer to the ground. The greater sag will also increase the available amount of negative fork travel (the amount the wheel can go down), which will help maintain tire traction in turns and when braking. Higher compression damping, while making the shock absorption slower, will still be fast enough to deal with isolated bumps, and it will eliminate the harshest bottoming out. Higher rebound damping will reduce the bouncing of the bike after the isolated bumps.

For courses that have a wide variety of smooth and rough sections, set up your suspension to perform best on the sections in which you have the most trouble for the most elapsed time. In other words, don't set up suspension for a tricky section you'll get through in a couple seconds; set it up for a challenging section on which you will spend half a minute. 🚲

Glossary

adjustable cup: the nondrive-side cup in the bottom bracket. This cup is removed for maintenance of the bottom-bracket spindle and bearings, and it adjusts the bearings. Term sometimes applied to top headset cup as well.

AheadSet: a style of headset that allows the use of a fork with a threadless steering tube. The name is a trademark of Dia-Compe and Cane Creek.

Allen key *(also known as Allen wrench and hex key):* a hexagonal wrench that fits inside a hexagonal hole in the head of a bolt.

all-terrain bike *(ATB):* another term for mountain bike.

anchor bolt *(also known as cable anchor and cable-fixing bolt):* a bolt securing a cable to a component.

axle: the shaft about which a part turns, usually on bearings or bushings.

ball bearing: a set of balls, generally made out of steel, rolling in a track to allow a shaft to spin inside a cylindrical part. May also refer to an individual ball.

barrel adjuster: a threaded cable stop that allows for fine adjustment of cable tension. Barrel adjusters are commonly found on rear derailleurs, shifters, brake levers, and road frame shift cable stops.

BB: see "bottom bracket" or "ball bearing."

bearing: see "ball bearing."

bearing cone: a conical part with a bearing race around its circumference. The cone presses the ball bearings against the bearing race inside the bearing cup.

bearing cup: a polished dish-shaped surface inside of which ball bearings roll. The bearings roll on the outside of a bearing cone that presses them into their track inside the bearing cup.

bearing race: the track or surface on which the bearings roll. It can be inside a cup, on the outside of a cone, or inside a cartridge bearing.

binder bolt: a bolt clamping a seatpost in a frame, a bar end to a handlebar, a handlebar inside a stem, or a threadless steering tube inside a stem clamp.

boot: a reinforcing patch at a tire cut. It is placed against the inner wall of a tire of prevent the inner tube from sticking out of the cut in the tire casing.

bottom bracket *(also known as BB):* the assembly that allows the crank to rotate. Generally the bottom-bracket assembly includes bearings, an axle, a fixed cup, an adjustable cup, and a lockring.

bottom-bracket shell: the cylindrical housing at the bottom of a bicycle frame through which the bottom-bracket axle passes.

brake boss *(also known as brake post or pivot, and cantilever boss, pivot, or post):* a fork- or frame-mounted pivot for a brake arm.

brake pad *(also known as brake block):* a block of rubber or another friction material used to slow the bike by creating friction on the rim, hub-mounted disc, or other braking surface.

brake post: see "brake boss."

brake shoe: the metal pad holder that holds the brake pad to the brake arm.

braze-on: a generic term for most metal frame attachments, including those that are welded or glued on.

brazing: a method commonly used to construct steel bicycle frames. Brazing involves the use of brass or silver solder to connect frame tubes and attach various "braze-on" items, including brake bosses, cable guides, and rack mounts, to the frame. Although rarely done, it is also possible to braze aluminum and titanium.

bushing: a metal or plastic sleeve that acts as a simple bearing on pedals, suspension forks, suspension swing arms, derailleur linkages and jockey wheels.

butted tubing: a common type of frame tubing with varying wall thicknesses. Butted tubing is thicker at the ends of the tube so as to accommodate the high stress points located there.

cable *(also known as inner wire):* wound or braided wire strands used to operate brakes and derailleurs.

cable anchor: see "anchor bolt."

cable end: a cap on the end of a cable to keep it from fraying.

cable-fixing bolt: an anchor bolt that attaches cables to brakes or derailleurs.

cable hanger: the cable stop on a fork- or seatstay-arch used to stop the brake cable housing for a cantilever brake.

cable housing: a metal-reinforced exterior sheath through which a cable passes.

cable housing stop: see "cable stop."

cable stop: a fitting on the frame, fork, or stem at which a cable housing segment terminates.

cage: two guiding plates through which the chain travels. Both the front and rear derailleurs have cages. The cage on the rear also holds the jockey pulleys. Also, a water-bottle holder.

Campagnolo: bicycle component manufacturer based in Vicenza, Italy. Maker of Ergopower shifters and Record, Chorus, and many other component lines.

cantilever boss: see "brake boss."

cantilever brake: a cable-operated rim brake comprised of two opposing arms pivoting on frame- or fork-mounted posts. Pads mounted to each brake arm are pressed against the braking surface of the rim via cable tension from the lever.

cantilever pivot: see "brake boss."

cantilever post: see "brake boss."

cartridge bearing: ball bearings encased in a cartridge consisting of steel inner and outer rings, ball retainers, and sometimes bearing covers.

cassette *(also called cogset):* the group of cogs that mounts on a freehub. Also the group of chainrings that mounts on a spiderless crankarm.

cassette hub: see "freehub."

chain: a series of metal links held together by pins and used to transmit energy from the crank to the rear wheel.

chain line: the imaginary line connecting the center of the middle chainring with the middle of the cog set. This line should in theory be parallel with the vertical plane passing through the center of the bicycle. This is measured as the distance from the center of the seat tube to the center of the middle chainring.

chain link: a single unit of bicycle chain consisting of four plates with a roller on each end and in the center.

chainring: a multiple-toothed sprocket attached to the right crankarm.

chainring-nut spanner: a tool used to secure the chainring nuts while tightening the chainring bolts.

chainstays: the frame tubes connecting the bottom-bracket shell to the rear hub axle.

chain suck: the dragging of the chain by the chainring past the release point at the bottom of the chainring. The chain can be dragged upward until it is jammed between the chainring and the chainstay.

chase, wild-goose: see "goose."

circlip *(also known as snapring and Jesus clip):* a c-shaped snapring that fits in a groove to hold parts together.

clincher rim: a rim with a high sidewall with a hook facing inward to constrain the bead of a clincher tire.

clincher tire: a tire with a bead, to hook into the rim sides. A separate inner tube is normally installed inside the tire, but tubeless clincher tires now provide another option.

clip-in pedal (also known as a clipless pedal): a pedal that relies on spring-loaded clips to grip a cleat attached to the bottom of the rider's shoe, without the use of toe clips and straps.

clipless pedal: see "clip-in pedal."

cog: a sprocket located on the drive side of the rear hub.

compression damping: the diminishing of the speed of the compression of a spring on impact by hydraulic or mechanical means.

cone: a conical part that serves to hold a set of bearings in place and also provides a smooth surface upon which those bearings can roll. Can refer to the conical (or male) member of any cup and cone ball bearing system. See "bearing cone."

countersteering: the act of initiating and modulating the lean angle of the bicycle in a corner by steering away from the corner, rather than toward it. See Block 24 for a thorough description of countersteering.

crankarm: the lever attached at the bottom-bracket spindle with a pedal on its opposite end used to transmit a rider's energy to the chain.

crankarm-fixing bolt: the bolt attaching the crankarm to the bottom-bracket spindle.

crankset: the assembly that includes a bottom bracket, two crankarms, a chainring set, and accompanying nuts and bolts.

cross three: a pattern used by wheel builders that calls for each spoke to cross three others in its path from the hub to the rim.

cup: a cup-shaped bearing surface that surrounds the bearings, as in a bottom bracket, pedal, headset, or hub. See "bearing cup."

damper: a mechanism in a suspension fork or rear shock that reduces the speed of the spring's oscillation.

damping: the reduction in speed of a spring's oscillation, as in a suspension fork or shock.

derailleur: a gear-changing device that allows a rider to move the chain from one cog or chainring to another while the bicycle is in motion.

derailleur hanger: a metal extension of the right rear dropout through which the rear derailleur is mounted to the frame.

disc brake: a brake that stops the bike by squeezing brake pads against a circular disc attached to the wheel hub.

dish: a difference in spoke tension on the two sides of the rear wheel so that the wheel is centered.

double: a two-chainring drivetrain setup (as opposed to a three-chainring or "triple" drivetrain setup).

down tube: the frame tube that connects the head tube and bottom-bracket shell.

drivetrain: the crankarms, chainrings, bottom bracket, front derailleur, chain, rear derailleur, and freewheel (or cassette).

drop: the vertical distance between the center of the bottom bracket and a horizontal line passing through the wheel hub centers. Also, the bend in a road bike's handlebar.

dropouts: the slots in the fork and rear triangle where the wheel axles attach.

dust cap: a protective cap that keeps dirt out of a part.

elastomer: a urethane spring used in suspension forks and swing arms.

endo: standing the bike up on the front wheel, or flipping over the front wheel, usually by stopping the front wheel suddenly either by pulling the brake or by dropping the wheel into a hole.

Ergopower: an integrated road brake/shift lever made by Campagnolo.

ferrule: a cap for the end of cable housing.

fixed cup: the unadjustable cup of the bottom bracket located on the drive side of the bottom bracket.

flange: the largest diameter of the hub where the spoke heads are anchored.

fork: the part that attaches the front wheel to the frame.

fork crown: the cross piece connecting the fork legs to the steering tube.

fork ends: see "dropouts."

fork rake *(also known as rake):* the perpendicular offset distance of the front axle from an imaginary extension of the steering tube centerline (or steering axis).

fork tips *(also known as fork ends):* see "dropouts."

frame: the central structure of a bicycle to which all of the parts are attached.

freehub: a rear hub that has a built-in freewheel mechanism to which the rear cogs are attached.

freewheel: the mechanism through which the rear cogs are attached to the rear wheel on a derailleur bicycle. The freewheel is locked to the hub when turned in the forward direction, but it is free to spin backward independently of the hub's movement, thus allowing the rider to stop pedaling and coast as the bicycle is moving forward.

front triangle *(main triangle):* the head tube, top tube, down tube, and seat tube of a bike frame.

goose chase, wild: see "wild."

granny gear: innermost chainring (lowest gear) on a triple crank.

Gripshift: a trademarked shifter manufactured by the SRAM corporation that is integrated with the handlebar grip of a mountain bike. The rider shifts gears by twisting the grip. See also "twist shifter."

hardtail: a mountain bike frame without a suspension system. Also a complete mountain bike without rear suspension.

headset: the cup, lockring, and bearings that hold the fork to the frame and allow the fork to spin in the frame.

head tube: the front tube of the frame through which the steering tube of the fork passes. The head tube is attached to the top tube and down tube and contains the headset.

hex key: see "Allen key."

hub: the central part of a wheel to which the spokes are anchored and through which the wheel axle passes.

hub brake: a disc, drum, or coaster brake that stops the wheel with friction applied to a braking surface attached to the hub.

hydraulic brake: a type of brake that uses fluid pressure to move the brake pads against the braking surface.

index shifter: a shifter that clicks into fixed positions as it moves the derailleur from gear to gear.

inner wire: see "cable."

Jesus clip: see "circlip."

jockey wheel *(also known as jockey pulley):* a circular cog-shaped pulley attached to the rear derailleur, used to guide, apply tension to, and laterally move the chain from rear cog to rear cog.

knobby tire: an all-terrain tire used on mountain bikes.

link: a pivoting steel hook on a V-brake arm that the cable-guide "noodle" hooks into. Also a pivoting rear suspension member. Also, see "chain link."

locknut: a nut that serves to hold parts in adjustment, as in a headset, hub, or pedal.

lockring: a large circular locknut. On a bottom bracket, the outer ring that holds the adjustable cup in position in the bottom-bracket shell. On a rear shock, the threaded ring that tightens the coil spring on a coil-over shock or is used to secure the fore-aft position of the shock body on some air shocks. On a cassette, the threaded ring that holds the cogs or chainrings in place.

lock washer: a notched or toothed washer that holds surrounding nuts in position.

master link: a detachable link that holds the chain together. The master link can be opened by hand without a chain tool.

mounting bolt: a bolt that mounts a part to a frame, fork, or component. See also "pivot bolt."

needle bearing: steel cylindrical cartridge with rod-shaped rollers arranged coaxially around the inside walls.

nipple: a thin nut designed to receive the end of a spoke and seat in the holes of a rim.

noodle: curved cable-guide pipe on a V-brake arm that stops the cable housing and directs the cable to the cable anchor bolt on the opposite arm.

outer wire: see "cable housing."

outer wire stop: see "cable stop."

pedal: platform on which the foot pushes to propel the bicycle.

pedal overlap: the overlapping of the toe with the front wheel while pedaling. Also known as "toe overlap" or "toe clip overlap."

pinch flat: a puncture in an inner tube that occurs when a tire is compressed down to the rim upon impacting an obstacle, pinching the tube between the tire and the rim. A pinch flat usually creates two small adjacent holes in the inner tube, called a "snake bite."

pin spanner: a wrench with pins protruding perpendicularly from one end. Often used for tightening the adjustable cup of a bottom bracket.

pivot: a pin about which a part rotates through a bearing or bushing. Found on brakes, derailleurs, and rear suspension systems.

pivot bolt: a bolt on which a brake, derailleur, or rear suspension part pivots.

preload: see "spring preload."

Presta valve: thin, metal tire valve that uses a locking nut to stop airflow from the tire.

quick release: (1) the tightening lever and shaft used to attach a wheel to the fork or rear dropouts without using axle nuts. (2) a quick-opening lever and shaft pinching the seatpost inside the seat tube, in lieu of a wrench-operated bolt. (3) a quick cable release on a brake. (4) any fixing bolt that can be quickly opened and closed by a lever.

quill: the vertical tube of a stem that inserts into the fork steering tube. It has an expander wedge and bolt inside to secure the stem to the steering tube.

race: (1) see "bearing race." (2) a speed competition.

rear triangle: the rear portion of the bicycle frame, including the seatstays, the chainstays, and the seat tube.

rebound damping: the diminishing of speed of return of a spring by hydraulic or mechanical means.

rim: the outer hoop of a wheel to which the tire is attached.

saddle (*also known as seat*): a platform made of leather and/or plastic upon which the rider sits.

Schrader valve: a high-pressure air valve with a spring-loaded air-release pin inside. Found on some bicycle tubes and air-sprung suspension forks as well as on adjustable rear shocks and automobile tires and tubes.

sealed bearing: a bearing enclosed in an attempt to keep contaminants out. See also "cartridge bearing."

seat: see "saddle."

seatpost: the post to which the saddle is secured.

seatstay: one of a pair of frame tubes that connect the rear dropouts with the seat tube.

seat tube: the frame tube that connects the top tube and seatstays to the bottom-bracket shell, and into which the seatpost is installed.

Shimano: Japanese bicycle-component company and maker of XTR, XT, LX, and STX component lines, as well as Rapidfire shifters, SPD pedals, and the STI shifting system.

sidepull cantilever brake: see "V-brake."

skewer: a long rod; a hub quick release; a shaft passing through a stack of elastomer bumpers in a suspension fork.

Slime: trademarked tire sealant consisting of chopped fibers in a liquid medium injected inside a tire or inner tube to fill small air leaks.

snake bite: the two adjacent holes created in an inner tube in a pinch flat.

snapring: see "circlip."

spider: a star-shaped piece of metal that connects the right crankarm to the chainrings.

spokes: rods that connect the hub to the rim of a wheel.

spring: an elastic contrivance, that, when compressed, returns to its original shape by virtue of its elasticity. In bicycle suspension applications, the spring used is normally either an elastic polymer cylinder, a coil of steel or titanium wire, or compressed air.

spring preload: the initial loading of a spring so part of its compression range is taken up prior to impact.

sprocket: a circular, multiple-toothed piece of metal that engages a chain. See also "cog" and "chainring."

SRAM: American bicycle-component company and maker of Gripshift, Half Pipe (shifters), and ESP (derailleurs). Owner of Sachs, a German bicycle component company.

standover clearance *(also known as standover height):* the distance between the top tube of the bike and the rider's crotch when standing over the bicycle.

star nut *(also known as star-fangled nut):* a pronged nut that is forced down into the steering tube and anchors the stem-cap bolt to adjust a threadless headset.

steering axis: the imaginary line about which the fork rotates.

steering tube: the vertical tube on a fork that is attached to the fork crown and fits inside the head tube.

STI *(Shimano Total Integration):* Shimano integrated brake/shift lever.

straddle cable: short segment of cable connecting two brake arms together.

straddle-cable holder: see "yoke."

swingarm: the movable rear end of a rear-suspension frame.

threadless headset: see "AheadSet."

three cross: see "cross three."

TIG welding: electric-arc welding using a tungsten electrode (from which the arc jumps) surrounded by a stream of an inert gas (such as argon) to prevent oxidation of the hot weld.

tire lever: a tool to pry a tire off of the rim.

tire sealant: see "Slime."

toe overlap *(also known as toe clip overlap):* see "pedal overlap."

top tube: the frame tube that connects the seat tube to the head tube.

triple: a term used to describe the three-chainring combination attached to the right crankarm.

tubular rim: a rim for a tubular tire. Is generally double-walled and concave on top. It is devoid of hook sides to constrain the beads of a clincher tire.

tubular tire *(also known as tubular, sew-up, and tub [British]):* a tire without a bead. The tube is surrounded by the tire casing, which is sewed together on the bottom. A layer of cotton base tape is usually glued over the stitching, and rim cement is applied to the base tape and the rim to bond the tire to the rim.

twist shifter: a rotating tubular handle that controls the derailleur by pulling a cable. Surrounds the handlebar adjacent the hand grip; it is twisted forward or back to cause the derailleur to shift. See also "Gripshift."

UST: tubeless-tire system originated by Mavic, Michelin, and Hutchinson in which the tire seals over a "hump" on the ledge inside a rim free of spoke holes on its outer circumference.

V-brake *(also known as sidepull cantilever brake):* a cable-operated cantilever rim brake consisting of two vertical brake arms pivoting on frame- or fork-mounted pivots pulled together by a horizontal cable. A brake pad is affixed to each arm, and there is a cable link and cable-guide pipe on one arm and a cable anchor on the opposite arm.

welding: the process of melting one metal surface to another to join them.

wheel base: the horizontal distance between the two wheel axles.

wild-goose chase: see "chase."

yoke: the part attaching the brake cable to the straddle cable, on a cantilever brake.

Gear Chart

The gear chart that follows is based on a 66cm tire diameter. This translates approximately to a 700cm x 19mm road tire or a 26" x 2.1" (inflated to 35psi and weighted) mountain bike tire. Your gear development numbers may differ slightly if the diameter of your rear tire, at inflation and with your weight on it, is not 66cm. Unless your bike has a nonstandard wheel size, however, these numbers will be very close.

If you want totally accurate gear development numbers for the tire you happen to have on your bike at the time, and at a certain inflation pressure, you can measure the tire diameter very precisely with the procedure below.

You can come up with your own gear chart by multiplying each number in this chart by the ratio of your tire diameter divided by 26" (the tire diameter we used, since this chart is in inches, and 66cm = 26"), or by plugging your tire diameter into the following gear development formula.

Gear = (number of chainring teeth) X (tire diameter) ÷ (number of cog teeth)

If you want the gear in inches, put in the tire diameter in inches. Multiply by π (3.14) to find how far you go with each pedal stroke.

Measuring the Diameter of Your Tire

1. Mark the spot on the rear rim that is at the bottom, and mark the floor adjacent to that spot.
2. Roll forward one wheel revolution (ideally, with your weight on the bike and the tire inflated to your preferred pressure), and mark the floor again where the mark on the rim is again at the bottom.
3. Measure the distance between the marks on the floor; this is the tire circumference.
4. Divide this number by π (pi)—3.14—to get the diameter.

Note: You can also use this roll-out procedure to measure wheel size when calibrating your bike computer (except do it on the front wheel for most computers).

Chainring gear teeth

Rear hub cogs	20	22	24	26	28	30	32	34	36	38	39	40	41
11	47	52	57	61	66	71	76	80	85	90	92	95	97
12	43	48	52	56	61	65	69	74	78	82	84	87	89
13	40	44	48	52	56	60	64	68	72	76	78	80	82
14	37	41	45	48	52	56	60	63	67	70	72	74	76
15	35	38	42	45	49	52	55	59	62	66	68	69	71
16	33	36	39	42	45	49	52	55	58	61	63	65	67
17	31	34	37	40	43	46	49	52	55	58	60	61	63
18	29	32	35	38	40	43	46	49	52	55	56	58	59
19	27	30	33	36	38	41	44	47	49	52	53	55	56
20	26	29	31	34	36	39	42	44	47	49	51	52	53
21	25	27	30	32	35	37	40	42	45	47	48	50	51
22	24	26	28	31	33	35	38	40	43	45	46	47	48
23	23	25	27	29	32	34	36	38	41	43	44	45	46
24	22	24	26	28	30	32	35	37	39	41	42	43	44
25	21	23	25	27	29	31	33	35	37	39	41	42	43
26	20	22	24	26	28	30	32	34	36	38	39	40	41
27	19	21	23	25	27	29	31	33	35	37	38	39	39
28	18	20	22	24	26	28	30	32	33	35	36	37	38
30	17	19	21	23	24	26	28	29	31	33	34	35	36
32	16	18	20	21	23	24	26	28	29	31	32	33	33
34	15	17	18	20	21	23	24	26	28	29	30	31	31
38	14	16	16	18	19	21	22	23	25	26	27	27	28
	20	22	24	26	28	30	32	34	36	38	39	40	41

Chainring gear teeth

42	43	44	45	46	47	48	49	50	51	52	53	Rear hub cogs
99	102	104	106	109	111	113	116	118	121	123	125	11
91	93	95	97	100	102	104	106	108	111	113	115	12
84	86	88	90	92	94	96	98	100	102	104	106	13
78	80	82	84	85	87	89	91	93	95	97	98	14
73	75	76	78	80	81	83	85	87	88	90	92	15
68	70	72	73	75	76	78	80	81	83	85	86	16
64	66	67	69	70	72	73	75	76	78	80	81	17
61	62	64	65	66	68	69	71	72	74	75	77	18
57	59	60	62	63	64	66	67	68	70	71	73	19
55	56	57	59	60	61	62	64	65	66	68	69	20
52	53	54	56	57	58	59	61	62	63	64	66	21
50	51	52	53	54	56	57	58	59	60	61	63	22
47	49	50	51	52	53	54	55	57	58	59	60	23
45	47	48	49	50	51	52	53	54	55	56	57	24
44	45	46	47	48	49	50	51	52	53	54	55	25
42	43	44	45	46	47	48	49	50	51	52	53	26
40	41	42	43	44	45	46	47	48	49	50	51	27
39	40	41	42	43	44	45	46	46	47	48	49	28
36	37	38	39	40	41	42	42	43	44	45	46	30
34	35	35	37	37	38	39	40	41	41	42	43	32
32	33	33	34	35	36	37	37	38	39	40	41	34
29	29	30	31	31	32	32	33	34	35	36	36	38
42	43	44	45	46	47	48	49	50	51	52	53	

The formula

Gear development = (number of teeth on chainring) x (wheel diameter) ÷ (number of teeth on rear cog). To find out how far you get with each pedal stroke in a given gear, multiply the gear development by 3.14159265 (π).

Index

About the Author

Lennard Zinn is a bike rider and racer, framebuilder, and technical writer. He grew up participating in and competing at cycling, skiing, and river running, as well as tinkering with mechanical devices, in Los Alamos, New Mexico. After receiving a B.A. in physics from Colorado College, he became a member of the U.S. Olympic Development (road) Cycling Team. While on the National Team, he built his first bicycle frame, and he later went on to learn more about the craft by working in Tom Ritchey's framebuilding shop. He has been producing custom road and mountain bike frames at Zinn Cycles since 1982. He supported the Zinn/Alfalfa's/Shimano/Mavic women's cycling team as a coach, manager, massage practitioner, and mechanic for many years and continues to coach riders and teach cycling to middle school students with his wife, a middle school teacher.

Zinn has been writing for *VeloNews* since 1989 and is currently the senior technical writer for *VeloNews, Inside Triathlon,* and *Ski Racing* magazines. Other books by Zinn are: *Zinn and the Art of Mountain Bike Maintenance* (VeloPress 1996, 1997, 2001), *Zinn and the Art of Road Bike Maintenance* (VeloPress 2000), *Mountain Bike Performance Handbook* (1998), and *Mountain Bike Owner's Manual* (VeloPress 1998). Lennard's work can be found online at www.zinncycles.com, www.velonews.com, www.insidetri.com, and www.velopress.com.